LEGAL NEGOTIATING

By

Gerald R. Williams
Marion G. Romney Professor of Law
Brigham Young University

Charles B. Craver
Freda H. Alverson Professor of Law
George Washington University Law School

AMERICAN CASEBOOK SERIES®

Mat #11576141

American Casebook Series and West Group are trademarks
registered in the U.S. Patent and Trademark Office.

© 2007 Thomson/ West
    610 Opperman Drive
    P.O. Box 64526
    St. Paul, MN 55164–0526
    1–800–328–9352

Printed in the United States of America

ISBN: 978–0–314–06606–0

TEXT IS PRINTED ON 10% POST
CONSUMER RECYCLED PAPER

Preface

This book is written primarily for law students who are learning negotiating skills in clinical courses involving live or simulated negotiations, but it will serve equally well for lawyers and others who are interested in the topic of negotiation. The materials are based upon empirical studies of the negotiating practices of lawyers, and they discuss negotiation in the context of lawyers' work. However, the principles of negotiation are equally valid for other settings, including business, labor, and government.

As recently as thirty years ago, the concept of negotiation was not in vogue; it was interesting to a handful of scholars, but the scholarly literature was quite manageable. Lawyers negotiated as much then as now, but the topic was neglected by the profession, and, with few exceptions, by law teachers. Its importance for attorneys was recognized by a few whose names are now familiar: James J. White, Andrew Watson, Cornelius Peck, and Robert Matthews, who were teaching negotiation skills in law school seminars and were actively encouraging others to study and teach this critical lawyering skill. Harry T. Edwards and James J. White performed a major service with the publication of *The Lawyer as a Negotiator: Problems, Readings, and Materials* (West 1977), which presented some of the better literature on negotiation from different scholarly disciplines in a format usable by the legal practitioner, teacher, and student.

Within the past three decades, however, there has been such a mushrooming of interest that we are faced with an embarrassment of popular literature on the topic. The general interest in negotiation has been nourished by a sizable increase in scholarly attention to the topic, particularly among economic and behavioral scientists. In the space of twenty-five to thirty years, the published literature has grown to impressive proportions.

Lawyers face several difficulties in applying this literature. One concerns the sheer volume of books and articles that have been published. Attorneys face a second problem in evaluating the reliability of the studies and their relevance to lawyering interactions. Most social psychological studies of bargaining encounters are based upon studies using college students to "negotiate" solutions in highly structured and narrowly limited simulation games. Lawyers must naturally be concerned about the applicability of the conclusions from these studies to bargaining interactions between professionals within the legal system.

Each school of negotiating has its own methods, assumptions, theories, and attitudes, which means that interested researchers or practitioners must spend most of their time reading literature from outside their own disciplines. Current knowledge embodied in such domains as decision theory, conflict theory, behavior exchange theory, learning theory, argumentation and persuasion theory, verbal and nonverbal communication research, and kinesics research has contributed substantially to our understanding of the negotiation process.

The methods and theories of traditional legal research do not lend themselves to a study of the negotiation behavior of lawyers. As a result, the methods and theoretical approaches of the behavioral sciences must be called upon. Behavioral studies of the legal profession require a joint effort between legal researchers and behavioral scientists. The field research reported in the first part of this volume is the result of such a joint effort, entitled the BYU Legal Negotiation Project. The behavioral expertise was provided by Larry C. Farmer and J. Lynn England of Brigham Young University and Murray Blumenthal of the University of Denver, who collaborated with Professor Williams in the research from which his findings are taken. The National Science Foundation provided generous financial support for this research.

After this data collection was completed and the findings were incorporated into legal negotiation courses, it became apparent that law students have difficulty envisioning the negotiating behavior being described. Because law students have done little or no work among professional negotiators, they cannot visualize the processes and dynamics described by the empirical findings. Professor Williams is indebted to Roger C. Croft, then of BYU's David O. McKay Institute, for providing the encouragement and impetus for capturing on videotape some very intense and authentic negotiations between experienced lawyers. He made the technical arrangements for professionally videotaping the spontaneous negotiation of seven cases by fourteen practicing lawyers from across the United States. He is indebted to the BYU Media Production Studio for producing the videotapes, and to the Studio and the J. Reuben Clark Law School at BYU for jointly providing the necessary funds. Special thanks are due to the attorneys who so kindly and expertly undertook the task of preparing and negotiating these cases under the warm glare of the television lights. Their efforts have provided the crucial means by which the research findings can literally be brought to life.

The efforts of these fourteen attorneys is representative of the quality and intensity of the assistance received from several hundred attorneys in Denver and Grand Junction, Colorado, and Phoenix, Arizona, over the two-and-one-half years of data collection, including approximately three hundred attorneys who provided detailed verbal reports of cases they were then handling. Officers of the bar associations and ethics committees gave much valuable support and counsel, as did the members of our attorney advisory committee in Denver. To all of these men and women, we extend our warmest thanks.

Almost twenty-five years after the BYU Legal Negotiation Project, Professor Andrea Kupfer Schneider replicated and amplified upon it using lawyers in the Milwaukee, Wisconsin, and Chicago, Illinois, areas.* She not only reported the changes in attorney styles that occurred during that time frame, but also explored other aspects of lawyer negotiating behavior.

Chapter 2 discusses the findings and implications of these empirical studies of negotiator motivations and behavior. We then use these empirical findings to examine the Dynamics of Cooperative/Problem-Solving and Competitive/Adversarial Negotiating in Chapter 3 and the relevance of lawyer styles in the Stages of the Negotiation Process in Chapter 4.

In Chapter 5, we describe the law of negotiation and settlement, and in Chapter 6 we explore the impact of economic and psychological factors on the decision-making process. Chapter 7 draws upon Professor Craver's studies of negotiation behavior and outcomes among law students to explore personal factors, such as race and gender, that may influence bargaining interactions.

GERALD R. WILLIAMS
CHARLES B. CRAVER

Provo, Utah
Washington, D.C.
May 2007

*

---

* Andrea Kupfer Schneider, *Shattering Negotiation Myths: Empirical Evidence on the Effectiveness of Negotiation Style*, 7 *Harv. Neg. L. Rev.* 143 (2002).

Acknowledgements

The longer we continue in the field of legal negotiating, the greater our indebtedness to others: to our colleagues, to teachers and scholars in many disciplines, to practicing lawyers, to law students, and to research and teaching assistants. After more than three decades apiece of reading articles and books, attending conferences and workshops, doing empirical research, preparing teaching materials, and receiving feedback from those we have taught, we fear it would be presumptuous to attempt to name here all those who have influenced us and have contributed significantly to our understanding. The names of those whose scholarly works have had the greatest impact upon our thoughts are listed in the bibliography. To them and to the many others who have contributed to our understanding of negotiation, we acknowledge our debt and express our continuing gratitude for being participants with so many exemplary individuals and organizations in learning and teaching the craft of legal negotiating.

*

Summary of Contents

Page

PREFACE v
TABLE OF CASES xvii

Chapter

One. Introduction to Legal Negotiation **1**
  I. Overview 1
  II. Lawyer Competency: Are Lawyers Adequately Trained in
      Negotiation Skills? 4
  III. Effectiveness in Legal Negotiation 6
  IV. What Cases Should Be Settled and What Cases Should Go to
      Trial? 8

Two. The Negotiating Patterns of Practicing Lawyers **12**
  I. Description of the Legal Negotiation Research Project 12
  II. How Lawyers Negotiate: Lessons From Attorneys 14

**Three. The Dynamics of Cooperative/ Problem–Solving
and Competitive/Adversarial Negotiating** **58**
  I. Introduction 58
  II. The Cooperative/Problem–Solving Strategy 59
  III. The Competitive/Adversarial Strategy 60
  IV. The Competitive/Problem–Solving Strategy 64
  V. Client Relations and Negotiation 65
  VI. Conflicts Between Attorneys and Clients 67

Four. Stages of the Negotiation Process **74**
  I. Introduction 74
  II. Discussion of the Stages 77
  III. The Interplay Between Legal Proceedings and the Negotia-
      tion Process 89
  IV. Pre–Bargaining Dynamics 90

Five. The Law of Negotiation and Settlement **93**
  I. Introduction: Is There a Law of Negotiation and Settlement .. 93
  II. The General Policy of the Law Toward Compromise and
      Settlement 93
  III. Contract Law as a Source of Negotiation Law 94
  IV. Ethical Constraints on Legal Negotiators 97
  V. Formation, Interpretation and Enforcement of Settlement
      Agreements 100
  VI. Defects in Compromise and Settlement Agreements 106
  VII. Special Rules Applicable to Insurers 107
  VIII. Rules of Evidence 108

                                                                    Page
Chapter
Six. The Impact of Economic and Psychological Factors on
       theDecision–Making Process --------------------------------- 111
    I. Introduction -- 111
   II. Economic Analysis of Cases: The Missing Lawyer Skill -------- 111
  III. Methods for Economic Case Evaluations --------------------- 116
   IV. An Objective Economic Method for Case Evaluation ---------- 120
    V. Decision-Making Influences ---------------------------------- 124

Seven. Personal Factors That May Influence Negotiator
        Performance -- 131

                            APPENDICES

Appendix I. Research Methodology: The BYU Legal Negoti-
       ation Project --- 153
Appendix II. Tables -- 157
Appendix III. Transcripts of student sexual harassment
       and personal injury negotiations ------------------------ 165

Bibliography --- 195
INDEX --- 217

Table of Contents

Page

PREFACE --- v
TABLE OF CASES -- xvii

Chapter One. Introduction to Legal Negotiation ------------ **1**
   I. Overview --- 1
      A. Transactions --- 2
      B. Civil Disputes --- 3
      C. Labor/Management Negotiations ------------------------------ 3
      D. Criminal Cases --- 3
   II. Lawyer Competency: Are Lawyers Adequately Trained in
      Negotiation Skills? --- 4
  III. Effectiveness in Legal Negotiation ----------------------------- 6
  IV. What Cases Should Be Settled and What Cases Should Go to
      Trial? -- 8
          Chapter Notes --- 10

**Chapter Two. The Negotiating Patterns of Practicing Law-
    yers** --- **12**
Introduction -- 12
Empirical Study Findings -- 12
1976 Study by Professor Williams -- 12
   I. Description of the Legal Negotiation Research Project ---------- 12
   II. How Lawyers Negotiate: Lessons From Attorneys --------------- 14
      A. Characteristics of Effective Negotiators ------------------ 17
         1. Effective/Cooperative Negotiators ----------------- 17
         2. Effective/Competitive Negotiators ----------------- 19
         3. Similarities Between the Two Effective Types ------ 21
      B. Characteristics of Average Negotiators ------------------- 25
         1. Average/Cooperative Negotiators ------------------- 25
         2. Average Competitive/Negotiators ------------------- 26
         3. Similarities Between the Two Average Types -------- 27
      C. Characteristics of Ineffective Negotiators --------------- 27
         1. Ineffective/Cooperative Negotiators --------------- 28
           a. Similarities Between Effective and Ineffective Co-
             operative Negotiators ---------------------------- 29
           b. Differences Between Effective and Ineffective Co-
             operative Negotiators ---------------------------- 29
         2. Ineffective/Competitive Negotiators --------------- 30
           1999 Study by Professor Schneider ------------------- 33
           *Andrea Kupfer Schneider, Shattering Negotiation Myths:
           Empirical Evidence on the Effectiveness of Negotiation
           Style* --- 33
           Which Approach Is More Effective -------------------- 52
           Competitive/Problem–Solving Style ------------------ 53

Page

II. How Lawyers Negotiate: Lessons From Attorneys—Continued
>>>>>> Which Type of Negotiator Are You? 54
>>>>>> Chapter Notes 55

Chapter Three. The Dynamics of Cooperative/Problem-Solving and Competitive/Adversarial Negotiating **58**
I. Introduction 58
II. The Cooperative/Problem–Solving Strategy 59
III. The Competitive/Adversarial Strategy 60
IV. The Competitive/Problem–Solving Strategy 64
V. Client Relations and Negotiation 65
VI. Conflicts Between Attorneys and Clients 67
>>>>>> Chapter Notes 68

Chapter Four. Stages of the Negotiation Process **74**
I. Introduction 74
>> A. Stage One: Preparation 74
>> B. Stage Two: Orientation and Positioning 75
>> C. Stage Three: Argumentation 76
>> D. Stage Four: Emergence and Crisis 76
>> E. Stage Five: Agreement or Final Breakdown 77
II. Discussion of the Stages 78
>> A. Stage One: Preparation 78
>>>> 1. Information Gathering 78
>>>> 2. Determining and Valuing Underlying Client Needs and Interests 78
>> B. Stage Two: Orientation and Positioning 79
>>>> 1. Orientation 79
>>>> 2. Positioning 79
>>>>>> a. Maximalist Positioning 80
>>>>>> b. Equitable Positioning 81
>>>>>> c. Integrative Positioning 82
>>>> 3. Inalterable Commitments to Opening Positions 83
>>>> 4. Duration of Stage Two 83
>> C. Stage Three: Argumentation 84
>>>> 1. Overview 84
>>>> 2. The Problem of Making Concessions 85
>> D. Stage Four: Emergence and Crisis 86
>>>> 1. Effect of Deadlines 86
>>>> 2. The Client, the Opposing Party, and the Negotiation Process 87
>> E. Stage Five: Agreement or Final Breakdown 88
>>>> 1. Agreement 88
>>>> 2. Final Breakdown 88
III. The Interplay Between Legal Proceedings and the Negotiation Process 89
IV. Pre–Bargaining Dynamics 90
>>>> Chapter Notes 91

Page

Chapter Five. The Law of Negotiation and Settlement 93
   I. Introduction: Is There a Law of Negotiation and Settlement .. 93
  II. The General Policy of the Law Toward Compromise and
      Settlement 93
 III. Contract Law as a Source of Negotiation Law 94
     A. The Notion of Good Faith in Bargaining 94
     B. The Use of Threats in Bargaining 95
  IV. Ethical Constraints on Legal Negotiators 97
   V. Formation, Interpretation and Enforcement of Settlement
      Agreements 100
     A. Offer and Acceptance 100
     B. Consideration 100
     C. Writings and Formalities 101
     D. Interpretation of the Agreement 102
     E. Conflict of Laws—Governing Law 103
     F. Federal Rules of Civil Procedure: Rule 68 Offers of Com-
        promise 103
     G. Court Supervision and Approval of Settlements 105
     H. Effect of Negotiations on Statutes of Limitations 105
  VI. Defects in Compromise and Settlement Agreements 106
     A. Introduction 106
     B. Fraud, Misrepresentation, and Mistake 106
     C. Mary Carter Agreements 106
 VII. Special Rules Applicable to Insurers 107
VIII. Rules of Evidence 108

Chapter Six. The Impact of Economic and Psychological
    Factors on theDecision–Making Process 111
   I. Introduction 111
  II. Economic Analysis of Cases: The Missing Lawyer Skill 111
 III. Methods for Economic Case Evaluations 116
  IV. An Objective Economic Method for Case Evaluation 120
     A. Introduction 120
     B. Time Value of Money 121
     C. The Appropriate Rate of Interest for Time–Value Calcula-
        tion Use 122
     D. The Tax Aspects of Settlement 123
   V. Decision-Making Influences 124
     A. Fixed Pie Assumption 124
     B. Egocentric/Self–Serving Bias 126
     C. Anchoring Impact of Initial Offers 126
     D. Gain–Loss Framing 127
     E. Reactive Devaluation 128
     F. Regret Aversion 129
        Chapter Notes 129

Page

Chapter Seven. Personal Factors That May Influence Negotiator Performance ----- **131**

    A. Abstract Reasoning Ability (IQ) vs. Emotional Intelligence (EI) ----- 131

       The Impact of Student Gpas and a Pass/Fail Option on Clinical Negotiation Course Performance ----- 132

    B. Impact of Gender ----- 136

       Gender and Negotiation Performance ----- 136

    C. Impact of Race ----- 144

       Race and Negotiation Performance ----- 144

       Chapter Notes ----- 150

Appendix I. Research Methodology: The BYU Legal Negotiation Project ----- **153**

Appendix II. Tables ----- **157**

Appendix III. Transcripts of Student Sexual Harassment and Personal Injury Negotiations ----- **165**

Bibliography ----- **195**

INDEX ----- **217**

Table of Cases

The principal cases are in bold type. Cases cited or discussed in the text are roman type. References are to pages. Cases cited in principal cases and within other quoted materials are not included.

August v. Delta Air Lines, Inc., 600 F.2d 699 (7th Cir.1979), 104

Booth v. Mary Carter Paint Co., 202 So.2d 8 (Fla.App. 2 Dist.1967), 107

City of (see name of city)
City Street Imp. Co. v. Pearson, 181 Cal. 640, 185 P. 962 (Cal.1919), 100, 101
Crisci v. Security Ins. Co. of New Haven, Conn., 66 Cal.2d 425, 58 Cal.Rptr. 13, 426 P.2d 173 (Cal.1967), 108

Davies v. Canco Enterprises, 350 So.2d 23 (Fla.App. 3 Dist.1977), 101
Delta Air Lines, Inc. v. August, 450 U.S. 346, 101 S.Ct. 1146, 67 L.Ed.2d 287 (1981), 104

General Motors Corp. v. Lahocki, 286 Md. 714, 410 A.2d 1039 (Md.1980), 106
Gregg v. Town of Weathersfield, 55 Vt. 385 (Vt.1883), 100

Jamestown Farmers Elevator, Inc. v. General Mills, Inc., 552 F.2d 1285 (8th Cir. 1977), 96

Kabatchnick v. Hanover–Elm Bldg. Corp., 328 Mass. 341, 103 N.E.2d 692 (Mass. 1952), 99

Kricar, Inc. v. General Acc., Fire and Life Assurance Corp., Ltd., 542 F.2d 1135 (9th Cir.1976), 108

Little Rock Packing Co. v. Massachusetts Bonding & Ins. Co., 262 F.2d 327 (8th Cir.1959), 100

Marek v. Chesny, 473 U.S. 1, 105 S.Ct. 3012, 87 L.Ed.2d 1 (1985), 104
Moore v. Gunning, 328 So.2d 462 (Fla.App. 4 Dist.1976), 101
Murphy v. I.R.S., 460 F.3d 79, 373 U.S.App. D.C. 143 (D.C.Cir.2006), 124

N.L.R.B. v. Waymouth Farms, Inc., 172 F.3d 598 (8th Cir.1999), 100

Posey v. Lambert–Grisham Hardware Co., 197 Ky. 373, 247 S.W. 30 (Ky.1923), 100, 101

Stoddard v. Mix, 14 Conn. 12 (Conn.1840), 100

Tucson, City of v. Gallagher, 108 Ariz. 140, 493 P.2d 1197 (Ariz.1972), 107

Wicker v. Board of Public Instruction of Dade County, Fla., 182 F.2d 764 (5th Cir.1950), 100

Young v. American Cas. Co. of Reading, Pa., 416 F.2d 906 (2nd Cir.1969), 107

*

LEGAL
NEGOTIATING

*

Chapter One

INTRODUCTION TO LEGAL NEGOTIATION

"The principal institution of the law in action is not trial; it is settlement out of court."[1]

I. OVERVIEW

Though we do not usually think of it in these terms, negotiating is the principal occupation of lawyers. It is so much a part of the fabric of daily law practice that past generations did not identify it as a distinct skill or process. Today, this perception is changing. Judicial statistics inform us that only a small percentage of legal disputes are resolved by court trial. For example, of all cases filed in U. S. District Courts in 2006, less than 2% reached trial; the remaining 98% were terminated without trial, in most cases by negotiated settlement agreements. Statistics are less precise for many state and local courts, but available figures indicate that for most jurisdictions, only 5% of all cases filed with the courts are resolved by trial verdicts.[2]

To say that most cases are settled does not imply that trials are unimportant; trials provide the leverage or threat that pushes opposing parties into settlement discussions and agreements. Lawyers also use predictions of probable trial outcomes as a basis for assigning dollar or other values to their cases. But as important as trials (and trial advocacy skills) may be in law practice, they are used in fewer than one case out of twenty. The remaining nineteen cases depend more importantly upon attorney negotiation skills.[3]

While settlement negotiations are an extremely important part of lawyering, negotiation is significant for lawyers in nondispute settings as

1. H. Laurence Ross, *Settled Out of Court* 3 (Aldine, 2d ed. 1980).

2. See Wayne Brazil, *Should Court-Appointed ADR Survive?* 21 Ohio St. J. Disp. Res. 241, 243–44 (2006); H. Samborn, *The Vanishing Trial*, A.B.A. J. 24 (Oct. 2002).

3. Even with respect to cases that are ultimately adjudicated, negotiation skills can be employed to stipulate legal and factual issues, and to structure discovery procedures.

well. American lawyers spend a major portion of their time in another area involving negotiation skills, which concerns the formation and execution of contractual transactions and relationships. In his major study of negotiation, Professor Eisenberg characterizes transactional negotiations as similar to private legislation in which parties develop rules to govern future conduct between them. He calls this "rulemaking-negotiation."[4] This work frequently involves lawyers in discussions within client corporations about matters of decision making, negotiation of various kinds of contractual undertakings with other parties, labor/management negotiations, and negotiation of agreements with representatives of various federal, state, and local governmental agencies. Contemporary business lawyers negotiate corporate deals with firms around the world, and these interactions often involve direct or indirect negotiations with different government departments.

Because negotiation settings vary so much, it is clear that general knowledge of negotiation skills must be supplemented by specialized knowledge of applicable law, customs, and practices. Negotiation settings can be roughly divided into four categories: transactions, civil disputes, labor/management relationships, and criminal matters. Each category has unique aspects and must be approached with these in mind.

A.   TRANSACTIONS

As a general rule, transactions are exchanges voluntarily arrived at by the parties, whether for purchase of real property, sales of goods, buying or selling a business, joint ventures, patent, copyright and trademark licenses, or any other kind of contractual undertaking. Attorneys must remind themselves that contractual relations are normally based upon a voluntary decision by both parties to do business with one another, sometimes in exchanges of short duration (in which interpersonal relationships are not very important), and sometimes in cooperative ventures of substantial duration (in which there is considerable interdependence). Contractual relationships are expected to be mutually beneficial, and particularly the longer-range relationships are based on the observance of customs and practices in the industry involved which help to prevent the kinds of manipulation and distrust that might undermine the good faith performance of agreements.

Lawyers trained in the Socratic classroom tend to see contract negotiations as adversarial, and they approach such undertakings with some apprehension. The adversarial approach is such a breach of etiquette in most transactional settings that lawyers are often seen as rude, nitpicking, and counterproductive. Obviously, lawyers face a dilemma in knowing how far to go in "protecting" clients in unfamiliar business contexts.

4. In his analysis, Professor Eisenberg compares dispute resolution by negotiation to adjudication, and calls it "dispute–negotiation." Eisenberg, *Private Ordering* *Through Negotiation: Dispute–Settlement and Rulemaking*, 89 Harvard L. Rev. 637, 638 (1976).

Transactions have many features in common, but they occur in virtually all of life's important settings, from sales of property between family members to commercial transactions to joint venture agreements between large corporations. A lawyer's effectiveness in each of these negotiating settings is enhanced in proportion to her understanding of the business facts associated with each type of transaction involved.[5]

B. CIVIL DISPUTES

These are distinguishable from transactions on several important grounds. In civil disputes, one party or the other has (or believes she has) legal rights against the other that are enforceable in court. If the parties cannot resolve the dispute, the complaining party can compel the reluctant party to participate in a judicial or arbitral proceeding. At this point, the defending side cannot walk away and find someone more pleasant to deal with. Since the two sides are forced to interact with one another, one or both can get away with much higher levels of aggressiveness and unreasonableness than would be tolerated in transactional settings.

C. LABOR/MANAGEMENT NEGOTIATIONS

These are hybrids: they have characteristics of transactions and of civil disputes.[6] They resemble transactions because they look to contractual agreements, they involve on-going relationships, and there is often no wrong for which there is a judicially cognizable remedy (at least not without exhaustion of administrative procedures mandated by labor and employment laws). On the other hand, labor/management negotiations resemble civil disputes in the sense that the parties have a legal duty to bargain.

The mandatory duty to bargain locks both sides into their seats at the bargaining table and requires them to negotiate in good faith. The adversarial aspects of the relationship give rise to elaborate and sophisticated bargaining strategies that may begin with psychological warfare long before talks begin and continue until the last issue is resolved.

D. CRIMINAL CASES

While criminal law often involves economic interests (theft, embezzlement, criminal destruction of property), it is primarily directed at the protection of society from criminal acts and the concurrent protection of accused persons from unjustified or overzealous prosecution or punishment.

Plea bargaining is a direct and explicit form of negotiation which has been singled out for attention on several counts. Approximately the same percentage of criminal cases settle as civil, but in the criminal

---

5. See James C. Freund, *Smart Negotiating* (New York: Simon & Schuster 1992); G. Richard Shell, *Bargaining for Advantage* (New York: Viking 1999).

6. See Richard E. Walton & Robert B. McKersie, *A Behavioral Theory of Labor Negotiations* (New York: McGraw–Hill 1965).

context a person's life or liberty is at stake. Plea bargaining by-passes many, if not all, of the formal constitutional protections built into the criminal justice system, and its pervasive use raises practical as well as philosophical concerns. For example, it is generally accepted that criminal court dockets are dependent on having 80 percent or more of the cases disposed of by plea bargain and that trial courts would be overwhelmed and paralyzed if all criminal defendants insisted upon a constitutionally guaranteed speedy trial in lieu of bargained pleas.

Most of what we learn about negotiation in civil contexts applies equally well to the criminal setting. However, criminal cases raise issues of justice, fairness, constitutional law, and public policy that are beyond the scope of this book.[7]

Despite their differences, these four contexts have one crucial element in common: they all involve negotiation. Most of the information and principles in this and the remaining chapters apply equally to all four settings. However, negotiation of civil disputes offers the most fertile ground for the focus of this book, because it includes a broad range of permissible behavior but stops short of the human rights issues raised by criminal law and the group dynamics issues raised by labor negotiations. For this reason, unless otherwise noted, the discussions in this book assume civil legal disputes.

II. LAWYER COMPETENCY: ARE LAWYERS ADEQUATELY TRAINED IN NEGOTIATION SKILLS?

There has been mounting concern within and without the legal profession about how lawyers perform skill-related functions such as negotiation. Two task forces of the ABA Section of Legal Education and Admissions to the Bar have recommended that law schools make training in negotiation and other skills available to all law students.[8]

---

7. For an introduction to the extensive literature on plea bargaining, see the Special Issue on Plea Bargaining, 13 Law and Society Review, Number 2, pp. 199–687 (1979), which includes articles reviewing historical patterns of plea bargaining, comparing practice in the U.S. to practices elsewhere, describing results of empirical research on plea bargaining, examining philosophical implications, and reviewing current literature on plea bargaining. For a lawyers' reference manual covering existing substantive and procedural law governing plea bargaining, see G. Nicholas Herman, *Plea Bargaining* (Newark: LexisNexis 2d ed. 2004) James E. Bond, *Plea Bargaining and Guilty Pleas* (New York: Clark Boardman Co. 2d ed. 1982) (with regular supplements). For a more anecdotal description of

plea bargaining that conveys the flavor of the courthouse, see Douglas W. Maynard, *Inside Plea* Bargaining (New York: Plenum 1984); Arthur Rosett and Donald R. Cressey, *Justice by Consent: Plea Bargaining in the American Courthouse* (Philadelphia: J.B. Lippincott Co. 1976).

8. *Legal Education and Professional Development* (ABA Section of Legal Education and Admissions to the Bar 1992); *Lawyer Competency: The Role of the Law Schools* (ABA Section of Legal Education and Admissions to the Bar 1979). See also *Law Schools and Professional Education* (Report and Recommendations of the Special Committee for a Study of Legal Education of the American Bar Association, 1980). The ABA Section of Legal Education and Admissions to the Bar recently adopted Standard

4

The reasons for this concern are not always apparent. Are lawyers deficient in their negotiating skills? If so, what problems does this cause and how can they be remedied? The most serious criticism of lawyer negotiating skills would be a finding that clients are receiving inadequate assistance of counsel as reflected in the dollar value of cases that settle. We can therefore pose the question: if a number of experienced lawyers were paired against each other and assigned to undertake settlement negotiations on identical cases, would the resulting settlements be substantially identical, or would there be considerable variation in the monetary outcomes? This question is vitally important. If results are about the same, we might conclude lawyers are already doing an adequate job at negotiation and there is little justification for concern about lawyer competency.

To test the question of lawyer negotiating outcomes, Professor Williams obtained the cooperation of 40 practicing lawyers in Des Moines, Iowa, who agreed to be divided into 20 pairs and to prepare and undertake settlement negotiations in a personal injury case. Approximately two weeks in advance of the negotiations, the attorneys were randomly assigned to represent either the plaintiff or the defendant (as counsel for his insurance company). Attorneys assigned to represent the plaintiff were given identical case files, as were attorneys assigned to the defense. Under the facts it was assumed the case arose in Iowa, Iowa law applied, and if the case went to trial it would be tried to a jury in Des Moines, Iowa. To assure comparability of predicted jury awards, photocopies of comparable jury awards from the Des Moines area were included in the case files for both sides, participating lawyers were informed that results of the negotiations would be published, with attorney names attached, among the participants at the workshop. This meant the attorneys had their professional reputations riding on their outcomes.

After two weeks preparation time, the attorneys came together and were given adequate time to reach settlements. They were then asked to fill out a form giving their names, the opening offers or demands made by each side, and the final outcomes (i.e. the dollar amount if settlement figures were agreed to, or notations of "impasse" if no agreements could be reached).

At the expiration of the time period, 14 of the 20 pairs were willing to submit their signed statement of results. The outcomes are shown in Table 1–1.

The results of this experiment were sobering to the participating attorneys. The outcomes ranged from a high of $95,000 to a low of $15,000; the average outcome was just over $47,000; and the remainder of the outcomes are scattered almost randomly between the two extremes. Whether or not these results are representative of the legal

302(a)(4) which provides that law schools should require all students to receive sub-   stantial instruction with respect to professional skills including legal negotiating.

profession as a whole, they give cause for concern. It is apparent that there were dramatic differences not only in the perceptions these law-yers had about the "value" of the case, but in the persuasiveness or skill with which they pursued their objectives. The study raises questions about how well lawyers are able to serve their own clients and/or the public interest through negotiated settlements.

Table 1–1.

Results of Des Moines Experiment

Attorneys	Plaintiff's Opening Demand	Defendant's Opening Offer	Settlement
Attorneys 1A and 1B	$32,000	$10,000	$18,000
Attorneys 2A and 2B	$50,000	$25,000	Impasse
Attorneys 3A and 3B	$675,000	$32,150	$95,000
Attorneys 4A and 4B	$110,000	$3,000	$25,120
Attorneys 5A and 5B	Unreported	Unreported	$15,000
Attorneys 6A and 6B	$100,000	$5,000	$25,000
Attorneys 7A and 7B	$475,000	$15,000	Impasse
Attorneys 8A and 8B	$180,000	$40,000	$80,000
Attorneys 9A and 9B	$210,000	$17,000	$57,000
Attorneys 10A and 10B	$350,000	$48,500	$61,000
Attorneys 11A and 11B	$87,500	$15,000	$30,000
Attorneys 12A and 12B	$175,000	$50,000	Impasse
Attorneys 13A and 13B	$97,000	$10,000	$57,500
Attorneys 14A and 14B	$100,000	Unreported	$56,875

Average Settlement $47,318

Since this Des Moines study, Professors Williams and Craver have taught continuing legal education courses on legal negotiating to approx-imately 100,000 practicing attorneys. They have had these course partici-pants engage in various legal negotiation exercises. These interactions continue to generate settlement terms as diverse—and, in some cases, even more diverse—than those reported in the Des Moines study. We believe that similar disparities affect actual dispute and transactional negotiations that are conducted every day by practicing lawyers through-out the United States and in countries around the world.

III.   EFFECTIVENESS IN LEGAL NEGOTIATION

What does it mean to be an effective negotiator? This question will be a major concern throughout the book. Is the effective negotiator the lawyer who obtained a $15,000 settlement on behalf of her client insurance company in the outcomes listed above? If so, what can be said of her opponent, who accepted on behalf of the injured plaintiff an amount $80,000 *below* the potential highest award and $32,000 below the *average* award? If the insurance company lawyer who obtained the $15,000 settlement is rated as an exceptionally skillful negotiator, what does that imply about the meaning of "effective"?

Or are the effective negotiators the attorneys who came closest to the average award in the experimental case? If they are the most effective negotiators, then what meaning is being given to the word "effective"? What criteria are being applied?

We have been examining negotiator effectiveness from a largely subjective point of view; attorneys and law students will naturally have their own opinions and values on this issue. But in arriving at an opinion, larger issues should be taken into account as well. For example, to what extent should a definition of negotiator effectiveness be reconcilable with one's view of justice and of the public interest? Clearly, any attempt to define "effectiveness" must consider the purposes and effects of the legal system as a whole and the role of lawyers working within that system. While individual attorneys may be justified in zealously pursuing the interests of their clients, even to the serious detriment of opposing parties, lawyers as members of the legal profession should adopt a wider perspective. The legitimate interests of each party, and of society at large, must be given full consideration.

Researchers studying negotiator effectiveness outside of the legal context have also wrestled with the problem of how to define it. Many researchers, for example, define negotiator effectiveness in terms of monetary units only. The effective negotiator is one who obtains the maximum amount of money from the other side. While not ignoring the relevance of a monetary measure of effectiveness, other researchers have argued that it fails to take account of other necessary considerations, such as the following:

1. What were the costs (in time, money, and social psychological terms) of resolving the problem? How do these compare to the costs of other methods that might have been used to process the dispute?

2. Were all of the issues resolved, or were some of them reserved for future action?

3. Is the agreement stable, or will one party or the other soon become dissatisfied with it and seek to overturn or dishonor it?

4. Does the agreement minimize the damage and maximize the benefits to both parties, or does it embody unnecessary costs or damage to one or both parties? Is the agreement economically efficient and socially productive?

5. To what extent were applicable rules, customs, and etiquette observed? What types of tactics (threats, promises, etc.) were used? To what extent did tactics increase the costs to one or

7

both parties? Would agreement have been possible through resort to other tactics?

6. Did the negotiators make efficient use of available resources (communication channels, cost reducing procedures, case management techniques, judicial resources)? Did they give proper consideration to alternative courses of action?

It should also be recognized that not all successful negotiations end in the settlement of lawsuits or the signing of business agreements. In business discussions, for example, talks may lead to the conclusion that neither party has what the other wants. If so, the discussions have achieved their purpose. By the same token, in civil or criminal disputes, negotiation may accomplish nothing more than clarifying the issues and preparing the case for a trial that both sides agree is necessary. Thus, the mark of a successful negotiation is not always a settlement or agreement; it may be nothing more than mutual recognition that trial (or some other approach, such as mediation or arbitration) is necessary.

IV. WHAT CASES SHOULD BE SETTLED AND WHAT CASES SHOULD GO TO TRIAL?

One of the major problems for lawyers is knowing which cases to settle and which cases to take to trial. As a national average, approximately 95% of cases settle. Using this norm as a guide, approximately 19 out of 20 cases are settled.

For strategic reasons, lawyers frequently pretend they have no interest in settling cases, thus implying to their opponents that they have absolute confidence they will prevail at trial. Opposing attorneys, not wanting to appear weak in the face of this tactic, also adopt the position that they will take their cases to trial, where they are equally certain of victory. Bluffing of this sort seriously distorts the real issues, because it precludes rational weighing of the decision whether to settle and puts an onus on the attorneys who open settlement negotiations. A later chapter will return to the strategic issues raised by bluffing. The objective in this chapter is to spell out considerations going to the question of whether to settle or try particular cases. Certainly bluffing is a weak reason for going to trial.

Advocates of settlement arrive at their positions from divergent points of view. Some dislike the adversarial combat of trial and see negotiated settlements as superior alternatives. Others admit the importance of trial as a forum of last resort, but argue that relatively few cases require (or deserve) going to that extreme. The reasons advanced below on behalf of settlement do not belong to any one school of thought.

In general, settlement offers the following potential advantages:

1. Avoids the delays associated with trial (whether the delay is occasioned by crowded court dockets or by trial tactics employed by one or both parties);

2. Avoids the economic costs of trial (attorneys fees in preparation for and conduct of the trial, court fees, additional discovery and expert witness fees, time lost by parties and non-expert witnesses in preparing for and attending trial, etc.);

3. Avoids social and psychological costs of trial (embarrassment to parties, further damage to the relationship between the parties, anxiety and stress over the spectacle of a public trial);

4. Avoids the uncertainty or unpredictability of trial outcomes, and allows the disputing parties to determine how their disagreement should be resolved;

5. Avoids the "winner-take-all" nature of most adjudicative procedures, providing the litigants with the opportunity to fashion a package in the best interests of both parties;

6. Reduces the pressure on trial courts, allowing more considerate treatment of cases that require adjudicative resolution;

7. Increases the number of cases attorneys can process;

8. Protects one or both sides from the risk of unfavorable interpretations of law and prejudicial admissions or findings of fact.

When deciding whether to attempt the settlement of cases, these factors should be explicitly reviewed with clients, so that the potential advantages of settlement can be explored and sound decisions made.

However, there are situations in which the presumption is against settlement. Certainly a case should be taken to trial when it is in the client's interest to do so and there are no compelling reasons not to. Cases occasionally involve critical legal issues the parties wish to have finally resolved by definitive judicial determinations.[9] The difficulty is knowing when adjudication is in the client's best interest. For example, attorneys have personal interests at stake too, particularly if they have a low volume of work and are dependent upon a small number of clients for their income. The temptation to pursue a case to trial for its fee creates a strong (if subtle) incentive to prolong the case. To continue a case (consciously or subconsciously) for the fees it generates is clearly improper. On the other hand, claimant attorneys who are generally employed on a contingent fee basis may encourage clients to settle cases quickly so they can handle and receive fees for more cases.

In general, there is a presumption in favor of trying cases under the following circumstances:

1. Where the suit against your client is a frivolous suit, brought only for its nuisance value;

---

9. See Owen Fiss, *Against Settlement*, 93 Yale L.J. 1073 (1984).

2. Where your client is seeking new developments or clarifications in the law and prefers the potential gain of trial and appeal to whatever settlement might be negotiated;

3. Where your client feels vindictive and the vindictiveness cannot be satisfied without letting the client have her "day in court";

4. Where the issue of liability or damages is so uncertain or difficult to evaluate that you want to shift the burden of evaluation to a judge or jury;

5. Where the opposing attorney is insufferably obnoxious and abusive, making meaningful dialogue impossible;

6. Where the other side is unwilling to compromise to an acceptable solution.

Items 3 through 6 involve factors the attorney has some power to control. For example, vindictive clients might receive more benefit from several hours of attorney time spent in counseling them than from one hundred hours invested in trials. In later chapters, we will devote considerable attention to these problems and suggest methods for dealing with them within the framework of negotiated solutions.

CHAPTER NOTES

1. *Alternatives to Settlement and Trial*

Discussion of negotiation and litigation as modes of dispute settlement is not meant to imply that all disputes cognizable in the legal system are resolved by these methods. Considering the numerous offenses to person and/or property that occur daily, only a tiny fraction develop into legal disputes. The process by which a comparatively few of these ripen into full-scale legal disputes is explored in Felstiner, Abel & Sarat, *The Emergence & Transformation of Disputes: Naming, Blaming, Claiming . . .* , 15 Law & Society Rev. 531 (1980–81). Of those offenses that do occur, most are ignored; the injured or offended party absorbs the loss, or the offender volunteers some compensatory assistance. If the offended party seeks some redress, it may come in many forms, from a simple request for an apology to some act of retribution. Methods most frequently cited include self-help, avoidance, mediation, voting, arbitration, and various types of non-governmental courts (religious courts, neighborhood courts, private organizations). *See* Alvin Goldman, *Processes for Conflict Resolution: Self–Help, Voting, Negotiation, and Arbitration* (BNA Labor Relations and Social Problems Series, 1972); William F. L. Felstiner, *Influences of Social Organization on Dispute Processing*, 9 Law & Society Rev. 63 (1974) and *Avoidance as Dispute Processing: An Elaboration*, 9 Law and Society Rev. 695 (1975). It is not only the offended who are troubled by these daily kinds of problems; many people who cause harm to persons or property feel a moral obligation to correct the wrong. This aspect of dispute resolution is explored by Stewart Macaulay & Elaine Walster in *Legal Structures and Restoring Equity* in

Law, Justice and The Individual in Society (June Lovin Tapp & Felice J. Levine, eds.) (New York: Holt, Rinehart and Winston 1977).

2. *Costs of Litigation and Problems of Court Congestion and Delay*

Trial expenses are not the only costs. The theory of trial is that one party is right and one is wrong. To obtain a favorable verdict, it isn't necessary for one party to be absolutely right; it is sufficient to be slightly right—to have a mere preponderance of the evidence in that party's favor. Preponderance means slightly more than a draw. But when one party or the other establishes its position by a preponderance of the evidence, the verdict goes entirely for her. Of course, there are mitigating doctrines like contributory negligence, comparative negligence, and various contract doctrines that may limit remedies to less than full damages. But the theory of remedies is that the person receiving the favorable verdict deserves her remedy; it is a theory of granting a whole remedy, or nothing at all. The idea of an all-or-nothing verdict (even when mitigated by various legal rules and by discretion of judge or jury) ignores what we know of human nature: rarely in human affairs is one person absolutely blameless and the other entirely at fault. An all-or-nothing verdict gives the more blameworthy party an opportunity to gamble. By going to trial, he may avoid entirely the consequences of his conduct, but at the risk of being held entirely accountable for the wrong. This reality has led some commentators to propose that the concept of equality would be better served in cases of uncertainty by a different approach, such as fifty-fifty apportionments of responsibility in cases where there is genuine doubt. See J. Coons, *Approaches to Court Imposed Compromise—The Uses of Doubt and Reason*, 58 Nw. U.L.Rev. 750 (1964) and J. Coons, *Compromise as Precise Justice* in *Compromise in Ethics, Law, and Politics* (J. Roland Pennock and John W. Chapman, eds.) (New York Univ. 1979).

The intensity of emotion and ill-will generated by litigation is frequently overlooked, particularly with respect to its effect upon the opposing attorneys. The level to which feelings rise was suggested in a report by co-counsel to the plaintiff in the Century City experimental mini-trial. He observed that: "Once an interparty decision has been made to pursue a mini-trial, *the transition is not easy from the contentiousness of pretrial discovery to a cooperative posture.*" He refers to hostility between the attorneys on each side, and notes that even within the protective confines of the non-binding mini-trial, if expressions of adversity should exceed the critical limit, "the rapport for settlement will be destroyed and the slugfest of full-scale litigation will resume." Byard B. Nilsson, *A Litigation Settling Experiment*, 65 A.B.A. J. 1818, 1819–20 (1979) (italics added).

11

Chapter Two

THE NEGOTIATING PATTERNS OF PRACTICING LAWYERS

INTRODUCTION

This chapter reports the results of two large-scale studies of the negotiating patterns of practicing attorneys. The objective throughout the chapter is very practical: to describe how lawyers actually negotiate, and to explore the impact of negotiator styles on bargaining interactions.

EMPIRICAL STUDY FINDINGS
1976 STUDY BY PROFESSOR WILLIAMS

I. DESCRIPTION OF THE LEGAL NEGOTIATION RESEARCH PROJECT[1]

The results of empirical research are no better than the methods used to collect them. For this reason, a brief outline of our research methods is presented in this chapter, followed by a discussion of the lawyer negotiating behavior described by the study. For those who are interested, a more detailed explanation of the research methodology is provided in Appendix I.

Four basic research methods were used. The first was the survey questionnaire, a standard feature of social science. It was prepared, and sent with a cover letter by the president of the pertinent bar association, to approximately two thousand attorneys practicing in Denver, Colorado and Phoenix, Arizona. Conducting research in two cities allowed us to test for significant differences in attorney perceptions or behavior between two metropolitan areas.

---

1. For a report of the research leading to the project proposal, see Gerald R. Williams, J. Lynn England, Larry C. Farmer, and Murray Blumenthal, *Effectiveness in* *Legal Negotiation* in Harry T. Edwards and James J. White, *The Lawyer as Negotiator* (West, 1977) (Hereinafter Williams et al. 1977).

After compiling the results of the mailed questionnaire, we returned to Denver, Colorado and conducted one-hour interviews with 45 attorneys. These were tape recorded and subsequently transcribed for analysis. The purpose of these interviews was to build on the base of data accumulated by the questionnaires.

We next used an original technique developed to investigate the dynamics of negotiation over time as viewed by both sides to the negotiation. Up to this point in the project, our data consisted only of reports by attorneys on characteristics of other attorney-negotiators and the negotiation process among attorneys. The next step was to learn how attorneys actually carried out the negotiation or litigation of particular cases. This information needed to come from attorneys on both sides of each case, so the perceptions, expectations, and actions of the opposing attorneys could be compared. Therefore, we asked attorneys on both sides of selected cases to maintain an oral, tape-recorded account of their actions as they moved step by step through the cases. With the approval of the Ethics Committee of the Bar Association, we tested the technique using four attorneys from our advisory committee. They each selected a case that was scheduled to go to trial within the next three months, obtained the client's permission and gave us the name of opposing counsel (so we could contact him and ask him to keep a similar record of his dealings with the case). Using tape recorders we provided, the attorneys then dictated an account of each significant step taken in handling the case (e.g., exchange of letters or telephone calls with opposing counsel, discovery, meeting with the client, legal research, pretrial procedures, etc.).[2]

After the research project was completed, it became apparent that we had overlooked a major source of information and understanding: videotaped recordings of experienced attorneys engaging in negotiations. To meet this need, we prepared a total of seven cases (personal injury, breach of contract, products liability, divorce, criminal law, land-tenant, and business transactions) for negotiation by experienced lawyers.

Fourteen attorneys from across the United States agreed to participate. They were given ten days to prepare their cases and were then brought together in pairs to conduct their negotiations on videotape. The attorneys received no coaching on how to proceed; they were simply asked to negotiate the cases exactly as they would do in a real situation. These seven videotaped negotiating sessions add a crucial visual dimension to the data received through the other research techniques by illustrating what those data mean in behavioral terms.

As we began our research, the questions foremost in our minds were these: What are the characteristics of effective legal negotiators? Are

---

2. To maintain confidentiality and prevent improper transfer of information between the two sides of each case by the researchers, the actual names of the clients were kept out of the record, and attorneys kept the records until both sides were satisfied that the case had been terminated to their satisfaction. Only then was the information made available to the researchers.

there identifiable patterns to their negotiating behavior? What strategies do lawyers most commonly use? What objectives do lawyers have in mind when they negotiate? What attitudes do they display? What combinations of traits are found in the most effective (and most ineffective) negotiators? What are their strong points, and what are their weak points?

The first phase of our research project was designed to answer these questions. The results are among the most dramatic and useful of the entire project.

In the Phoenix version of the survey questionnaire, which was conducted in 1976 and is reported here, attorneys were asked to think of their most recently completed case or transaction, to briefly describe the matter, to think of the attorney representing the other party in the matter, and to describe that attorney according to 137 characteristics listed in the questionnaire. When they had completed the descriptive ratings, they were asked to rate the negotiating effectiveness of the attorney they had described. This rating scale was divided into three categories: ineffective, average and effective.

The results were compiled and analyzed according to standard statistical routines, including the standard R-factor analysis, Q-factor analysis, multiple regression analysis, and discriminate analysis. The results reported here were obtained by means of the Q-factor analysis.[3]

II. HOW LAWYERS NEGOTIATE: LESSONS FROM ATTORNEYS

The Q-factor analysis was used to look for stable patterns in the negotiating behavior of attorneys. The results indicate that legal negotiations proceed quite consistently within the parameters of two basic approaches. Both approaches are described in considerable detail by the analysis, providing powerful insights into the nature of bargaining interactions generally and the behavior of individual negotiators in particular. The pattern identified in a majority of the negotiators (65%) is best described as a *cooperative* approach to negotiation, while the second pattern (identified in 24% of attorneys) represents a *competitive* approach. These labels, *cooperative* and *competitive,* will be used to refer generally to attorneys of each type. Toward the end of the discussion it will become apparent that these labels are somewhat imprecise and that finer distinctions can be made. Knowledge of these two basic patterns

3. Steven R. Brown, *Political Subjectivity: Applications of Q Methodology in Political Science* (New Haven & London: Yale University Press 1980). Q-factor analysis is an exceptionally impartial method of analysis, because it avoids biases the researchers might have about what patterns will be found to exist. There is no attempt to tell the computer what kind of patterns to find, or to give special emphasis to one set of characteristics or another. The program merely looks for any identifiable patterns in the descriptions of attorneys. It ignores the pet theories and preferences of the researchers in favor of a more free form of analysis.

provides a powerful tool for analyzing and understanding how individuals operate in negotiation situations.

The strength of the two styles was so pervasive that only 11% of the attorneys failed to identify with one or the other. The analysis failed to identify any consistent pattern in the characteristics of this latter (11%) group of attorneys, suggesting that they do not represent a third pattern of negotiation. A complete listing of results of the Q-factor analysis is given in Appendix II, while the most important findings are described in the text and tables below.

The distribution of attorneys among all categories is shown in Diagram 2–1. As indicated in the Diagram, neither style has an exclusive claim on effectiveness. Use of the cooperative style does not guarantee effectiveness, any more than does the use of the competitive approach. An attorney can be very effective or very ineffective within the constraints of either. Nonetheless, the higher proportion of cooperative attorneys who were rated effective (58.5%) does suggest it is more difficult to be an effective competitive negotiator (25%) than an effective cooperative.

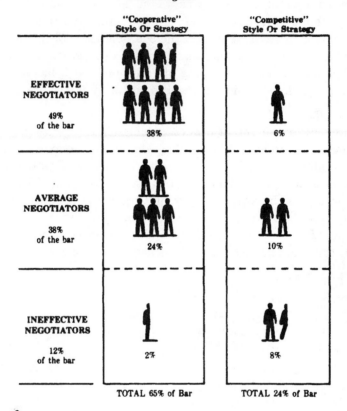

Diagram 2-1
Percentage of Each
Negotiator Type Among the
Practicing Bar

	"Cooperative" Style Or Strategy	"Competitive" Style Or Strategy
EFFECTIVE NEGOTIATORS 49% of the bar	38%	6%
AVERAGE NEGOTIATORS 38% of the bar	24%	10%
INEFFECTIVE NEGOTIATORS 12% of the bar	2%	8%
	TOTAL 65% of Bar	TOTAL 24% of Bar

 = Approximately 5% of the Bar

Note: Eleven percent of the rated attorneys did not fall within either of these two catagories.

Note: The silhouette figures are male because less than 3% of the sample was female. This percentage is too low to provide reliable statistics on distribution of women among these categories. None of the females in the sample were rated as ineffective, however.

Persons concerned about lawyer competency will be interested to observe that in our random sample of attorneys, 49% were rated as effective negotiators, 38% were rated as average negotiators, and 12% were rated ineffective.

The value of these findings comes in learning the major components of each style. What are the characteristics of the effective negotiators of each type? What do they do that differentiates them from the average and ineffective negotiators? How are the effective styles different from each other, and how are they similar?

16

To answer these questions we selected the most strongly-rated descriptors of each group and sorted them into logical clusters to make their meaning more apparent. The following analysis demonstrates this method. For more detailed information about the data, see Appendix II.

A. CHARACTERISTICS OF EFFECTIVE NEGOTIATORS

1. Effective/Cooperative Negotiators

The highest-rated characteristics of effective/cooperative negotiators fall into six informal clusters. The first cluster describes, in order of importance, their motivational objectives:

CLUSTER ONE

Conducting Self Ethically

Maximizing Settlement for Client

Getting a Fair Settlement

Meeting Client's Needs

Avoiding Litigation

Maintaining or Establishing a Good Personal Relationship with Opponent

It is surprising to find the predominant concern is with *ethical conduct.* This theme recurs among cooperative negotiators at all levels of effectiveness. The second concern is with *maximizing settlement for the client,* but this must be interpreted in light of item number 3, concern for *getting a fair settlement.* Attorneys of this type feel constrained in their conduct by a standard of fairness and ethical dealing. They want to know their clients' needs and, if possible, meet those needs through ethical behavior and without the necessity of litigation. They are also concerned with maintaining good personal relationships with opposing attorneys.

Their strategy for meeting these goals is straightforward, as reflected in the following descriptors:

CLUSTER TWO

Accurately Estimated the Value of the Case

Knew the Needs of the Client

Took a Realistic Opening Position

Probed Opponent's Position

Knew the Needs of Opponent's Client

Willing to Share Information

Forthright

Trustful

Willing to Move from Original Position

Objective

Fair–Minded

Reasonable

Logical (Not Emotional)

Did Not Use Threats

CLUSTER THREE

Courteous

Personable

Friendly

Tactful

Sincere

CLUSTER FOUR

Organizing

Wise

Careful

Facilitating

Cooperative

The third cluster relates to personableness: effective/cooperative negotiators are seen as friendly, personable, courteous, and tactful. However, some degree of caution is called for in interpreting these words. A person unfamiliar with legal negotiation is likely to picture a "soft" negotiator who is, as a consequence of personableness, a pushover. This cannot be a correct interpretation, because the adjectives describe *effective* negotiators at work in the legal context. A richer sense of meaning will develop as additional adjective clusters are considered.

Effective/cooperative attorneys are also seen as fair, objective, reasonable, logical, and willing to move from their established positions. Interpretation of these adjectives is aided by the other Cluster Two descriptors, which indicate these attorneys establish realistic opening positions, support their positions with facts, and are forthright.

While these traits are quite general, there are a number of descriptors that specifically relate to negotiating situations. For example, effective/cooperatives seek to facilitate agreement, they avoid the use of threats, they accurately estimate the value of cases they are working on, they are sensitive to the needs of their clients, and they are willing to share information with their opponents. It appears from these items that their strategy is to approach negotiations in an objective, fair, trustworthy way, and to seek agreements by the open exchange of information.

They are apparently as concerned with getting settlements that are fair to both sides as they are with maximizing the outcomes for their own clients.

The attitude of effective/cooperatives is reflected in attorney comments. For example, one attorney wrote: "The vital item in negotiation for me is trust in the other attorney. If an attorney has a good reputation and/or I have dealt with him before and found him honest, I can and will negotiate pragmatic settlements, hopefully to the long term benefit of both parties." In a similar vein, another attorney said, in speaking of his relationship with opposing counsel, "our relationship was constructive ... we both tried to reach a fair settlement, which we did without trial." Finally, an attorney described his opponent (an effective/cooperative) in these words: "The attorney I negotiated with is highly ethical and [is] respected as a trial attorney. He has considerable experience as a prosecutor as well as for the defense."

2. Effective/Competitive Negotiators

The differences in approach between cooperative and competitive attorneys is most quickly illustrated by comparing motivational objectives. In order of their importance, effective/competitives have as their goals:

CLUSTER ONE

Maximizing Settlement for Client

Obtaining Profitable Fee for Self

Outdoing or Outmaneuvering the Opponent

Obviously, the goal of getting a maximum settlement value for the client means something different to a competitor than to a cooperator. To competitors, the goal includes a reward to self both in monetary terms and in satisfaction from outdoing opponents. The difference in view between these two types becomes more apparent from examining other competitor traits. They are seen as:

CLUSTER TWO

Tough

Dominant

Forceful

Aggressive

Attacking

CLUSTER THREE

Ambitious

Egotist

Arrogant

19

Clever

CLUSTER FOUR

Made a High Opening Demand

Took Unrealistic Opening Position

Used Take-It-or-Leave-It Approach

Rigid

Disinterested in Needs of Opponent's Client

Did not Consider Opponent's Needs

Unconcerned about How Opponent Would Look to His Client

Willing to Stretch the Facts

Knew the Needs of Own Client

Careful about Timing and Sequence of Actions

Revealed Information Gradually

Used Threats

Obstructed

Uncooperative

In contrast to the friendly, trustworthy approach of effective/cooperatives, effective/competitives are seen as dominating, competitive, forceful, tough, arrogant, and uncooperative. They make high opening demands, they use threats, they are willing to stretch the facts in favor of their clients' positions, they stick to their positions, and they are parsimonious with information about their cases. They are concerned not only with maximizing the outcomes for their own clients, but also appear to take a gamesmanship approach to negotiation seeking to outdo or outmaneuver their opponents. Thus, rather than seeking outcomes that are "fair" to both sides, they want to outdo their opponents and to score clear victories.

Fees are obviously important to this type of negotiator. Obtaining profitable fees is rated as the second highest priority on their agenda, a priority that can lead to conflicts. One attorney, describing an effective/competitive opponent, said the case would have settled if the other attorney had approached the matter "from a realistic standpoint, i.e., the welfare of the children and future relationships of the parties (the divorcing parents) instead of being primarily interested in increasing his fee."

Effective/competitives are careful about the timing and sequence of their actions, which underscores the gamesmanship element of competitive negotiating behavior. This reflects a high level of interest in tactical or strategic considerations, suggesting that they orchestrate their cases for best effect. One effective/competitive attorney laughed when his cooperative opponent said the objective of negotiation was to achieve a just outcome. He said, "This is a poker game, and you do your best to put the best front on your case and you try to make the other fellow think that his weaknesses are bigger than he really ought to consider them." Another attorney reported that the insurance defense attorney opposing him "could have appraised the case more on injury to the plaintiff rather than on difficulty of plaintiff in putting on a good case at trial." These comments show the unbridgeable gap in perceptions and attitudes between cooperative and competitive attorneys. Cooperatives feel that cases should be evaluated objectively, on their merits, and that both sides should seek to find fair outcomes. Competitive attorneys view their work as a game in which they seek to outwit and out-perform the other side. The tension between these two styles raises major ethical, moral, and public policy questions, many of which will be dealt with later in this book.

This description of effective/competitives makes them sound somewhat Machiavellian, in the "gunslinger" image of lawyers, just as the description of effective/cooperatives makes them sound surprisingly "soft". However, the descriptions in both instances are incomplete, because they describe only the extreme differences between the two patterns without including the similarities. As indicated below, the additional information creates a more balanced picture of both types.

3. Similarities Between the Two Effective Types

While there are clear differences in approach between effective/cooperatives and effective/competitors, both negotiation styles are rated as highly effective. Our interest is in what makes such seemingly different negotiators effective—what traits do they have in common. Common traits are particularly important, since law students and attorneys can seek to understand and emulate them regardless of which approach they prefer to follow.

COMPARISON ONE: THE ADJECTIVE CHECKLIST

	Effective/ Cooperative Rankings	Effective/ Competitive Rankings
Experienced	(1)	(2)
Realistic	(2)	(10)
Ethical	(3)	(15)
Rational	(4)	(4)
Perceptive	(5)	(3)
Trustworthy	(6)	(20)
Convincing	(7)	(1)
Analytical	(8)	(5)
Creative	(10)	(6)
Self–Controlled	(11)	(12)
Versatile	(12)	(18)
Adaptable	(14)	(17)
Poised	(17)	(14)
Legally Astute	(20)	(16)

COMPARISON TWO: THE BIPOLAR SCALES

	Effective/ Cooperative Rankings	Effective/ Competitive Rankings
Honest	(1)	(11)
Adhered to Customs and Courtesies of the Bar	(2)	(14)
Intelligent	(3)	(4)
Thoroughly Prepared on the Facts of the Case	(12)	(7)
Thoroughly Prepared on the Law of the Case	(18)	(15)
Effective Trial Attorney	(22)	(3)
Skillful in Reading Opponent's Cues	(23)	(18)
Active	(24)	(8)

COMPARISON THREE: OBJECTIVES

	Effective/ Cooperative Rankings	Effective/ Competitive Rankings
Conducting Himself Ethically	(1)	(4)
Maximizing Settlement for Client	(2)	(1)
Satisfaction in Exercise of Legal Skills	(5)	(5)

These descriptors apply to effective negotiators regardless of which style they employ. They reliably describe the characteristics of effective legal negotiators. Assuming that we all wish to improve our effectiveness as negotiators, it is important to learn the meaning of these terms.

Both types of effective negotiators are ranked as highly experienced. This comes as no surprise, since we normally assume that negotiating effectiveness improves with experience. Its meaning here is illuminated by the comment of a responding attorney, who wrote: "it is important to have enough experience in order that you have confidence in yourself and be able to convey that confidence." This statement reflects the fact that more confident negotiators tend to induce less confident negotiators to reconsider their positions in favor of the positions being articulated by the more certain participants.

More importantly, both types are seen as ethical, trustworthy and honest, dispelling any doubt about the ethical commitments of effective/competitives. However, the priority of these traits is ranked much higher for cooperatives (3rd, 6th and 1st in priority) than for competitives (15th, 20th and 11th in priority). Given the current interest and concern about professional responsibility in the Bar, the high ratings on ethical and trustworthy behavior for both effective groups are significant. Although literature on professional responsibility generally argues that high ethical standards are a precondition to success in practice, many law students and some practicing attorneys continue to believe or suspect that they must compromise their ethical standards to effectively represent their clients and attain success in practice. The findings of this survey suggest such compromises are not only unnecessary, but actually counterproductive to one's effectiveness in negotiation situations.

In the same vein, we see that both types are careful to observe the customs and courtesies of the bar. While some attorneys have argued that there are tactical advantages in deliberately departing from the etiquette of the profession, as a general rule effective negotiators conduct themselves professionally. The Model Code of Professional Responsibility indicates lawyers have an ethical duty to "follow local customs of courtesy or practice" unless they give timely notice to opposing counsel of their intention not to do so (EC 7–38). Although the more-recently drafted Model Rules do not include a similar provision, Comment 1 to Rule 1.3, which states that "a lawyer shall act with reasonable diligence ... in representing a client", indicates that: "The lawyer's duty to act with reasonable diligence does not require the use of offensive tactics or preclude the treating of all persons involved in the legal process with courtesy and respect."

Although effective/competitives were seen as taking unrealistic opening positions, in general they share with effective/cooperatives the traits of being realistic, rational, and analytical. These three attributes become very important in interpreting negotiator behavior. They mean more than the idea of "thinking like a lawyer"; they impose limits on how far a negotiator may credibly go in such things as interpretation of facts, claims about damages and other economic demands, and levels of emotional involvement in the case.

Both effective types are seen as thoroughly prepared on the facts and the law of the case. They are also described as legally astute. This, again, is something to be expected. But it bears emphasis because, as we shall see, ineffective negotiators lack these qualities. One attorney had these traits in mind when he wrote, "In my experience, the most important part of negotiation is thorough preparation and a complete knowledge of the strengths and weaknesses of your position.... I feel individual personality traits (e.g. loud, forceful, quiet, reserved) are unimportant."

Legal astuteness means they have not only done their homework by informing themselves about the legal and procedural ramifications of the case, but they also have acquired good judgment about how and when to act with respect to this information.

Both types of effective attorneys are rated as creative, versatile, and adaptable. This is true even though effective/competitives are also labeled rigid. Apparently there is a distinction between being tough (which competitive attorneys are) and being obstinate. Attorneys should not be so rigid that they are unable to seek creative solutions to problems. The flavor of the terms is suggested in a comment by an attorney representing a party who was involved in a very acrimonious dispute with a neighbor over an irrigation ditch. He wrote, "Our problem was solved by a simple relocation agreement executed by the parties and recorded. The opposition attorney and myself, after great study and much effort, came up with the simple solution of simply relocating the ditch."

Both types are self-controlled. This is not a phrase all will immediately consider an attribute of effectiveness, but they will appreciate its meaning and importance after we consider the characteristics of ineffective negotiators.

One of the more important marks of effective negotiators is skill in reading opponent cues. This refers not only to the ability to judge opponent reactions in negotiating situations, but also to affirmatively learn from opponents. The old saying is that experience is the best teacher. Experience is only a good teacher for those who are skillful at learning from it. In the course of interviews connected with Denver attorneys, they were routinely asked what they did when they were faced with an inexperienced opponent—an opponent fresh out of law school. Their responses were very informative. One group of attorneys would get sly grins on their faces, their eyes would light up, and they would say "I hammer them into the ground". By far the larger number of attorneys responded quite differently, however. They said that when they had "green" opponents, they slowed the cases down, tried to spell everything out as they went along, and tried generally to show the younger attorneys the right way to go about handling cases.

Consider this problem from the perspective of law graduates recently admitted to the bar. During the first few months of practice, they encounter some attorneys who hammer them into the ground, taking advantage of them at every turn, and others who try to teach them how to be good lawyers. The experience is not calculated to engender trust in fellow officers of the court. Rather, the tendency in young lawyers is to develop a mild paranoia and to distrust everyone. This is unfortunate, because *some* opponents are providing valuable information, albeit in subtle ways. The key is to learn to observe and "read" opposing attorneys and know who can be trusted and who cannot and learn from both types without being misled by persons seeking to exploit their inexperience.

Effective/competitives and effective/cooperatives are rated as perceptive, a term that goes hand in hand with skill in reading cues. It relates in part to the ability to perceive opponents' strategies and their subjective reactions to your strategies. It also has a larger connotation, referring to the accuracy of one's perception of the whole case. One attorney in our study gave a telling description of his perception of a recently completed case: "I lost the case. Though my opponent was ineffective in preparation and presentation—and was a drunk—the judge *disbelieved* my key witness, a fundamentalist Minister, and the plaintiff got every cent he had wrongly demanded from my client."

Finally, it must be stressed that both types of effective negotiators are also rated as effective trial attorneys. As mentioned earlier, the alternative to settlement is trial. If attorneys are known as weak trial lawyers, it will often be more profitable for their opponents to take them to trial than agree to reasonable settlements. This creates an awkward and troublesome dynamic, because the weak trial attorneys know that their clients would be poorly served by inept trials of their cases. The weak attorneys often feel compelled to discount their cases as an inducement to opponents to settle and avoid the costs (and benefits) of trial. The interplay between fear of trial and discounting of cases is not healthy. There appears to be only one solution: to be taken seriously, lawyers who negotiate legal disputes (as opposed to non-actionable matters) must either develop substantial expertise as trial attorneys, or openly associate themselves (whether by partnership, a referral system, or some other way) with effective trial counsel.

B. CHARACTERISTICS OF AVERAGE NEGOTIATORS

As we move down the effectiveness scale from the "effective" to the "average" negotiator level, we find that differences between the two negotiating styles are much more pronounced. They differ from each other with respect to 13 of the 20 adjectives, 25 of the 26 bipolar pairs, and all but 2 of the motivational objectives.

1. Average/Cooperative Negotiators

Selected characteristics from the adjective checklist that distinguish average/cooperative negotiators from their average/competitive counterparts include the following:

SELECTED CHARACTERISTICS: AVERAGE/COOPERATIVES

Realistic

Self–Controlled

Careful

Discrete

Objective

Analytical

Fair

Loyal

Perceptive

Helpful

Deliberate

Experienced

Organizing

Average/cooperative attorneys possess many of the characteristics of effective/cooperative attorneys, such as trustworthy, experienced, ethical, and realistic, and their high ratings with respect to these factors raise the question of why they were seen as only average negotiators. Part of the answer may lie in their lower ratings on such characteristics as analytical, perceptive, convincing, and legally astute. In addition, they are noted for their caution, discretion, sociability, and obliging behavior, some of which may have a dampening effect on their effectiveness.

In describing an average/cooperative opponent, one attorney wrote, "The lawyer is a sincere, honest member of the bar with 15 years of practice; but [has only] moderate legal and intellectual ability."

2. Average Competitive/Negotiators

In contrast, the average/competitive negotiator has the following characteristics:

SELECTED CHARACTERISTICS: AVERAGE/COMPETITIVES
Argumentative

Ambitious

Demanding

Bluffer

Egotist

Evasive

Suspicious

Greedy

Headstrong

Impatient

Complaining

Quarrelsome

Unpredictable

Average/competitive attorneys show a dramatic shift in the quality of the characteristics noted, since all the adjectives describing them have predominantly negative connotations: bluffer, demanding, headstrong, argumentative, and irritating. Interestingly, the behavior connoted by these adjectives is associated with public interest advocacy and persons supporting particular "causes." The fact that these adjectives occur for the first time in the average groupings should not be taken as a demonstration of their effectiveness or ineffectiveness as negotiation styles, since one's approach may vary according to the demands of particular situations. It is probable, for example, that strong and even irritating tactics may be highly effective when selectively used. However, the preponderance of these characteristics in the average and ineffective range of competitive attorneys suggests that as a matter of routine style or approach, they seriously detract from one's effectiveness.

In trying to understand the personality of average/competitive negotiators, it may be seen that greed, ambition, and egotism are associated with their style. None of these selfish or self-centered characteristics are seen as characterizing either of the effective groups, but rather were seen as decidedly *uncharacteristic* of effective attorneys.

One attorney described his average/competitive opponent in this way: "Obviously, this was an unpleasant and poor attorney, and I should say that he is in a minority; he just happened to be [my most recent opponent] ... and unfortunately, there are still too many [like him]."

3. Similarities Between the Two Average Types

Of the 20 highest characteristics from the adjective checklist scales, only 7 are shared by both types. Since the most interesting comparisons come at the ineffective level, relatively little discussion will be given about average negotiators. The listing of characteristics, with their rank orderings, is sufficient.

	Average/ Cooperative Rankings	Average/ Competitive Rankings
Ethical	(1)	(7)
Trustworthy	(2)	(19)
Rational	(3)	(20)
Personable	(4)	(15)
Cautious	(5)	(12)
Sociable	(10)	(6)
Legally Astute	(12)	(9)

There are substantial differences in the strengths of these characteristics in the two average types, with average/cooperatives being rated as more ethical, trustworthy, rational, personable, and cautious, while average/competitives were ranked as more sociable and more legally astute.

C. CHARACTERISTICS OF INEFFECTIVE NEGOTIATORS

The two ineffective types are a study in contrasts. We did not see this degree of difference between cooperatives and competitives at the effective level because they had a crucial similarity: they were *effective negotiators*. At the bottom level, the two types do not share that critical trait. What we have, then, is a description of the extremes of both styles, with both approaches being ineffective, but in opposite ways. The ineffective extremes hold essential clues to the underlying dynamics of the cooperative and competitive strategies. Assuming that negotiators at the effective level have somehow discovered aspects of each strategy that are successful, we can assume that negotiators at the ineffective level either omit essential aspects of their respective strategies, or else they defeat their own strategies by going too far with them or otherwise negating their effectiveness.

1. Ineffective/Cooperative Negotiators

Ineffective/cooperatives are characterized by many socially desirable traits.

SELECTED CHARACTERISTICS: INEFFECTIVE/COOPERATIVES

Honest

Forthright

Trustful

Willing to Share Information

Courteous

Adhered to Customs and Courtesies to the Bar

Sincere

Friendly

Cooperative

Knew the Needs of his Client

Logical

Did not Use Threats

Facilitated

Tactful

Was Willing to Move from Original Position

Intelligent

Reasonable

Got to Know My Personality

Thoroughly Prepared on the Factual Elements

Flexible

Informal

Emotionally Detached

Probed My Position

Revealed Information Early

Modest

Accurately Estimated the Value of the Case

OBJECTIVES

Conducting Himself Ethically

Maximizing Settlement for His Client

Meeting His Client's Needs

Getting a Fair Settlement

Maintaining or Establishing a Good Personal Relationship with Opponent

Satisfaction in Exercise of Legal Skills

Ineffective/cooperatives do not have the skills or attitudes of effective/cooperatives, such as being perceptive, convincing, or having the reasonableness cluster (realistic, rational, and analytical). Nor are they creative, self-controlled, versatile, objective, organizing, or legally astute. The ineffectives are apparently unsure of themselves or of the value of their cases (conservative, staller, cautious, deliberate). They are torn between being gentle, obliging, patient, moderate, and forgiving, on the one hand, and demanding, "masculine", and argumentative on the other, and tend to be idealistic. Their idealism may account for their lack of versatility, adaptability, creativity, and wisdom.

a. Similarities Between Effective and Ineffective Cooperative Negotiators

Effective and ineffective cooperatives share five important characteristics. They are both seen as ethical, trustworthy, fair, personable, and experienced.

Selected Comparisons

	Effective/ Cooperative Rankings	Ineffective/ Cooperative Rankings
Ethical	(3)	(1)
Personable	(13)	(3)
Fair	(9)	(4)
Trustworthy	(6)	(7)
Experienced	(1)	(14)

Since these traits are shared by effective/cooperatives and ineffective/cooperatives, their presence does not guarantee negotiation success. Rather, they should be interpreted as notable characteristics of the cooperative style of negotiation.

b. Differences Between Effective and Ineffective Cooperative Negotiators

It is helpful to compare the differences between effective/cooperatives and ineffective/ cooperatives:

SELECTED DIFFERENCES

Effective/ Cooperative Rankings		Ineffective/ Cooperative Rankings	
Realistic	(2)	Complaining	(2)
Rational	(4)	Gentle	(5)
Perceptive	(5)	Conservative	(6)
Convincing	(7)	Masculine	(8)
Analytical	(8)	Staller	(9)
Creative	(10)	Obliging	(10)
Self–Controlled	(11)	Demanding	(11)
Versatile	(12)	Cautious	(12)
Adaptable	(14)	Deliberate	(13)
Wise	(15)	Patient	(15)
Objective	(16)	Moderate	(16)
Poised	(17)	Forgiving	(17)
Careful	(18)	Argumentative	(18)
Organizing	(19)	Idealist	(19)
Legally Astute	(20)	Sociable	(20)

2. Ineffective/Competitive Negotiators

Ineffective/competitive attorneys are characterized by negative traits, and can be generally described as *irritating*. The strength of this irritating characteristic (2.80 on a 3.00 scale) compares with the strength of the outstanding characteristics of effective attorneys: trustworthy for effective/cooperatives (2.82), and experienced for effective/competitives (2.83).

Ineffective/competitives represent types of persons we have all met (perhaps trapped in low-level bureaucratic positions making life miserable for all around them) and have occasionally emulated. Like ineffective/cooperatives, they are complaining. They are also, in rank order:

CLUSTER ONE

Headstrong

Impatient

Intolerant

Rigid

Loud

CLUSTER TWO

Greedy

Demanding

Unreasonable

Uncooperative

Arrogant

Tactless

CLUSTER THREE

Complaining

Sarcastic

Insincere

CLUSTER FOUR

Devious

Conniving

Impulsive

Unpredictable

Evasive

CLUSTER FIVE

Suspicious

Distrustful

Unskillful in Reading My Cues

CLUSTER SIX

Unsure of Value of the Case

Took Unrealistic Opening Position

Made a High Opening Demand

Used Take–It-or-Leave–It Approach

Narrow Range of Bargaining Strategies

Bluffer

Unwilling to Share Information

Disinterested in Opponent's Position

Took One Position and Refused to Move From It

Used Threats

Emotional

Quarrelsome

Rude

Hostile

Obstructive

CLUSTER SEVEN

Ineffective Trial Attorney

CLUSTER EIGHT

Disinterested in the Needs of My Client

Did Not Consider My Needs

Disinterested in My Personality

Unconcerned About How Opponent Would Look in the Eyes of His Client

CLUSTER NINE

Maximizing Settlement for Client

Outdoing or Outmaneuvering You

Obtaining Profitable Fee for Self

Ineffective/competitives share only *one* trait with their effective/competitive counterparts: egotist. The problem of the ineffective/competitives is relatively easy to define: they are obnoxious. These negotiators rate extremely low on such professionally-mandated standards as ethical and trustworthy. They are also rated extremely low in rational, perceptive, realistic, and convincing.

The reason ineffective/competitive attorneys are seen as irritating may be explained in part by the nature of their other notable characteristics: they were seen as hostile, intolerant, argumentative, demanding, bluffing, headstrong, egotistical, and quarrelsome. Because these adjectives typify socially undesirable behavior, a question arises as to whether there may be other elements lacking from their behavior which account for their ineffectiveness. This question is brought into better focus by considering the ratings of the ineffective/cooperative attorneys. Unlike ineffective/competitives, they are seen as ethical, trustworthy, fair, personable, and self-controlled, which are traits they share in common with effective/cooperative attorneys. In addition, they are considered gentle, patient, obliging, adaptable, sociable, dignified, and forgiving. Since ineffective/cooperative attorneys appear to observe the social graces and yet are still seen as ineffective negotiators, it appears that it is not their regard or disregard of the social graces which determines an attorney's negotiating effectiveness.

In describing an ineffective/competitive, one lawyer wrote, "My experience with this attorney was not typical of most. Other negotiations have been open and candid with generally favorable or reasonable results." Reflecting on his negotiations with an ineffective/competitive, another attorney said, "In my opinion, ... negotiations break down or are fruitless and futile when the opposing attorney's attitude is arrogant, self-serving, unbending, and unrealistic." A similar view is reflected by the attorney who wrote, in describing his opponent, "In his initial evaluation of the merits, the inept negotiator sells himself on the virtues of his position, sets unrealistic objectives, and falls in love irreversibly with his position.''

The adjectives we have considered here suggest a possible hypothesis as to what makes ineffective/competitives ineffective. They lack such characteristics as perceptive, analytical, realistic, convincing, rational, experienced, and self-controlled, which both types of effective attorneys share in common. Indeed, it may be due to the positive effects of these attributes that effective/competitive attorneys are seen as ambitious, forceful, and dominant in their assertiveness rather than egotistical, argumentative, and bluffing. What is suggested here is that forceful persons who have low regard for social amenities may function effectively as legal negotiators *if* they can show themselves to be perceptive, analytical, realistic, and self-controlled. On the other hand, if the same forceful persons do not demonstrate the skills of perceptiveness, analytical ability, and realistic evaluation of their positions, yet try to maximize their positions by competitive tactics, they will be seen as argumentative, quarrelsome, and irritating, and as persons who, in lieu of skilled preparation, resort to bluffing, bullying, or evasive tactics in an effort to maximize their outcomes.

Somehow, effective/competitive legal negotiators are able to apply their expertise without being seen as greedy or conniving, but rather as reasonable and realistic. Again, these comparisons seem to point to the quality of the legal work being performed, including the expertise with which attorneys have investigated the facts of their cases, studied and understood the legal rules applicable to them, taken realistic positions with respect to case values, and presented their positions in ways that other attorneys accept as being rational, fair, and persuasive (convincing). It may follow that attorneys in this posture have little cause to be argumentative, quarrelsome, rude, and hostile, since they are prepared to effectively go forward on the merits of their positions rather than to seek advantage by being personally offensive to opposing attorneys, or by stalling, bluffing, or quarreling.

1999 STUDY BY PROFESSOR SCHNEIDER

ANDREA KUPFER SCHNEIDER, SHATTERING NEGOTIATION MYTHS: EMPIRICAL EVIDENCE ON THE EFFECTIVENESS OF NEGOTIATION STYLE

7 HARV. NEG. L. REV. 143, 146–48, 151, 160, 163–71, 176–79, 181–89 (2002)*

* * *

Articles advocating adversarial behavior confirm the latent fears of most young lawyers—what if I am too nice? While there are plenty of tales of lawyers being taken advantage of—they were too nice, they just wanted to get along, etc.—we do not have similar tales about the dangers of being unpleasant or combative. Few law students are afraid of being too adversarial. After all, society (and clients) seems to expect this behavior. Given the choice between being too soft and too hard, most lawyers would opt for being too hard. They might be unpleasant jerks, but at least they did "what they were supposed to do."

* * *

This article provides a current look at how lawyers actually negotiate and should serve to shatter the myth that adversarial bargaining is more effective and less risky than problem-solving. The data reported herein is based on a wide-ranging study that asked lawyers to evaluate the negotiation styles and the resulting effectiveness of other lawyers. First, the study shows that effective negotiators exhibit certain identifiable skills. For example, the research indicates that a negotiator who is assertive and empathetic is perceived as more effective. The study also reveals distinctive characteristics of ineffective negotiators, who are more likely to be stubborn, arrogant, and egotistical. Furthermore, when this adversarial negotiator is unethical, he is perceived as even less effective. Third, the study found that problem-solving behavior is perceived as highly effective. This information should help focus negotiation training toward the task of learning these new skills or modifying ineffective habits.

The first section of this article reviews the original Williams study examining negotiation styles conducted in 1976.[20] This is followed by an outline of relevant changes in the negotiation field since that time and the corresponding revisions made to the original study intended to reflect those changes.... The third section analyzes the substantive results of the survey employed.... The fourth section compares this study's results with those from Williams' 1976 study. The comparison indicates that adversarial attorneys have become more extreme and less effective in the last twenty-five years....

I. MEASURING NEGOTIATION EFFECTIVENESS

* * *

As the body of negotiation-related literature grows, we are beginning to experience label confusion. Williams divided the lawyers in his study into two groups—cooperative and competitive. Other negotiation literature has also referred to two different styles or techniques of negotiating, but it does not always use the same terminology. Carrie Menkel–Meadow divided behaviors into problem-solving and adversarial.[29] David Lax and

---

20. GERALD R. WILLIAMS, LEGAL NEGOTIATION AND SETTLEMENT 15–46 (1983).

29. Carrie Menkel–Meadow, *Toward Another View of Legal Negotiation: The Structure of Problem Solving*, 31 U.C.L.A. L. REV. 754 (1984).

James Sebenius categorized negotiation strategies as value-creating and value-claiming.[30] Roger Fisher outlined three types of behavior: the hard bargainer, the soft bargainer, and the preferred alternative of principled bargaining.[31] Donald Gifford also lists three types of behavior: competitive, cooperative and integrative.[32] In the new book *Beyond Winning*, the authors outline four types of behavior—accommodating, avoiding, competing, and problem-solving.[33] . . .

II. BACKGROUND AND POPULATION CHARACTERISTICS

A. Administration of the Survey

The survey was sent to 1,000 lawyers in Milwaukee and 1,500 lawyers in Chicago in January 1999. . . . 727 attorneys returned their surveys for an overall response rate of 29%, . . .

Of the 690 matters discussed in this article, 71% were potential or actual litigation disputes. The remaining 29% were transactional negotiations. The majority of the 490 disputes were resolved prior to a trial verdict. Sixty-six reached a mediated settlement (13.5%) and 291 reached a negotiated settlement (59.4%). Seven were decided on summary judgment (1.4%) and fifty-one were decided by trial verdict (10.4%). . . .

III. SUBSTANTIVE RESULTS OF THE NEW STUDY

A. Problem-Solving and Adversarial Styles of Negotiating

* * *

The survey results divided the assessed attorneys into two clusters of approximately 64% and 36%, which, given their respective characteristics, I have labeled problem-solving and adversarial.[58]

1. Adjective Ratings

The table below is a list of the 20 most frequently selected adjectives for each cluster.

30. DAVID A. LAX & JAMES K. SEBENIUS, THE MANAGER AS NEGOTIATOR: BARGAINING FOR COOPERATION AND COMPETITIVE GAIN (1986).

31. ROGER FISHER, WILLIAM URY & BRUCE PATTON, GETTING TO YES: NEGOTIATING AGREEMENT WITHOUT GIVING IN (2d ed. 1991).

32. Donald Gifford, *A Context–Based Theory of Strategy Selection*, 46 OHIO ST. L.J. 41, 43 (1985).

33. ROBERT MNOOKIN, SCOTT PEPPET & ANDREW TULUMELLO, BEYOND WINNING NEGOTIATING TO CREATE VALUE IN DEALS AND DISPUTES 50–68 (2000).

58. I changed the names of Williams' original labels of "competitive" and "cooperative" for two reasons. First, I believe that the label "cooperative" has come to imply a level of passivity that is not reflective of what Williams' study actually showed. Someone labeled "cooperative" is more likely to be associated with soft-bargaining (roll-over-and-play-dead) in common usage, a very different conception than what these adjectives actually describe. Second, "problem-solving" and "adversarial" are labels more in current use in the negotiation literature.

TOP 20 ADJECTIVES PER CLUSTER

	Problem–Solving Adjectives	Adversarial Adjectives
1.	Ethical	Stubborn
2.	Experienced	Headstrong
3.	Personable	Arrogant
4.	Rational	Assertive
5.	Trustworthy	Irritating
6.	Self–Controlled	Argumentative
7.	Confident	Egotistical
8.	Agreeable	Confident
9.	Realistic	Demanding
10.	Accommodating	Quarrelsome
11.	Sociable	Ambitious
12.	Fair–Minded	Experienced
13.	Dignified	Firm
14.	Communicative	Tough
15.	Perceptive	Forceful
16.	Adaptable	Suspicious
17.	Astute About the Law	Manipulative
18.	Poised	Hostile
19.	Careful	Masculine
20.	Helpful	Evasive

The problem-solving adjectives encompass several different elements of behavior. The problem-solving negotiator is upstanding (ethical and trustworthy), pleasant (personable, agreeable, sociable) and interested in the other side (fair-minded, communicative, perceptive, helpful). The problem-solver is also flexible (accommodating, adaptable) and prepared (experienced, rational, confident, realistic, astute, poised).

The adversarial adjectives stand in strong contrast. The adversarial negotiator is inflexible (stubborn, assertive, demanding, firm, tough, forceful) and self-centered (headstrong, arrogant, egotistical). This negotiator likes to fight (irritating, argumentative, quarrelsome, hostile) and the method of fighting is suspect (suspicious, manipulative, evasive). Only two adjectives appear completely positive—confident and experienced—and these are the only two adjectives also ascribed to problem-solving negotiators. Thus, two very different approaches to negotiation appear from the descriptors alone.

2. *Bipolar Ratings*

The bipolar rating scale can offer more insight into the particular negotiation strategies employed in each approach because the pairs are more descriptive of behavior. A list of the most frequently selected behaviors for each cluster appears below.

TOP BIPOLAR RATING PER CLUSTER

	Problem–Solving Bipolars	Adversarial Bipolars
1.	Did not Make Derogatory Personal References	Disinterested in My Client's Needs
2.	Interested in His Client's Needs	Extreme Opening Demand
3.	Courteous	Unrealistic Initial Position
4.	Did Not Use Offensive Tactics	Interested in His Client's Needs
5.	Honest	Arrogant
6.	Zealous Representation Within Bounds	Unconcerned How I Look
7.	Pursued Best Interests of Client	Rigid
8.	Intelligent	Aggressive
9.	Friendly	Had a Fixed Conception of the Problem
10.	Adhered to Legal Courtesies	Narrow View of Problem
11.	Reasonable	
12.	Tactful	
13.	Cooperative	
14.	Prepared	
15.	Forthright	
16.	Accurate Representation of Position	
17.	Sincere	
18.	Trustful	
19.	Facilitated	
20.	Did Not Use Threats	

At first glance, the problem-solving bipolars contain descriptions that fit our general expectations of what constitutes a good negotiator. An attorney should be assertive while remaining ethical and following the standards of the bar, intelligent, and prepared. Problem-solving negotiators also appear to understand their clients very well (interested in the needs of the client, actions were consistent with the best interests of the client, accurately represented client's position), are easy to work with as seen on the adjective ratings (courteous, friendly, tactful, cooperative), and are ethical (honest, forthright, trustful, sincere, represented client zealously and within the bounds of the law). We also see a description that highlights communication (facilitated the negotiation). Finally, a problem-solving negotiator does not make unfair representations, use haranguing or offensive tactics, make threats, or advance unwarranted claims.

The picture of the adversarial negotiator is also further clarified by these bipolar descriptions. Leading the descriptions of this negotiator is the impression that an adversarial negotiator is not concerned with the other side (not interested in my client's needs, and unconcerned how I would look in the eyes of my client). Second, there is evidence that this negotiator acts in a classic adversarial mode by being rigid, aggressive and starting off high (made extreme opening demand and took an unrealistic initial position). As indicated in the adjective ratings, this negotiator is also arrogant. Again, the survey responses point to clear differences in the approaches taken by lawyers in each cluster.

3. Goals

Negotiators' goals can give us additional insight into their respective approaches. This next table relates the goals most frequently attributed to the assessed attorneys in each cluster.

TOP GOALS PER CLUSTER

	Problem–Solving Goals	Adversarial Goals
1.	Ethical Conduct	Maximizing Settlement
2.	Maximizing Settlement	Outdoing You
3.	Fair Settlement	Profitable Fee
4.	Meet Both Sides' Interests	Meeting Client's Needs
5.	Meeting Client's Needs	
6.	Avoiding Litigation	
7.	Good Relations with you	

The first thing to note is that both types of negotiators want to serve their clients well. Maximizing the settlement for the client and seeing that the client's needs were met are goals for both groups of negotiators. The remaining goals highlight the difference in approaches. For problem-solving negotiators, the highest goal is conducting oneself ethically. This is consistent with findings in the other two scales, which both showed an emphasis on ethical behavior. The goal of obtaining a settlement that is both fair and that meets the underlying interests of both sides is exactly what one would expect from a problem-solving negotiator. The goal of good relations between the attorneys is consistent with the results of the other scales and also with negotiation literature highlighting how good relationships between the lawyers can serve the client. Avoiding litigation is also consistent with problem-solving behavior.

The second and third goals (outdoing the other side and obtaining a profitable fee) attributed to adversarial negotiators reveal quite a lot about these lawyers. Both are self-centered rather than client-centered and raise concern about the difference in interests between attorneys and the clients they ostensibly serve. If the negotiation becomes focused on ego or making money for the lawyer, one could legitimately wonder if the client's interest is being well served.

4. Effectiveness Ratings

The following comments both describe effective behavior, but very different styles:

"The attorney was realistic, had a good grasp of the law and of the practical (or in this case impractical) aspects of taking the case to litigation as opposed to negotiating a settlement. He was also firm and represented his client's position well, but was courteous and straightforward at all times, which created a productive basis for reaching settlement when the time came for negotiations."

"He was effective because he wore us down. He used all types of dirty tactics such as having various attorneys contact the state's Attorney, bringing in an attorney who was friendly with the judge, and filing numerous meritless motions."

The following table groups all lawyers by effectiveness and style, and is just as revealing.

NUMBER OF LAWYERS PER GROUP BY EFFECTIVENESS

	Ineffective	Average	Effective
Problem–Solving	14	166	213
Adversarial	120	84	21

Several items stand out from these results. Only 9% of those lawyers seen as adversarial were rated as effective by their peers and only 9% of all effective lawyers were described as adversarial. Furthermore, 90% of lawyers perceived as ineffective were also adversarial. In contrast, 91% of lawyers seen as effective took a problem-solving approach to negotiation. More than half of problem-solving lawyers were seen as effective and only 4% of these problem-solving lawyers were seen as ineffective. Contrary to the popular (student) view that problem-solving behavior is risky, it would seem instead that adversarial bargaining represents the greater risk. A lawyer is much more likely to be viewed as effective when engaging in problem-solving behavior.

B. *Judging the Effectiveness of Problem–Solving Behavior*

"He advocated for his client—kept coming back to the table—and proposing alternatives—was effective in making emotional appeal—got a good deal—was friendly and courteous—never took it personally."

"I felt the attorney was effective because she was assertive and aggressive in attempting to maximize the settlement for her client, but at the same time she was a good listener and kept an open mind regarding my proposals. She was willing to be accommodating while not forsaking her client's goal."

* * *

1. *Two Cluster Analysis*

The following charts show the most frequently selected adjectives, bipolar descriptions and goals for problem-solving bargainers, grouped according to their level of perceived effectiveness.

a) Adjective Ratings

TOP 20 PROBLEM–SOLVING ADJECTIVES

	Ineffective	Average	Effective
1.	Self–Controlled	Ethical	Ethical
2.	Ethical	Personable	Experienced
3.	Sociable	Experienced	Personable
4.	Personable	Self–Controlled	Rational
5.	Trustworthy	Agreeable	Trustworthy
6.	Experienced	Confident	Realistic
7.	Fair–Minded	Accommodating	Confident
8.	Dignified	Trustworthy	Perceptive
9.	Accommodating	Rational	Communicative
10.	Agreeable	Realistic	Fair–Minded
11.	Confident	Sociable	Dignified
12.	Discreet	Fair–Minded	Self–Controlled
13.	Moderate	Dignified	Accommodating
14.	Poised	Adaptable	Astute About the Law
15.	Communicative	Communicative	Agreeable
16.	Patient	Patient	Sociable
17.	Rational	Flexible	Adaptable
18.			Poised
19.			Careful
20.			Wise

There are several adjectives attributed to effective problem-solvers, but not to ineffective problem-solvers, which should give us some insight into what makes the difference. Four of these adjectives—realistic, astute, careful and wise—are traits of an experienced and prepared negotiator. None of these appear on the ineffective top twenty list, and only realistic appears for average negotiators. Two other adjectives—perceptive and adaptable—highlight important elements of problem-solving behavior. If one is going to come up with integrative solutions, understanding the other side and being flexible in how one meets the client's interests are crucial skills. Perceptive was not listed for either ineffective or average negotiators, and adaptable was not attributed to ineffective negotiators.

b) Bipolar Ratings

The bipolar descriptions attributed to each group of problem-solving negotiators continue to highlight their differences.

TOP PROBLEM–SOLVING BIPOLARS

	Ineffective	Average	Effective
1.	Did Not Make Derogatory Personal References	Did Not Make Derogatory Personal References	Interested in His Client's Needs
2.	Honesty	Interested in His Client's Needs	Did Not Make Derogatory Personal References

	Ineffective	Average	Effective
3.	Adhered to Legal Courtesies	Did Not Use Offensive Tactics	Honesty
4.	Courteous	Courteous	Courteous
5.	Friendly	Zealous Representation within Bounds	Intelligent
6.	Did not Use Offensive Tactics	Pursued Best Interests of Client	Did Not Use Offensive Tactics
7.	Zealous Representation within Bounds	Honesty	Pursued Best Interests of Client
8.	Accurate Representation of Position	Adhered to Legal Courtesies	Zealous Representation within Bounds
9.	Did not Use Threats	Friendly	Friendly
10.	Forthright	Intelligent	Tactful
11.	Interested in his Client's Needs	Reasonable	Reasonable
12.	Inaccurately Estimated Case	Cooperative	Adhered to Legal Courtesies
13.	Narrow Range	Forthright	Prepared
14.	Sincere	Tactful	Cooperative
15.			Forthright
16.			Sincere
17.			Trustful
18.			Accurately Represented Own Client's Position
19.			Facilitated
20.			Did Not Make Unwarranted Claims
21.			Viewed Negotiation as Possibly Having Mutual Benefits

.... As with the adjectives, the effective negotiator was perceived as better handling the case in terms of intelligence, acting in their client's best interests, and preparation. He was also described as cooperative, facilitating the negotiation and viewing the negotiation as a mutually beneficial process. Finally, the effective problem-solver was distinguished for being reasonable, trustful, and for not advancing unwarranted claims.

In contrast, both the ineffective and average negotiators only received fourteen highly rated bipolar pairs out of the sixty-one listed. The two bipolar descriptions listed exclusively on the ineffective negotiator's list are inaccurately estimating the value of the case and having a narrow range of bargaining strategies....

c) Goals

Finally, we turn to the different goals attributed to problem-solving negotiators.

TOP PROBLEM–SOLVING GOALS

	Ineffective	Average	Effective
1.	Maximizing Settlement	Ethical Conduct	Ethical Conduct
2.	Ethical Conduct	Maximizing Settlement	Maximizing Settlement
3.	Fair Settlement	Fair Settlement	Fair Settlement
4.	Meeting Client's Needs	Meeting Client's Needs	Meet Both Sides' Interests
5.	Use Legal Skills Well	Avoiding Litigation	Avoiding Litigation
6.		Meet Both Sides' Interests	Meeting Client's Needs
7.		Good Relations with You	Good Relations with You
8.			Use Legal Skills Well
9.			Good Relations Between Parties

The differences on the following charts invite three interesting observations. Only the effective and average negotiators were interested in reaching an agreement that met the underlying interests of both sides, avoiding litigation and having good relations with the other negotiator. The absence of these goals from the ineffective list negates my previous hypothesis that ineffective negotiators were too concerned with relationships and a fear of litigation. The ineffective negotiator also failed to show the goal of reaching a mutually satisfying agreement. Either the ineffective negotiator was not sufficiently assertive on his own behalf to protect his interests or he paid no heed to the interests of the other side. Given the descriptions from the earlier ratings scales, we can hypothesize that one reason ineffective negotiators are so is their failure to search for mutually beneficial solutions.

One of the effective negotiator's goals not shared by the average negotiator was taking satisfaction in the exercise of legal skills. Might this difference in legal skills be the difference between effective problem-solvers who can successfully execute their negotiation strategies and average problem-solvers who cannot quite manage to do so? In other words, perhaps both the ineffective and average problem-solvers are not really problem-solvers in the true sense of the term. They may aspire to employ that strategy, but may lack the traits that make problem-solving effective.

* * *

C. Judging the Effectiveness of Adversarial Behavior

"The attorney did a good job of preparing for trial, then taking a blistering and extreme position in negotiations and then, upon seeing a favorable settlement, pressured the client to settle immediately."

* * *

1. Two Cluster Analysis

The charts below highlight the differences among those negotiators falling into the adversarial categories based on levels of perceived effectiveness.

42

a) Adjective Ratings

TOP 20 ADVERSARIAL ADJECTIVES

	Ineffective	Average	Effective
1.	Stubborn	Headstrong	Egotistical
2.	Irritating	Assertive	Demanding
3.	Headstrong	Stubborn	Ambitious
4.	Arrogant	Arrogant	Experienced
5.	Argumentative	Argumentative	Confident
6.	Assertive	Confident	Assertive
7.	Egotistical	Egotistical	Forceful
8.	Confident	Demanding	Arrogant
9.	Demanding	Irritating	Headstrong
10.	Quarrelsome	Experienced	Tough
11.	Ambitious	Ambitious	Firm
12.	Firm	Quarrelsome	Irritating
13.	Experienced	Tough	Stubborn
14.	Manipulative	Adaptable	Argumentative
15.	Suspicious	Forceful	Dominant
16.	Hostile	Masculine	Manipulative
17.	Forceful	Suspicious	Masculine
18.	Evasive	Firm	Quarrelsome
19.	Tough	Hostile	Suspicious
20.	Complaining	Complaining	Bluffer

We can examine the few adjectives that do not appear in all three categories to see if this provides any insight into the difference in effectiveness. Unlike the difference among the problem-solvers, these different adjectives are all listed at or near the bottom of the lists, implying that they have less significance. The two adjectives listed for an effective adversarial negotiator that are not on the other two lists are dominant and bluffer, numbers 15 and 20 from the effective list, respectively. The difference in effectiveness could be related to how well the negotiator controlled the negotiation in general or through the particular tactic of bluffing. On the other hand, the two adjectives listed on the ineffective and average lists but not on the effective list are hostile and complaining. This difference seems to be based on the degree to which the adversarial bargainer was difficult. Being egotistical, arrogant, irritating and quarrelsome can be viewed as effective as long as you are not additionally annoying by complaining or being overly hostile.

b) Bipolar Ratings

The bipolar descriptions highlight the differences in effectiveness more clearly.

TOP 20 ADVERSARIAL BIPOLARS

	Ineffective	Average	Effective
1.	Disinterested in My Client's Needs	Interested in His Client's Needs	Disinterested in My Client's Needs
2.	Extreme Opening Demand	Disinterested in My Client's Needs	Interested in His Client's Needs
3.	Unrealistic Initial Position	Unconcerned How I Look	Arrogant
4.	Rigid	Arrogant	Aggressive
5.	Fixed Conception of the Problem	Unrealistic Initial Position	Pursued Best Interest of Client
6.	Negotiation = Win/Lose	Extreme Opening Demand	Intelligent
7.	Narrow View of Problem	Aggressive	Active
8.	Narrow Range of Strategies		Extreme Opening Demand
9.	Unconcerned How I Look		Zealous Representation Within Bounds
10.	Arrogant		
11.	Fixed on Single Solution		
12.	Inaccurately Estimated Case		
13.	Unmovable Position		
14.	Used Take It or Leave It		
15.	Aggressive		
16.	Interested in His Client's Needs		
17.	Obstructed		
18.	Did Not Consider My Needs		
19.	Unreasonable		
20.	Uncooperative		

The bipolar descriptions focus more on the strategies chosen by the negotiators and demonstrate some very important differences among the effectiveness levels. First, only the effective adversarial negotiator was perceived as acting in the best interests of his or her client. We can hypothesize that the ineffective adversarial bargainer was perceived as allowing his strategies or ego to get in the way of the client's needs. Second, the effective adversarial bargainer was perceived as representing the client zealously and within the bounds of the law. While this is not the same as being perceived as ethical, it is as close as we get to a recognition that effective adversarial bargainers understand the ethical limits while other adversarial bargainers do not. Finally, the effective adversarial bargainer was also perceived as intelligent and active. This could relate to the difference noted above in terms of controlling the course of the negotiation.

On the other hand, the ineffective adversarial bargainer is perceived as engaging in all sorts of tactics that his effective peers do not. Both the average and ineffective adversarials start high (extreme opening demand and unrealistic initial position) and are particularly uninterested in the other attorney (unconcerned how I would look in the eyes of my client). The ineffective adversarial bargainer also was perceived as viewing the case narrowly (fixed conception of the problem, narrow view of case) and bargaining in a positional manner (rigid, fixed on single solution, took one position and refused to move, used take it or leave it, narrow range of bargaining strategies). They ultimately viewed negotiation as a case of winners and losers and, therefore, did not feel the need to work with the other side (did not consider my needs, uncooperative, obstructed the negotiation.) Finally, the ineffective adversarial negotiator was perceived as unreasonable and to have inaccurately estimated the value of the case. We can hypothesize that the extreme forms of adversarial behavior make this type of negotiator appear ineffective rather than average or effective.

c) Goals

TOP ADVERSARIAL GOALS

	Ineffective	Average	Effective
1.	Maximizing Settlement	Maximizing Settlement	Maximizing Settlement
2.	Outdoing You	Outdoing You	Outdoing You
3.	Profitable Fee	Profitable Fee	Profitable Fee
4.	Improving Firm Reputation	Meeting Client's Needs	Meeting Client's Needs
5.	Meeting Client's Needs	Use Legal Skills Well	Use Legal Skills Well

The difference in goals sheds a little more light on the differences among the effectiveness ratings. The one goal listed for an ineffective negotiator not listed for the other two categories is that this negotiator is concerned with improving his or her reputation among the members of the law firm. This goal bolsters our earlier hypothesis that ineffective adversarials are more concerned with themselves at the expense of their clients. In addition, the goal listed for average and effective negotiators but not listed for the ineffective negotiator is taking satisfaction in the exercise of legal skills. We can infer that the ineffective bargainer is perceived as having few legal skills in general.

2. [Two] Cluster Analysis

* * *

[Professor Schneider divided lawyers described as adversarial negotiators into "ethical adversarials" and "unethical adversarials."]

a. Adjective Ratings

TOP 20 ADJECTIVES

Ethical Adversarial	Unethical Adversarial
1. Confident	Irritating
2. Assertive	Stubborn

Ethical Adversarial	Unethical Adversarial
3. Arrogant	Headstrong
4. Headstrong	Argumentative
5. Experienced	Quarrelsome
6. Demanding	Arrogant
7. Egotistical	Egotistical
8. Ambitious	Manipulative
9. Stubborn	Assertive
10. Argumentative	Demanding
11. Tough	Complaining
12. Irritating	Hostile
13. Forceful	Suspicious
14. Firm	Conniving
15. Quarrelsome	Greedy
16. Masculine	Rude
17. Dominant	Angry
18. Ethical	Confident
19. Deliberate	Ambitious
20. Hostile	Deceptive

.... The top five adjectives in the ethical group are confident (number 18 in the unethical group), assertive (number 9 in the unethical group), arrogant (number 6 in the unethical group), headstrong (number 3 in the unethical group and therefore the only overlap between the categories' top five lists), and experienced (not listed for the unethical group). Furthermore, unlike the other groups, the ethical group is *not* described as manipulative, conniving, deceptive, evasive, complaining, rude, angry, intolerant, sarcastic, greedy or stern. The ethical adjectives therefore are not particularly negative nor do they suggest the table-banging style of negotiation.

b) *Bipolar Ratings*

TOP 20 BIPOLARS

	Ethical Adversarial	Unethical Adversarial
1.	Interested in His Client's Needs	Not Interested in My Client's Needs
2.	Unrealistic Initial Position	Rigid
3.	Extreme Opening Demand	Arrogant
4.	Not Interested in My Client's Needs	Unreasonable
5.	Aggressive	Single Solution
6.	Arrogant	Uncooperative
7.	Prepared	Narrow Range of Strategies
8.		Narrow View of Problem
9.		Extreme Opening Demand
10.		Did Not Consider My Needs
11.		Negotiation = Win/Lose
12.		Unrealistic Initial Position
13.		Unconcerned How I look

	Ethical Adversarial	Unethical Adversarial
14.		Aggressive
15.		Inaccurately Estimated Case
16.		Insincere
17.		Fixed Conception of Problem
18.		Distrustful
19.		Obstructed
20.		Inflicted Needless Harm

A review of the bipolar pairs further shows the difference between the two adversarial groups. Attorneys falling in the unethical adversarial group had numerous adjectives and behavior ascribed to them that were not ascribed to attorneys in the ethical adversarial group. First, attorneys in the unethical adversarial group were unpleasant: discourteous, unfriendly, and tactless. Second, they were untrustworthy: insincere, devious, dishonest and distrustful. Third, these attorneys were uninterested in the client or lawyer on other side: no understanding of the opposing client, unconcerned how opposing counsel would look, no consideration of opposing counsel's needs, infliction of needless harm. Fourth, these attorneys were inflexible in their view of the case and their strategies: narrow view of case, rigid, took one position, narrow range of strategies, focused on a single solution, fixed concept of negotiation. Fifth, they used manipulative tactics: attacked, used take it or leave it, inaccurate case estimate, advanced unwarranted claims. Finally, their general view of the negotiation process was competitive: uncooperative, unreasonable, viewed negotiation as win-lose, obstructed the negotiation. The ethical adversarials, as compared to the unethical adversarials, had a broader view of the case, a different negotiation style, and were more pleasant.

c) Goals

TOP GOALS

	Ethical Adversarial	Unethical Adversarial
1.	Maximizing Settlement	Maximizing Settlement
2.	Improving Firm Reputation	Outdoing You
3.	Outdoing You	Profitable Fee
4.	Meeting Client's Needs	Improving Firm Reputation
5.	Use Legal Skills Well	Meeting Client's Needs
6.	Ethical Conduct Use	Legal Skills Well
7.	Profitable Fee	Improving Bar Reputation
8.	Fair Settlement	
9.	Avoiding Litigation	
10.	Improving Bar Reputation	
11.	Good Relations With You	

Finally, in a comparison of the goals for these two adversarial groups, the ethical adversarials have two significant additions to those goals they have in common. First, attorneys in the ethical adversarial group were interested in exercising their legal skills well. Second, and more notably, they were also interested in conducting themselves ethically.

These differences in adjective descriptions, bipolar pairs, and goals suggest a qualitative difference in the type of negotiator being assessed in the ethical adversarial group. These negotiators may still be adversarial in the traditional definition of hard bargainers (assertive, demanding, tough, firm, etc.), but they are also ethical. The lawyers falling in this cluster did not engage in manipulative tactics or deception, nor were they mean or nasty.

* * *

IV. CHANGES IN EFFECTIVE NEGOTIATING OVER THE PAST 25 YEARS

After looking at the results for the new study, it is important to compare the behavioral traits of those negotiators perceived as effective today to the traits that were revealed in the earlier Williams study. Have the characteristics of "effective" lawyers changed over the years? What are the characteristics of effective problem-solvers and effective adversarials? Simply showing that the problem-solvers are generally perceived as more effective is insufficient; attorneys need to understand why problem-solving is effective.

A. Effective Problem–Solving

The following tables compare the adjective rankings from the new study to the placement of the same adjectives in the Williams study.

EFFECTIVE PROBLEM–SOLVING–TOP 20 ADJECTIVES

Rank Ranking	Adjective in the New Study	Placement of Adjective in Williams
1	Ethical	3
2	Experienced	1
3	Personable	13
4	Rational	4
5	Trustworthy	6
6	Realistic	2
7	Confident	New Item Added
8	Perceptive	5
9	Communicative	New Item Added
10	Fair–Minded	9
11	Dignified	Did Not Make Top 20
12	Self–Controlled	11
13	Accommodating	New Item Added
14	Astute About the Law	20
15	Agreeable	New Item Added
16	Sociable	Did Not Make Top 20
17	Adaptable	14
18	Poised	17

Rank Ranking	Adjective in the New Study	Placement of Adjective in Williams
19	Careful	18
20	Wise	15

The lists are very similar and describe a negotiator who is both assertive (experienced, realistic, fair, astute, careful, wise) and empathetic (perceptive, communicative, accommodating, agreeable, adaptable).... Furthermore, the effective problem-solver is also good (ethical and trustworthy) and offers enjoyable company (personable, sociable, poised). It should be no surprise that this negotiator is seen as effective.

The fact that the description of effective problem-solving behavior has not really changed suggests some interesting insights. First, it appears that the negotiation literature advocating problem-solving behavior as effective close to twenty years ago was accurately describing behavior then and is worthy of consideration now. Second, despite the public perception of lawyers, it appears that close to two-thirds of lawyers continue to engage in non-adversarial modes of communication and that these lawyers are perceived as highly effective by their peers.

B. *Effective Adversarial*

The following table shows the top twenty adjectives for the small percentage of attorneys who were perceived as both adversarial and effective, along with corresponding rankings from the Williams study.

EFFECTIVE ADVERSARIAL–TOP 20 ADJECTIVES

Rank Ranking	Adjective in the New Study	Placement of Adjective in Williams
1	Egotistical	Did Not Make Top 20
2	Demanding	Did Not Make Top 20
3	Ambitious	7
4	Experienced	2
5	Confident	New Item Added
6	Assertive	New Item Added
7	Forceful	9
8	Arrogant	New Item Added
9	Headstrong	Did Not Make Top 20
10	Tough	11
11	Firm	New Item Added
12	Irritating	Did Not Make Top 20
13	Stubborn	New Item Added
14	Argumentative	Did Not Make Top 20
15	Dominant	8
16	Manipulative	Did Not Make Top 20
17	Masculine	Did Not Make Top 20
18	Quarrelsome	Did Not Make Top 20
19	Suspicious	Did Not Make Top 20
20	Bluffer	Did Not Make Top 20

Unlike the similarity in problem-solving adjectives, the adjectives describing the effective competitive or adversarial negotiator have changed greatly. The new study includes five completely new adjectives and ten adjectives that were below the top twenty in the Williams study. The new adjectives are, by and large, negative.

The competitive negotiator described by Williams was not nearly so unpleasant and negative. The top five adjectives describing the effective competitive negotiator in the Williams study were: (1) convincing; (2) experienced; (3) perceptive; (4) rational; and (5) analytical. None of these adjectives has a particularly negative connotation. In fact, perceptiveness can demonstrate interest in one's opponent's position. Now the top five adjectives describing an effective adversarial negotiator are: (1) egotistical; (2) demanding; (3) ambitious; (4) experienced; and (5) confident. Clearly things have changed for the worst when the most important description given to a lawyer is egotistical. In fact, the rest of the top twenty list is even more undesirable. Out of the entire list of adjectives, over half have negative connotations. Lawyers therefore have a poor view of their adversarial opponents despite their negotiation effectiveness.

C. Effective Behavior on the Goals Ratings

EFFECTIVE PROBLEM–SOLVING–TOP GOALS

Rank Ranking	Goal in the New Study	Placement of Goal in Williams
1	Ethical Conduct	1
2	Maximizing Settlement	2
3	Fair Settlement	3
4	Meet Both Sides' Interests	New Item Added
5	Avoiding Litigation	6
6	Meeting Client's Needs	4
7	Good Relations with You	7
8	Use Legal Skills Well	5

We can also compare the goals attributed to the assessed attorneys in each study. As with the adjectives, the goals for problem-solvers appear to be similar across time. The only new goal, to meet the interests of both sides, is consistent with the idea of an integrative negotiation.

EFFECTIVE ADVERSARIAL–TOP GOALS

Rank Ranking	Goal in the New Study	Placement of Goal in Williams
1	Maximize Settlement	1
2	Meeting Client Needs	6
3	Outdoing You	3
4	Profitable Fee	2
5	Exercising Legal Skills	5

The effective adversarial also appears to have changed little in goals with one key exception. In Williams' study, the goal of ethical conduct was ranked fourth for an effective adversarial bargainer. Here that goal is no longer in the top five and has fallen to seventh.

D. Effectiveness Regardless of Style

Another type of analysis is to compare the similarities and differences among those negotiators perceived as effective regardless of their negotiation style. There is relatively little overlap between adjectives describing effective problem-solving behavior and adjectives describing effective competitive behavior. In the Williams study, fourteen adjectives made the top twenty in both groups. This provided helpful advice to lawyers because, regardless of their overall styles, as long as they displayed these characteristics, they would be considered effective. In the new study only two adjectives overlap: experienced and confident. This lack of overlap suggests that the two styles of negotiation have clearly diverged in the last twenty-five years and that it is unlikely for a negotiator to be able to move between these antithetical types of negotiation styles.

There are several common strategies revealed by the top bipolar descriptions, however. Both effective problem-solvers and effective adversarials were perceived as being interested in the needs of their client, acting consistently with the best interests of their client, and representing their client zealously and within the bounds of the law. Both were also perceived as intelligent. Finally, the goals in common were maximizing the settlement for the client, seeing that the client's needs were met, and taking satisfaction in the exercise of legal skills. It is easy to see that what effective lawyers have in common. They are assertive, smart, and prepared.

E. Comparing Effectiveness Ratings over Time

Finally, we can compare the effectiveness rating of Williams' two groups to this study.

Compared to the Williams study, the percentage of problem-solving negotiators who were deemed to be effective has dropped from 59% to 54%. The change in the percentage of adversarial bargainers, however, is much more striking. Twenty-five percent of competitive negotiators were seen as effective in the Williams study as compared to 9% in this study. Alternatively, only 33% of competitive negotiators were seen as ineffective in the Williams study while 53% were in this study. [On the other hand, the percentage of cooperative/problem-solvers rated ineffective rose from 3% in the Williams study to only 4% in this study.]

* * *

51

WHICH APPROACH IS MORE EFFECTIVE

Individual negotiators may not have much choice about the basic approach they use, which may be determined largely by their own personality and experience. Attorneys should probably be more concerned with improving effectiveness within their style of preference than with changing styles.

Still one wonders whether one approach or the other is more effective. The answer provided by Professor Williams' Phoenix study and Professor Schneider's Milwaukee and Chicago study is that there is no difference in degree of effectiveness attributed to effective/cooperatives and effective/competitives. They received comparably high ratings for effectiveness. It does not appear, therefore, that either approach has the edge when it comes to obtaining the highest (as compared to greatest number) of effectiveness ratings. On the other hand, there are a substantially greater number of effective attorneys of the cooperative type than of the competitive type.

Professor Williams found that 59% of cooperative/problem-solvers were considered effective negotiators, while Professor Schneider found that 54% of such lawyers are considered effective. Professor Williams found that 25% of competitive/adversarials were effective negotiators, but Professor Schneider found that only 9% of such attorneys are considered effective negotiators. These data would clearly indicate that individuals using the cooperative/problem-solving style are much more likely to be viewed by their peers as effective negotiators than their competitive/adversarial cohorts. Using the more recent Schneider data, cooperative/problem-solvers are six times more likely (54% vs. 9%) to be considered effective negotiators than their competitive/adversarial colleagues. On the other hand, while Professor Williams found that 33% of competitive/adversarials were ineffective, Professor Schneider found that 53%—more than half–of such attorneys are now rated ineffective. These figures should be contrasted with the fact that the percentage of ineffective cooperative/problem-solvers rose from 3% in Professor Williams' study to only 4% in Professor Schneider's study. These data indicate that thirteen times as many competitive/adversarials are considered ineffective negotiators than their cooperative/problem-solving colleagues.

A critical factor undoubtedly contributed to the significant increase in the percentage of ineffective competitive/adversarial negotiators between the 1976 Williams study and the 1999 Schneider study. Competitive/adversarial lawyers are characterized more negatively now than when Professor Williams administered his study. They behave less professionally and more rudely. When we encounter overtly competitive opponents who evidence a lack of respect for us and the interests of our clients, we are unlikely to become docile targets for exploitation. We instead work harder to protect our clients and to avoid exploitation. We minimize our information disclosures to counteract their lack of openness, and we carefully monitor our opening positions and concession patterns to be sure we are not being taken advantage of. As a result, our competitive/adversarial opponents will find it difficult to gain a negotiation edge. Such interactive pairs will probably reach fewer agreements than cooperative/problem-solving negotiators. When they do reach agreements, their lack of openness is likely to make their final accords less efficient than those that could have been attained through more cooperative behavior.

COMPETITIVE/PROBLEM–SOLVING STYLE

Effective cooperative/problem-solver negotiators and effective competitive/adversarial negotiators share one trait that is most often associated with competitive/adversarial bargainers—they hope to *maximize settlements* for their *own clients*. This may suggest that many effective negotiators are not entirely cooperative/problem-solving or competitive/adversarial, but a combination of both styles. These individuals seek to advance client interests (competitive/adversarial goal), but do so in a courteous and professional manner (cooperative/problem-solving approach). They are also concerned about the interests of opposing parties and hope to achieve agreements that maximize the joint returns enjoyed by both sides (cooperative/problem-solving goal). This hybrid approach may account for the fact that lawyers rated far more cooperative/problem-solvers as effective negotiators than competitive/adversarials. If we could create a third category consisting of *competitive/problem-solvers*, this group might encompass a substantial portion of the lawyers labeled effective cooperative/problem-solvers.

This is the approach that we consider to be the most effective over the long run. We believe that attorneys should work diligently to advance the interests of their own clients, but should not allow this objective to negate other equally important considerations, such as behaving ethically and professionally and seeking fair settlements that maximize the joint returns achieved by both sides. Once negotiators obtain what they think is appropriate for their own clients, they should look for ways to accommodate the non-conflicting interests of their opponents. They should seek what Ronald Shapiro and Mark Jankowski call "WIN-win" results–both parties obtain beneficial results, but their side obtains more generous terms.[4] They should do this not only for altruistic reasons, but also for their own benefit. First, they have to provide opponents with sufficiently generous terms to induce those parties to accept agreements over their non-settlement alternatives. Second, they hope to ensure that opponents will not develop post-negotiation "buyer's remorse" and try to overturn the agreements reached. Finally, they are likely to interact with opposing counsel in the future. If they are remembered favorably, their subsequent encounters are likely to be pleasant and mutually productive. On the other hand, if they are remembered negatively as nasty competitive/adversarials who

---

4. Ronald M. Shapiro & Mark A. Jankowski, *The Power of Nice* 45–61 (2001).

sought to exploit and even embarrass their opponents, those lawyers will seek retribution during their future interactions with these difficult negotiators.

WHICH TYPE OF NEGOTIATOR ARE YOU?

As you studied the various negotiating styles and levels of effectiveness, you probably began to ask yourself what type of negotiator you tend to be. This is an important question. For many people, the answer is clear. Some recognize (as one of the authors did) a clear tendency to be a milquetoast, a classic ineffective cooperative/problem-solver. Some see themselves as fair-minded, professional negotiators who work to advance the interests of their own side while striving to simultaneously enhance the benefits obtained by their opponents. These persons are either effective cooperative/problem-solvers or effective competitive/problem-solvers. Others see a clear pattern of successful gamesmanship, characteristic of effective competitive/adversarial negotiators. A few may realize that their overly-aggressive and occasionally offensive approach may place them in the ineffective competitive/adversarial group. Even if these persons continue their competitive/adversarial style, we would urge them to limit their use of offensive tactics, recognizing that a courteous and professional approach would enable them to be more effective in their regular interactions. But many people are not so sure. In some situations they are likely to be cooperative/problem-solvers, while in other circumstances they can be competitive/adversarials. In fact, the evidence suggests that most of us can all shift from one style to another or anywhere in between under sufficient encouragement or provocation.

Law students and attorneys often have strong feelings about the propriety of shifting "roles". Cooperative/problem-solvers are particularly prone to believe that it is dishonest to calculate which role to play; that the honest person must respond "naturally" to a situation, rather than plan in advance how to gain an advantage. However, the data suggest that many effective attorneys have developed the capability to adopt either style convincingly. This is especially true for individuals who use a cooperative/problem-solving or a competitive/problem-solving approach, depending upon the particular interaction involved. If this is true, then this kind of versatility is probably something to be desired. One attorney said, "Being a compromising person at heart, I am becoming more impressed all the time how much more one can get by being mean and nasty (within bounds)." If some attorneys are learning to be "mean and nasty" to get their own way, then all attorneys need to learn to deal effectively with that strategy. It is not enough to rely on pure instincts. It is not enough to get mad and fight back with a vengeance. The effective negotiator needs to develop an approach that satisfies two conditions: (1) it should protect and be compatible with the interests of clients and society; and (2) it should provide adequate protection against the gamesmanship of others. This is why Professor Craver likes the competitive/problem-solving approach in which attorneys seek to enhance their own side's interests while working to expand the overall pie to be divided and ensure beneficial results for opposing parties.

Versatility is more of an issue for lawyers than other professionals, because their primary function is to represent the legitimate interests of other people. If attorneys feel morally obligated to be irritating, hostile, and intolerant in all their dealings on behalf of clients, they will rarely serve client interests well because they are locking themselves into a generally ineffective mode. Similarly, if attorneys feel morally obligated to be gentle, forgiving, patient, and unassertive in every situation (no matter how tough the opponent), they will be unable to protect their clients from opponents who are dealing with them in an unscrupulous or overbearing way.

CHAPTER NOTES

1. Further Thoughts About Negotiator Effectiveness

The lack of consensus in the literature about the meaning of "effectiveness" in negotiation creates a problem for every researcher and practitioner. Anyone searching the authorities for definitions is forced to choose between inconsistent definitions and assumptions. In preparing their research, Professors Williams and Schneider developed a set of hypotheses about effectiveness, and where they found conflicting theories they opted for those favoring a cooperative/problem-solving model of effectiveness. These hypotheses are important *NOT* because they were correct (they were not all correct), but because they led us to the classic error that virtually all researchers and commentators in the field of negotiation have generally made: The error of taking observations or hypotheses that are valid for *SOME* negotiators, and generalizing from them as if they were valid for all negotiators. Our hypotheses make this error in favor of "cooperative/problem-solving" behavior. Because they are fairly good statements of cooperative/problem-solving assumptions, they are worth reproducing here.

Among effective attorneys the following informal rules are observed:

A. *Dynamics.* Both sides will:

1. make serious attempts to reach agreements (*i.e.*, will bargain in good faith);

2. when presenting client positions, represent them accurately;

3. avoid undue emotionalism;

4. maintain trust, candor, confidentiality, and flexibility;

5. be thoroughly prepared on the facts, the applicable law, and other relevant considerations;

6. avoid deception, insults, flagrant lies, and impolite acts;

7. avoid interrupting or obstructing the routinized aspects of interpersonal relations; and

8. avoid causing other attorneys to lose face.

B. *Effectiveness Traits.* Effective legal negotiators can be distinguished from their less effective colleagues by superior ratings on traits such as:

1. legal acumen (skill in knowing and applying the law);

2. thorough preparation;

3. reputation and ability as capable trial attorneys;

4. creativity (ability to invent or create innovative alternatives);

5. skillful use of tactics such as commitment, toughness, reciprocation, initial offers, and control of information flow; and

6. awareness of and skillful use of the strength of their positions.

C. *Objectives.* In examining the objectives or end results lawyers try to achieve in negotiations, we hypothesized that, for effective negotiations, the dollar value of client outcomes would be important, but that they would also take into account such concerns as:

1. the overall needs, interests, and desires of their clients;

2. the need for favorable economic returns to the negotiators; and

3. the need to maintain favorable reputations within the legal community.

D. *Variations Within the Bar.* We also hypothesized that there are more specific or technical expectations among practicing lawyers, and that these develop in unique ways within geographic areas and within legal specialties. For example, attorneys specializing in personal injury work in a particular city or region of the country develop a set of informal practices and assumptions different from the informal practices of lawyers working in other regions or within other specialties. This creates difficulties for attorneys who are not specialized, who are new to practice, or who come from other regions of the country, because their failure to know and observe these unwritten rules reduces attorney negotiating effectiveness.

2. Research on Negotiation in Other Disciplines

Outside of the legal context there has been an explosion of interest in the phenomenon of negotiation. Over the past thirty years, the concept of negotiation has grown from that of an ethereal art practiced discretely by diplomats to that of a fundamental decision-making process in democratic societies. In this short time span, the amount of scholarly attention paid to negotiation in such disciplines as economics, sociology, psychology, communications, political science, and international relations has increased significantly. Although this interest is still relatively recent and much of the literature is still somewhat removed from practical application, it has nevertheless produced a wealth of experimental and theoretical work that is of potential value to all lawyers. Equally important, this work has brought with it the development of research techniques that can be directly applied by legal scholars to the legal negotiating context. The leading books and articles are set forth in the Bibliography at the conclusion of this book.

Some of the particularly useful collections are:

J. Rubin & B. Brown, *The Social Psychology of Bargaining* (1975)

H. Raiffa, *The Art and Science of Negotiation* (1982)

R. Fisher, W. Ury & B. Patton, *Getting to Yes* (2d ed. 1991)

K. Arrow, R. Mnookin, L. Ross, A. Tversky & R. Wilson, *Barriers to Conflict Resolution* (1995)

G. Kennedy, *Kennedy on Negotiation* (1998)

R. Shell, *Bargaining for Advantage* (1999)

R. Mnookin, S. Peppet & A. Tulumello, *Beyond Winning: Negotiating to Create Value in Deals and Disputes* (2000)

H. Raiffa (with J. Richardson & D. Metcalfe), *Negotiation Analysis* (2003)

D. Kolb & J. Williams, *Everyday Negotiation* (2003)

M. Latz, *Gain the Edge: Negotiating to Get What You Want* (2004)

R. Lewicki, D. Saunders & B. Barry, *Negotiation* (2005)

L. Thompson, *The Mind and Heart of the Negotiator* (3d ed. 2005)

D. Lax & J. Sebenius, *3–D Negotiation* (2006)

3.   Predictability of Negotiating Behavior

All human beings have characteristic patterns of behavior. We see evidence of this in the habits and mannerisms of close friends and family members. We would see evidence of these patterns in others if we could observe them long enough and with sufficient attention to detail.

Coaches in college and professional football take advantage of this principle, and the better prepared among them apply it when preparing for each team they meet. The way they discover the patterns of opposing coaches is not necessarily by studying these coaches, but by studying recent films of their games and charting the offensive and defensive plays executed by their teams in different situations. Coaches typically have a rather small number of basic plays, and their games are built around variations on those plays. One coach has referred to this set of plays as the "comfort zone", which consists of the plays a team does best and the coach feels most comfortable using.

Lawyers can apply this concept to negotiations, and begin to look for the patterns followed by the different opponents they face. These patterns generally represent "comfort zones" for those negotiators, within which they are likely to want to function during their negotiations. The more attorneys can predict how particular opponents will behave in specific bargaining situations, the more effectively they can interact with those individuals.

Chapter Three

THE DYNAMICS OF COOPERATIVE/ PROBLEM–SOLVING AND COMPETITIVE/ADVERSARIAL NEGOTIATING

"It is disgraceful, after much trouble, much display, and much talk, to do no good at all." Hippocrates

I. INTRODUCTION

The descriptions of cooperative/problem-solving and competitive/adversarial negotiators provide a basis for evaluating our personal negotiating patterns and those of negotiators we may encounter in practice. But the descriptions do not directly address the question of *how the cooperative/problem-solving and competitive/adversarial strategies work: what are the dynamics of each strategy, and what determines the effectiveness or ineffectiveness of negotiator applications of the different strategies?* Negotiator effectiveness is *NOT* determined by the patterns they follow, but rather by what they do with those patterns. The objective of this chapter is to describe the underlying dynamics of the cooperative/problem-solving and competitive/adversarial styles and determine, as much as possible, the principles that govern the effectiveness of each.

Until recently, there was no reliable way of knowing how to interpret and apply social scientific literature on bargaining to the actual negotiating practices of lawyers. One interpretive difficulty concerned the dichotomy between cooperative/problem-solving and competitive/adversarial negotiating preferences in the literature. No one knew which of these styles was most applicable to actual bargaining interactions among lawyers. The finding that *both* approaches are routinely used by lawyers and that neither pattern has a monopoly on effectiveness helps shift the debate from the question of which method is best to the more constructive question of *how each pattern works.*

II. THE COOPERATIVE/PROBLEM-SOLVING STRATEGY

Cooperative/problem-solving negotiators move psychologically *toward* opposing attorneys. They seek common ground. They communicate a sense of shared interests, values, and attitudes, using rational, logical persuasion to encourage mutual cooperation. They openly disclose the underlying interests of their clients, seeking to expand the overall pie and achieve mutually efficient agreements. They promote a trusting atmosphere, appearing to seek no special advantage for themselves or their clients. Their explicit goal is to reach fair resolutions of conflicts based on objective analyses of the underlying facts and law.

Many cooperative/problem-solving negotiators show their own trust and good faith by making unilateral concessions. Making unilateral concessions is risky, but cooperative/problem-solving negotiators believe it creates a moral obligation in those with whom they interact to reciprocate. The cooperative/problem-solving strategy is calculated—consciously or subconsciously—to induce other parties to reciprocate: to cooperate in openly and objectively resolving the problem; to forego aggression; and to make reciprocal concessions until solutions are reached.

Cooperative/problem-solving negotiators feel a high commitment to fairness, objecting to the competitive view of negotiation as a game. To cooperative/problem-solvers, gamesmanship is considered ethically suspect. They feel that to move psychologically *against* other persons to promote their own interest is manipulative and an affront to human dignity. On the other hand, cooperative/problem-solvers move psychologically *toward* other people to achieve their preferred outcomes. Competitive/adversarial negotiators have reason to ask whether this approach is any less manipulative. Their manipulations are designed to induce or permit opponents to trust, cooperate with, and make concessions cooperative/problem-solving manipulators find beneficial.

Cooperative/problem-solving strategies are often more effective than tough strategies for two primary reasons. First, they produce fairer and more efficient outcomes. Second, they result in fewer bargaining breakdowns.

The cooperative/problem-solving strategy, like the competitive/adversarial approach, has limitations. Its major disadvantage is its vulnerability to exploitation, a problem compounded by the apparent inability of some cooperative/problem-solving types to recognize when they are being fleeced. When cooperative/problem-solving negotiators attempt to establish cooperative, trusting atmospheres, in negotiations with tough, noncooperative opponents, the cooperative attorneys have an alarming tendency to ignore the lack of cooperation being reciprocated and to pursue their cooperative strategy unilaterally. Their strategy requires them to continue discussing the relevant issues openly, fairly and objectively, to make concessions about the weaknesses of their cases, and to refrain from self-serving behavior. In such situations, the tough negotiators are free to accept all of the fairness and cooperation being extended to them without giving anything in return. One might reasonably suggest that it would be irrational to do anything else. On these facts, the cooperative/problem-solvers have placed themselves at a serious disadvantage. They have foregone attacking their opponents' positions, they have conceded the weaknesses of their own positions, and they have received no reciprocal concessions in return.

The problem for cooperative/problem-solving negotiators does not end here. Competitive/adversarial negotiators interpret cooperation as a sign of weakness. From their viewpoint, people who have strong positions do not make concessions or admit to weakness. When opponents act cooperatively with them, they actually increase their demands and raise their expectations about what they will be able to obtain.

Some attorneys argue that cooperative/problem-solving attorneys should not fear looking weak early in bargaining encounters, because this approach induces tough opponents to overplay their hands and expose their selfish objectives. However, reason suggests this is a risky approach.

Cooperative/problem-solvers can effectively minimize their exposure to exploitation by competitive/adversarial opponents by moving slowly at the beginning of bargaining interactions. They should always be courteous and professional when they interact with others. At the outset, they should release *some* information regarding the underlying needs and interests of their clients. If these actions are reciprocated, they should continue their disclosures and begin to look for ways to achieve agreements that are mutually efficient. On the other hand, when their openness is not reciprocated, they must become less forthright. They should not create information imbalances that favor their manipulative opponents.

Cooperative/problem-solvers who initially encounter minimal disclosures by their opponents should seek to generate greater openness. They should ask open-ended questions designed to elicit more candor. They might politely point out that their openness is not being reciprocated. If these efforts fail, they should reduce their own disclosures to avoid unfair exploitation. While they should continue to look for trades that would enhance the interests of both sides, they should be careful to avoid unilateral concessions that only benefit their manipulative adversaries.

III. THE COMPETITIVE/ADVERSARIAL STRATEGY

The researchers who argue that tough negotiators are the most effective are supported by a variety of interesting studies. Experiments conducted by Siegel & Fouraker[1] on the process of making demands and counter-demands in bargaining indicated that tough negotiators obtain higher payoffs than negotiators who do not behave that way. These results have been duplicated in a number of experimental settings.[2]

The indicia of the "tough" approach include:

1. making high initial demands;

2. maintaining a high level of demands during the course of negotiations;

3. making few concessions;

4. making small concessions—when concessions are made; and

5. having high aspirations.

These tactics are so consistent with the behavior patterns of competitive/adversarial attorneys described in the preceding chapter that we can propose that most of the social scientific literature on toughness in bargaining is relevant to understanding how competitive/adversarial attorneys negotiate.

In *Persuasion: Understanding, Practice and Analysis* 133–134 (1976), Herbert W. Simmons observed that the underlying dynamic of combative strategies is to move psychologically *against* opponents by words and action. Videotapes of competitive/adversarial lawyers engaged in negotiating show a definite pattern of their moving psychologically against non-competitive attorneys. They make very high demands and few, if any, concessions. They use exaggerations, ridicule, threats, bluffs, and accusations to create high levels of tension and exert pressure on their opponents.

What are the effects of these tactics? If used effectively, the tactics cause opposing attorneys to lose confidence in themselves and their cases, to reduce their expectations of what they will be able to obtain, and to accept less than they otherwise would as bargaining outcomes. As Simons observed, the combative approach is employed by manipulative negotiators to intimidate opponents into accepting their one-sided demands.

Experimental studies of bargaining interactions have shown that in many settings, use of toughness increases gains for the tough negotiator.[3] Professor Williams' Q-factor analysis showed that maximizing settlement value is the primary concern of competitive negotiators.

1. Siegel, S. & L. Fouraker, *Bargaining and Group Decision Making* (McGraw–Hill, 1960).

2. See, *e.g.*, D. Hartnett, L. Cummings & W. Hamner, "Personality, Bargaining Style and Payoff on Bilateral Monopoly Bargaining Among European Managers," 36 *Sociometry* 325 (1973).

3. The classic work is S. Siegel and L. Fouraker, *Bargaining and Group Decision Making* (McGraw–Hill, 1960). Other experiments have confirmed this finding. See, e.g., Harnett, Cummings, & Hamner, *Personality, Bargaining Style and Payoff in Bilateral Monopoly Bargaining Among European Managers*, 36 Sociometry 325 (1973).

Professor Schneider's data reinforced this perspective. But these negotiators are not only after money. They take satisfaction in winning—in outdoing or outmaneuvering their opponents.

Other researchers have tested the effectiveness of the tough or competitive/adversarial strategy and have identified several limitations. These limitations are important for lawyers to know, because this approach will only be effective if its limitations are known and minimized.

Kahn and Kohls[4] found that when negotiators lack sufficient information with which to negotiate they compensate by behaving more competitively. However, use of toughness in these circumstances does not increase negotiator gains. This finding correlates nicely with data from the last chapter. Ineffective competitive/adversarial negotiators are rated as unprepared on the facts and the law, which means they lack sufficient information with which to negotiate. If the findings by Kahn and Kohls apply to lawyers, lack of preparation by ineffective competitive/adversarial negotiators increases their toughness (pushing them into the hostile, strident category) and reduces their effectiveness.

Even when used by effective negotiators who are well prepared, competitive/adversarial behavior creates other problems as well. Osgood[5] found that the use of toughness and unilateral commitment in bargaining encounters generates a marked increase in tension and mistrust between the negotiators. The tension and mistrust create additional effects which may impact negatively on the negotiations. One immediate effect is to distort the communications between the parties. As early as 1956, Mellinger found that when people communicate under conditions of distrust, they tend to overstate the extent of agreement or the extent of disagreement.[6] Both have negative consequences. In the first case, tough negotiators are led to believe that their opponents are closer to agreements than is actually true, and they move on to the next items on the agenda or, if the agenda is completed, they seek closure, only to find that their opponents are in serious disagreement and will not commit themselves to the anticipated agreements. Such discoveries often precipitate bargaining breakdowns, and, in actionable cases, resort to trials.

Misunderstandings can have other serious effects for competitive/adversarial negotiators and their opponents. When tough negotiators wrongly sense agreement in their opponents, they often increase their demands and expectations.

Tension and mistrust can distort communication in the opposite direction as well, creating the appearance of *more disagreement* and causing the parties to think they are further apart than they actually

4. A. Kahn & J. Kohls, "Determinants of Toughness in Dyadic Bargaining," 35 *Sociometry* 305 (1972).

5. C. Osgood, *An Alternative to War or Surrender* (Univ. of Illinois Press 1962).

6. G. Mellinger, "Interpersonal Trust as a Factor in Communication," 52 Journal of Abnormal Social Psychology 304 (1956).

are. The result may be a complete bargaining breakdown, or at best, it will take substantial effort by both sides to overcome the misunderstandings that separate them. Since some of the distance between them is illusory, efforts to overcome their misunderstandings may be futile. Unless some means is found to correct the misperceptions through more accurate communication, these negotiations will end in stalemates.

The effects of toughness on party perceptions are crucial to the success of the competitive/adversarial strategy. In psychological terms, toughness works on the emotions of opposing parties, causing them to become preoccupied with emotional issues and lose sight of the objective merits of their positions. This may induce them to accept less beneficial agreements than the merits would dictate.

When emotions run high, the danger of impasse increases. If the correlation between the experimental literature on toughness and our empirical descriptions of competitive/adversarial attorneys is as strong as we believe, we should find evidence of the same effects among competitive/adversarial lawyers.

Data from the Williams questionnaire research of several hundred Phoenix attorneys showed the rate of impasse was significantly higher for effective competitive than for effective cooperative negotiators. Effective cooperatives obtained settlement agreements in 84% of their cases and went to trial with the remaining 16%. By contrast, effective competitives settled only 67% of their cases and faced breakdown and trial in 33%

The Williams Phoenix data also allowed comparison of trial percentages of average and ineffective negotiators of both types. Here the data were more subtle and complex. Average cooperative negotiators settled 62% and tried 38% of their cases, which was a higher trial rate than effective competitives, but their trial rate was lower than the rate for their fellow average competitives, who settled 50% and went to trial with 50%.

The statistics on ineffective negotiators show a contrary tendency. Ineffective cooperatives, whom we suspected of giving their cases away, took an extraordinary 64% of their cases to trial (a settlement rate of only 36%), while their ineffective competitive counterparts went to trial only 33% of the time, a rate that compared favorably with the trial rate of effective competitives. One explanation of this reversal is that ineffective cooperatives *know* they are too soft and, as a defense, feel compelled to protect their clients by trying the cases—a dubious protection, however, given their low ratings on trial effectiveness. On the other hand, ineffective competitives depend upon the bluff. They are, as we saw in the last chapter, not prepared on the facts or the law, not legally astute, and not effective negotiators. They rely on extreme demands, quarrelsomeness, hostility, rudeness, and other ploys to coerce opponents into settlements. If their bluffs do not work, as is generally the case, they face a particularly excruciating problem. As ineffective trial attorneys, if they are forced try their cases they will be publicly exposed as bluffers. Their safest bet is to bluff to the last minute, then cave in. If ineffective competitives follow this pattern, it helps to explain why so many of their cases settled during the last moments before trial.

When emotions run high and impasses occur, the offended parties are often filled with righteous indignation at what they consider unfair treatment. They retaliate against their tough opponents by working harder on the case and creating as many obstacles and costs as possible.

A fourth consequence of toughness is its damage to long-term relationships that depend upon mutual trust. Where attorneys are likely to encounter each other frequently over the years, tension and mistrust generated in one case will influence the dynamics and outcomes of later cases against the same opponents. This effect is magnified as attorney reputations become known throughout the local bar.

The liabilities of the tough approach provide important clues to why so few attorneys use it effectively. Its effectiveness depends upon creating enough pressure and tension to induce emotional reactions and reduced expectations in opposing parties. But if the pressure is excessive, or is maintained too long, the strategy backfires and trials result.

IV. THE COMPETITIVE/PROBLEM–SOLVING STRATEGY

As noted in chapter 2, effective cooperative/problem-solvers and effective competitive/adversarials share a critical common goal—they seek to maximize the gains for *own clients*. This quintessential competitive objective may suggest the existence of a third negotiating style that is often overlooked—the competitive/problem-solving approach. These persons seek to advance their own side's interests, but simultaneously strive to obtain mutually beneficial results which maximize the joint returns achieved by both sides. They always try to behave in a pleasant and professional manner, which misleads opponents into labeling them "cooperative/problem-solvers" instead of hybrid "competitive/problem-solvers."

Competitive/problem-solvers are relatively open with respect to client interests, but they are not as open as true cooperative/problem-solvers. They are a bit exploitative, but not to the degree of competitive/adversarial negotiators. These are WIN-win attorneys who seek beneficial terms for their own clients, while trying to maximize opponent gains once their primary objectives have been accomplished.

By being quite forthright and courteous, competitive/problem-solvers induce both cooperative/problem-solving opponents and some competitive/adversarial opponents to lower their guards and release more client information than those persons would ever release against openly competitive/adversarial negotiators. Their bargaining interactions are almost always pleasant, and they work to leave opponents with the sense they obtained good agreements. As a result, when opponents have future interactions with competitive/problem-solvers, they anticipate enjoyable encounters and look forward to working with them.

If we are correct in this regard, it might account for the greater percentage of cooperative/problem-solvers regarded by opponents as effective negotiators. Many of the persons placed in this category are most likely skilled competitive/problem-solvers who behave like wolves in sheepskin. Opponents enjoy interacting with them so much, they try to satisfy their basic needs. In addition, opponents can hardly wait to meet them in the future to demonstrate their capacity to give them what they really want.

V. CLIENT RELATIONS AND NEGOTIATION

Two major issues in lawyer-to-lawyer negotiations recur with considerable force in the attorney-client relationship. One is the issue of negotiation as a decision-making process; the other is the issue of manipulation.

We have been assuming that the attorney and client on each side of a civil dispute were of one mind; that they were agreed on what course to pursue, and the value at which they would be willing to settle. In practice, attorney-client relationships with this degree of mutual understanding and harmony require a great deal of skill and patience on the part of the attorneys. There are many potential sources of conflict and misunderstanding. Attorneys have specialized knowledge of the law, the legal system, and the dynamics of negotiation—areas not usually understood by clients. Clients have their own perceptions of their problems and motives for pursuing their matters, not all of which are communicated to the attorneys representing them.

In a sample of approximately 150 cases Professor Williams studied in Phoenix, Arizona, the impact of attorney-client misunderstandings was the single largest factor in determining what cases went to trial instead of settling. This information came from attorneys whose cases actually went to trial. When asked to identify the reason why their cases did not settle, over 50% of the attorneys said it was *due to the unwillingness of one or the other of the clients to accept settlement figures recommended by their own attorneys.*

This perspective on attorney-client relations is troubling. It suggests that attorneys are not good at communicating with their clients. We have already noted that negotiation is a decision-making process, and that the decisions are made over time as facts and other persuasive factors influence attorney's perceptions of cases. It is easy to see how attorneys might fail to keep their clients informed not only of events occurring in the processing of their cases, but of developments and changes in their own case assessments. If the clients are left behind in this way, they will naturally resist settlement offers based on case developments they have no knowledge of.

There is a larger issue implicit in these findings: if attorneys are managing cases without fully informing the clients involved, we must conclude these clients are not participating meaningfully in their own cases. Lack of client involvement in and ultimate control over their own cases may seriously reduce their satisfaction with respect to case outcomes,[7] and there is convincing evidence that it may actually result in a lower dollar value conclusions.

The importance of client participation in cases was highlighted in a study of personal injury cases in New York City by Douglas Rosenthal. He found that the dollar outcomes of personal injury cases were consistently higher when lawyers kept their clients not only informed about the cases, but also actively involved in the resolution process.[8]

Most clients have had little exposure to the legal system and they have no idea of what they can do to help move their cases toward successful conclusions. Keeping clients informed and participating in their cases requires extra effort by attorneys, and involves some risk. However, attorneys have been found to work more effectively on behalf of *informed* clients than uninformed ones. Attorneys should take the time to reach mutual understandings with clients on fee arrangements, the scope of attorney undertakings (e.g. does the contingent fee cover the cost of taking their cases on appeal), the factual and legal issues posed by their cases, the probable time frame for processing their cases, the potential for and difficulties likely to be encountered in negotiating out-of-court settlements, the psychological difficulty in (and risk inherent in) signing releases from liability at the time of settlement (or, if the clients are defendants, of paying over the money or otherwise performing the settlement agreements), and the possibility of having the cases go to trial with their attendant uncertainties and unpleasantness.

Once clients have some understanding of the legal process, attorneys should involve them in preparation of their cases. Good attorneys will explain what factual information will be needed, and give clients specific assignments to assist them in gathering the necessary documentation and other materials. Clients should be informed of the kinds of records (medical reports, expenses, lost earnings, etc.) they should be keeping, and how their actions may affect their claims. In personal injury cases, plaintiffs should be advised not to make any statements about their cases without first informing their lawyers, and not to sign anything related to their cases without their lawyer's advice.

7. The importance of a client involvement in and control over the processing of their cases is discussed in M. Spiegel, *Lawyering and Client Decisionmaking: Informed Consent and the Legal Profession*, 128 U. Pa. L. Rev. 41 (1979) and W. Lehman, *The Pursuit of a Client's Interest*, 77 Mich. L. Rev. 1078 (1979).

8. Douglas E. Rosenthal, *Lawyer and Client: Who's In Charge?* (Russell Sage Foundation: 1974).

Straightforward discussion of cases and of client responsibilities helps prepare clients for what is to come. At the same time, it creates the opportunity to counsel clients not only on the legal aspects of their cases, but also on the medical, emotional, employment, family, and financial aspects. These are all non-legal areas that may have a direct bearing on their claims—what doctors to see, when to return to work, when and how to pay medical bills, how to finance the period of recuperation, and how to adjust emotionally.

Finally, clients must be kept constantly informed of the case developments. There should be a steady stream of information flowing from the attorney to the client by way of letters, telephone calls, e-mails, copies of documents, etc. to inform the clients of every important development. This helps clients and attorneys, because the clients can often prevent costly mistakes such as forgotten aspects of their claims, misplaced information, incorrect assumptions about the facts, etc. As stated in Ethical Consideration 7–8:

> A lawyer should exert his best efforts to insure that decisions of his client are made only after the client has been informed of relevant considerations. A lawyer ought to initiate this decision-making process if the client does not do so.... A lawyer should advise his client of the possible effect of each legal alternative. A lawyer should bring to bear upon this decision-making process the fullness of his experience as well as his objective viewpoint.

This is similar to the obligations attorneys have under Model Rules 1.4 and 1.2. Rule 1.4(a) provides that "[a] lawyer shall (1) promptly inform the client of any decision or circumstance with respect to which the client's informed consent ... is required ... (2) reasonably consult with the client about the means by which the client's objectives are to be accomplished; (3) keep the client reasonably informed about the status of the matter; [and] (4) promptly comply with reasonable requests for information ..." Rule 1.4(b) states that "[a] lawyer shall explain a matter to the extent reasonably necessary to permit the client to make informed decisions regarding the representation." Model Rule 1.2 provides, in relevant part, that "[a] lawyer shall abide by a client's decision whether to settle a matter."

VI. CONFLICTS BETWEEN ATTORNEYS AND CLIENTS

Lawyers adopt cooperative/problem-solving, competitive/problem-solving, or competitive/adversarial styles. Our data do not reveal whether clients divide along similar lines, but other evidence suggests that they do. If these classifications are valid with respect to clients, it follows that cooperative/problem-solving clients will generally seek "fair" or equitable "win-win" results achieved through open discussions and reliance upon objective criteria, while competitive/adversarial clients will desire "win-lose," personally maximizing outcomes which wreak as much havoc on the other side as possible. Competitive/problem-solving clients will strive for "WIN-win" results which favor their own interests, but maximize the joint returns achieved by the parties. A client's personal approach to bargaining interactions will have a crucial and potentially dominating influence on negotiations. It can cause attorney-client misunderstandings and conflicts with respect to the objectives being sought, the bargaining strategy to be employed, interactions with the other side, and expectations about ultimate outcomes.

Competitive/adversarial clients with cooperative/problem-solving lawyers may feel that their lawyers are too mushy, naive, and uncertain. Cooperative/problem-solving clients with competitive/adversarial lawyers may feel that their attorneys are too pushy and demanding, and that the lawyers have taken complete control over their cases. In either of these situations, the clients and the attorneys must work together—before serious discussions commence with opposing parties—to develop strategies and goals both the clients and the lawyers can comfortably and effectively follow. Clients with competitive/problem-solving attorneys should find it easier to work with these representatives regardless of their own cooperative or competitive leanings, due to the capacity of effective competitive/problem-solving lawyers to adapt to the wishes of their clients and to the particular styles of opposing attorneys. By being alert to these stylistic differences between attorneys and clients, attorneys can establish and maintain more satisfactory client relationships.

CHAPTER NOTES

1. *Individuals Differ in Their Definitions of Justice*

A useful insight into your own bargaining objectives as well as those of your opponent comes with recognition that people (including lawyers) have different ideas about what constitutes "justice". A negotiator's view of the justice of a cause will be reflected in his approach to negotiation.

Consider the effect upon negotiations of each of the following four conceptions of justice:[9]

A. *Absolute Justice.* Under this perspective, persons believe that they represent "truth" and "justice", and that compromise is therefore wrong because it represents a departure from undeviating enforcement of correct principles.

This is the position of a factory owner who would rather shut down the factory and go out of business (and risk being found in violation of national labor law) than be compelled to bargain with a newly-formed labor union representing his workers, not because the union's demands are inappropriate, but because he believes labor unions are evil and cannot be condoned.

9. The ideas for these categories come from I. W. Zartman, *The 50% Solution* 38– 41 (Anchor Press 1976), although the labels used here are new.

While few law students or lawyers would adopt such an extreme position on an issue such as unionization, most people have sets of values they believe to be "true" and not susceptible to compromise. In the legal setting, cases would rarely go to trial if one or both sides did not believe they were substantively "right".

B. *Conciliatory Justice.* Under this perspective, people assume that in most disputes the parties are acting in good faith and there is merit in the claims of both sides. Conciliatory justice points toward finding the good faith interests of both sides and adopting the midpoint between those benchmarks as the fairest and most "just" solution.

C. *Compassionate Justice.* This perspective acknowledges merit in the good faith claims of both sides, but, rather than viewing midpoints between party positions as appropriate solutions, it prefers outcomes determined according to the needs of the parties.

Compassionate justice allows weaker sides to use their inferior positions as an argument for more favorable treatment. The moral force of these arguments is evidenced in some affirmative action programs which give temporary preferential treatment to groups traditionally denied equal opportunities.

D. *Power Justice.* This perspective is the reverse-image of compassionate justice. It assumes that disputed goods or benefits should be distributed, not to those with greater need, but to those with greater power.

Most people have not stopped to analyze which concepts of justice they apply when they make decisions about the distribution of scarce resources. This lack of insight into motives sometimes causes people anxiety when, after they have argued in favor of particular positions, they are suddenly confronted with exposure of their underlying assumptions about justice.

How would you respond in the following situations?[10] Which concept of justice are you applying?

1. Two friends, one rich and one poor, are walking down the street, and the rich one finds some money lying on the sidewalk. What should they do?

   a. They should divide it equally.

   b. The finder should keep most or all of it.

   c. The finder should offer to give most or all of it to her friend due to that person's greater economic need.

2. A teacher has been given some story books to give to the students in his class, but not quite enough for everyone. Should he:

   a. Give them to the children who don't have enough money to buy such books.

   b. Draw lots, so everyone has an equal chance to get them.

---

10. Questions developed by Daniel Druckman, an active researcher on bargaining and editor of *Negotiations: Social–Psychological Perspectives* (SAGE, 1977).

   c. Give them to everyone except those who make a lot of noise and/or cause trouble.

3. Two sisters are invited to a friend's party. One of them can't go because she is sick. The other goes, does very well in many games, and wins a large number of prizes. Their mother says that the two sisters should divide the prizes. How should they divide them?

   a. The sister who went should get most of them.

   b. The sister who didn't go should get most of them.

   c. They should divide them equally.

4. A girl in a science club is working on a project, and wants to look at some things through a microscope and make drawings of them. She starts to sit down at the microscope just as a boy, who also wants to use it, comes over. What should she do?

   a. Tell the boy to wait until she finishes.

   b. Let the boy use it first.

   c. Talk it over with the boy and decide together who should use it first.

5. A school has been given a large box of candy. Each class elects someone to enter a dart-throwing contest to see how much of the candy he or she can win for the class. The winner of the contest gets 5 boxes for his or her class, with each of the other classes getting 2 boxes. The winner comes back to her class with 5 boxes. Should she:

   a. Get the same as everyone else in the class.

   b. Get more than everyone else in the class.

   c. Get less than everyone else in the class.

In thinking about one's concept of justice, it is helpful to consider the meaning of the word "compromise". For some, the word has a pejorative meaning; for others it embodies some of humankind's highest ideals. In the legal context, compromise means a settlement of differences in which each side makes concessions. Compromise is so important to the idea of settlements that legal encyclopedias and other reference works discuss legal rules governing settlement agreements under the heading of "compromise and settlement".

The requirement of compromise is consistent with each of the above definitions of justice except the first, which sees compromise (at best) as a necessary evil much to be avoided. But the meaning of compromise is general enough to accommodate those who feel the division of interests ought to favor one side (whether the needier side or the stronger side) as well as those who believe it should be equal.

A fear of compromises or concessions is not irrational. Everyone can recall occasions when they have made concessions only to find later that they were duped by the other side into giving up much more than they should have, or occasions where they have performed their side of a bargain only to have the other side accept the benefit then refuse to perform their part of the agreement. In international relations there are continuing debates about whether it is safe to make concessions to an enemy, and when concessions are made there are always those who cry it was a "sell out".

The fear of being exploited, concern about undiscovered facts, and the uncertainty about the credibility of evidence, combine to make compromise an uncomfortable act. Much of the art of negotiation is learning when, how, and why to compromise.

2. *The Importance of Context and Objectives in Legal Negotiation*

Negotiations may arise in a wide range of settings, each requiring a somewhat different set of strategies. Effective negotiation is situation specific. There is no single approach or strategy that will function optimally in all negotiation settings. The simplest way to illustrate the relationship between strategy and setting is to consider the dynamics called into play by the following representative negotiating tasks.

A. You are counsel to the Salvation Army, which sends you from New York to Texas to negotiate the terms of a $5,000,000 charitable contribution by the 85–year old widow of a Texas oil millionaire. Her children are divided over the advisability of such a contribution, and want to discuss it with you.

B. You are counsel to United Air Lines, which sends you to negotiate the terms of two-year contract for the purchase of jet fuel from a major petroleum company.

C. You are counsel to the Metropolitan Daily Express (an influential regional newspaper). The President of the corporation which publishes the *Express* retains you to represent her in a divorce. One of her major concerns is that there be *no* publicity.

D. You are an attorney with a public interest law firm. You agree to represent the tenants of a decaying central city apartment house. The apartment house is in the pathway of an urban renewal project, and your first task is to represent the tenants in eminent domain hearings before the City Council.

E. You represent the plaintiff (or, if you prefer, the defendant insurance company) in a personal injury case. The judge calls you and opposing counsel in for a pretrial settlement conference.

F. You are called in by a local trial judge and assigned to represent a person accused of rape.

G. You are counsel to a major labor union and one of your duties is to participate (as a member of the five person union team) in the negotiation of a new two-year contract with a hostile employer. When the current contract was negotiated, two years ago, both sides engaged in bitter, intense negotiations for over three months without reaching agreement. The union had been forced to strike and the workers were off the job for nearly four weeks before a federal mediator was able to help the parties come to an agreement. In anticipation of expiration of the contract, both sides have started a propaganda campaign as they seek a bargaining advantage for the upcoming talks.

WHAT USEFUL DISTINCTIONS CAN BE MADE BETWEEN THESE DIFFERENT TYPES OF SITUATIONS?

1. *Transactions vs. disputes* (planning relationships and preventing legal problems vs. resolving disputes or problems once they have arisen.)

2. *Motives of principals* involved may include:

   a. donative intent;

   b. economic exchange (profitability);

   c. avoid personal embarrassment;

   d. maximize/minimize dollar recovery;

   e. public good/political expediency;

   f. punish a wrongdoer.

3. *Arena* in which the negotiations will take place:

   a. Living room of wealthy donor;

   b. Business offices;

   c. Law firm offices;

   d. City Council or other administrative chambers;

   e. Judge's chambers;

   f. Trial court;

   g. Conference room of an office building or hotel.

4. *Legal rules* applicable to the transaction or dispute.

It should be clear that no single set of skills is going to carry an attorney safely through each of these situations. In fact, an attorney may be highly competent in two or three of the situations, but utterly ineffective in the others.

3. *Some Questions About Choice of Strategy*

The Williams and Schneider data suggest that negotiators will have competitive/adversarial opponents about 25% of the time. What strategies are available to negotiators who want to interact cooperatively (in the problem solving mode) for discovering, in the early stages of the negotiation, whether their opponents are dealing cooperatively or competitively?

Since the data suggest that some—perhaps most—attorneys have the ability to negotiate using either style, is there a possibility that negotiators can, by their own conduct, influence opponent behavior in favor of cooperation?

4. *Use of Facts in Bargaining: Strategic Issues*

A central issue in bargaining literature concerns the role of information in the process and outcome of bargaining. Most economic and game theoretic models of negotiation assume that both parties to a negotiation have "perfect" or "complete" information, which means that they have full knowledge of (1) the facts of the problem; (2) the rules governing resolution of the problem; (3) the range of alternatives or strategies available to each of them; and (4) the utility function of each of them (i.e. the importance or value to each party of each item in the payoff matrix). Most of these models further assume that neither side will change its utility functions over the course of the bargaining.

Economic and game theoretic models also assume that negotiators and their opponents will both make decisions on the basis of rational choice, which is a formal concept meaning that (1) individuals evaluate alternatives in their environment on the basis of their personal preferences among those options, (2) their preference orderings are consistent and transitive, and (3) they always choose the preferred alternatives. *These assumptions define away some of the major problems indigenous to legal negotiations.*

The central problem for lawyers is the inverse of these two sets of assumptions including lack of complete information and lack of knowledge about how opponents will act and react.

For lawyers, the problem of information becomes a problem of obtaining sufficient (or adequate) information and presenting it is a way which does justice to its truth (i.e. credibility). The skills involved in gathering, analyzing, and persuading with facts are complex and varied. Some relate to the insight and creativity required in knowing what to look for and where to look (e.g. in a products liability case, how do you prove negligent manufacture?) Other skills relate to the mechanics of discovery: knowing how, when, and why to use the various procedural devices available in a particular jurisdiction. Sometimes the choice of jurisdiction may be dictated by the quality of discovery rules available—as between federal and state courts, for example. Additional, and more sophisticated, skills are required in making the strategic choices about when, where, and how to obtain information. On one hand, there is a danger of alienating the other side, polarizing the parties, and creating unnecessary delay, costs, and animosity by overly aggressive or burdensome discovery tactics. On the other hand, there is a concomitant danger of under-discovery, of overlooking or failing to track down the crucial evidence or information upon which the case depends.

Finally, there are strategic decisions which must be made. When and how should you disclose facts to give them their best impact? Many trial attorneys recommend that you save your best facts and your most persuasive arguments, so you can introduce them as surprises at trial. The difficulty of that position—however effective it may be if the case does go to trial—is that on the average, only about 1 case in 20 goes to trial. If attorneys reserve their best facts and arguments for use at trial *and* settle 19 out of 20 cases, then they are settling cases on *less than their best facts and arguments,* which strongly suggests they are getting less than full value for their clients with respect to the vast majority of matters they dispose of through negotiated agreements.

Chapter Four

STAGES OF THE NEGOTIATION PROCESS

I. INTRODUCTION

Negotiation is a repetitive process that follows reasonably predictable patterns. Yet in legal disputes, so much of attorney attention and energy is absorbed by pretrial procedures and approaching trial dates that they fail to recognize the identifiable patterns and dynamics of the negotiation process.

A useful description of the dynamics of legal negotiations can be developed by selectively applying the insights and observations available in the legal and non-legal literature describing negotiation and through videotaped examples of legal negotiating. Based on such analyses, five negotiation stages can be identified.

A. STAGE ONE: PREPARATION

1. Information Gathering

   a. Attorneys must ascertain the relevant factual, legal, economic, medical, cultural, etc. information.

   b. Attorneys must develop discovery plans designed to elicit information from opponents that can not be unilaterally obtained.

2. Determining and Valuing Underlying Client Needs and Interests

   a. Attorneys must ask clients detailed questions to ascertain real client desires—not necessarily what they *say* they want, but what they really hope to achieve from this matter.

   b. Attorneys and clients must assign priorities to the different issues involved.

      (i) What are the *essential items* clients must obtain if the bargaining interactions are to be successful?

      (ii) What are the *important issues* the clients would like to obtain, but which are not essential to an acceptable agreement?

      (iii) What are the *desirable items* the clients would be willing to exchange for essential or important items?

    c. Attorneys and clients must jointly determine the relative values of the items within each category so they can know which should be given up for other items within that same general category.

3. Attorneys must develop logical and objective arguments—and occasionally emotional appeals—to support client demands for the particular items involved.

4. Attorneys must carefully estimate the underlying needs and interests of the *other side* by trying to place themselves in the shoes of *opposing parties*.

    a. What are their essential, important, and desirable items?

    b. How strongly are opponents likely to value each of those items?

    c. What are the items the parties could possibly exchange to enhance the value of agreement to both sides (*e.g.*, giving up an important item for an essential item or a desirable item for an important item)?

5. Attorneys must develop principled opening positions which they can rationally defend and which provide them with a reasonable amount of bargaining flexibility.

6. Attorneys must determine their side's aspiration level for *each item* to be discussed, recognizing that there is a direct correlation between aspiration levels and bargaining outcomes.

7. Attorneys and clients must determine their Best Alternatives to Negotiated Agreements (BATNAs)[1]—i.e., the lines they will not go above or below, preferring their non-settlement alternatives to less beneficial agreements.

B. STAGE TWO: ORIENTATION AND POSITIONING

1. Orientation

    a. Opposing attorneys begin dealing with each other.

---

1. R. Fisher & W. Ury, *Getting to Yes* (2d ed. 1991). Parties who view their negotiation options from a negative perspective often call this their WATNAs, for Worst Alternatives to Negotiated Agreements. See also R. Mnookin, S. Peppet & A. Tulumello, *Beyond Winning; Negotiating to Create Value in Deals and Disputes* (Belknap/Harvard 2000).

       b.   Relationships are defined and established.

       c.   The tone for the bargaining interaction is developed.

2. Positioning

       a.   Negotiators talk primarily about the strengths or merits of their side of the case (often in very general terms).

       b.   Negotiators work to establish their opening positions. Possible positions include:

          (i) *Maximalist Position.* Asking for much more than they expect to obtain.

          (ii) *Equitable Position.* Taking a more reasonable opening position.

          (iii) *Integrative Position.* Presenting or seeking to discover alternative solutions to the problem as a means of putting together the most attractive package for all concerned.

       c.   Both sides create the illusion of being inalterably committed to their opening positions.

C.   STAGE THREE: ARGUMENTATION

1. Each side seeks to present its case in the strategically most favorable light.

2. Each side seeks to discover the *real* positions of the other, while trying to avoid disclosing its own real positions:

       a.   Issues become more clearly defined.

       b.   Underlying client needs and interest are explored to allow the participants to look for ways to expand the pie and generate jointly efficient exchanges.

       c.   The strengths and weaknesses of each side become more apparent.

3. Each side seeks to discover and reduce the real positions of the other.

4. The expectations of each side with respect to what can be obtained in the case undergo substantial changes.

5. Concessions are made by one or both sides as they look for trades that may simultaneously benefit both parties.

D.   STAGE FOUR: EMERGENCE AND CRISIS

1. Negotiators experience the pressure of approaching deadlines.

2. Each side realizes that one or both of them must make major concessions, present new alternatives, or admit dead-

lock and resort to their non-settlement alternatives (trials for litigators).

3. Each side seeks and gives clues about areas in which additional concessions might be given.

4. Innovative alternatives are proposed, and more concessions are made.

5. Crisis is reached:

    a. Neither side wants to give any more.

    b. Both sides are wary of being exploited or taken advantage of.

    c. Both sides have given up more than they initially planned to concede.

    d. Both sides know they must stop somewhere.

    e. The deadline is upon them—one of the parties must accept the other's final offer or there is a breakdown and impasse.

    f. The client worries whether to accept the attorney's recommendation to accept the other side's finally proposed terms.

E. STAGE FIVE: AGREEMENT OR FINAL BREAKDOWN

1. If the parties achieve a settlement, Stage Five includes:

    a. Working out the specific details of the final accord.

    b. Justifying and reinforcing each other and the clients about the desirability of the agreement.

    c. Formalizing the agreement.

2. If the negotiations break down and are not revived, the case goes to trial (or transactional parties seek others with whom to interact).

As simple as this outline is, it becomes a surprisingly powerful tool for bargaining lawyers. Inexperienced attorneys often misperceive which stage of the process the case is in and use tactics that are unnecessary or even harmful to the dynamics of the negotiation. One example is the tendency of cooperative/problem-solving attorneys to move psychologically through the stages more quickly than competitive/adversarial opponents. When no agreement is forthcoming, they assume that the final stage has been reached, and they envision final breakdowns in the bargaining process.

77

II. DISCUSSION OF THE STAGES

A. STAGE ONE: PREPARATION

1. Information Gathering

The most important stage of most bargaining interactions takes place before the parties even begin their serious discussions. This is where the negotiators initially ascertain the relevant factual, legal, economic, medical, cultural, and other information. If they hope to appreciate their own side's true bargaining situations, lawyers must try to understand the strengths and weaknesses of their own clients' circumstances. This will allow them to accurately assess their bargaining power, and enable them to enhance their strengths and diminish the negative influence of their possible weaknesses.

2. Determining and Valuing Underlying Client Needs and Interests

When most clients seek legal assistance, they ask for terms they think lawyers are likely to get for them. Attorneys need to go behind these initial positions and ascertain their real underlying needs and interests. What do the clients truly want to achieve through the impending bargaining interactions? What are their *essential* items, their *important* items, and their *desirable* items? How do they prioritize the different items within each category? For someone who has been discharged, do they want reinstatement to their former position, or would they prefer a cash buyout? Does a severely injured claimant prefer an immediate monetary settlement or a structured arrangement that would provide them with payouts over a number of years? Would a corporate seller accept stock or goods/services instead of cash? Once attorneys appreciate client values and priorities, they can begin to understand which items should be exchanged for higher priority terms.

Attorneys have to develop logical factual, legal, and even emotional arguments to support the positions they plan to take. This approach is designed to enhance the confidence the lawyers will have in their positions once they begin to interact with opponents. Individuals who are able to exude real confidence in their positions often induce less prepared and less confident opponents to reassess their situations in favor of the positions being articulated by the more confident participants.

Less effective negotiators frequently evaluate their own client situations quite well, but fail to look across the bargaining table and endeavor to place themselves in the shoes of their opponents. What are the underlying needs and interests of the *opposing side*? What are their viable leverage factors, and what are their weaknesses? How can their strengths be countered, and how might their weaknesses be exploited?

Many negotiators concede more bargaining power to their opponents than they deserve. They become intimately familiar with their own side's weaknesses, but fail to appreciate the other side's vulnerabilities. They thus accord the other side more leverage than they deserve. It is only through a thoughtful and thorough comparison of their own side's strengths and weaknesses with those of their opponents that lawyers can ascertain their actual bargaining strength.

Once attorneys have gathered the relevant client and opponent information, they have to determine three critical issues. First, what should be their *opening positions* and how can they logically defend those positions? It is critical to remember the importance of establishing principled opening positions that can be logically explained, since wholly irrational positions lack credibility and turn off other parties. Second, what are their side's *aspirations* with respect to *each issue* to be negotiated? When in doubt, their goals should be higher rather than lower, recognizing the direct correlation between aspiration levels and final outcomes. Finally, what is their *bottom line* below which they will not go? What are their Best Alternatives to Negotiated Agreements (BATNAs)? It is vital for lawyers to acknowledge that bad deals are worse than no deals when the negotiated terms are worse than their non-settlement alternatives.

B. STAGE TWO: ORIENTATION AND POSITIONING

1. Orientation

Stage Two of the negotiation process involves two interrelated dynamics, described as orientation and positioning. Orientation is the less obvious of the two. In routine matters, it is the natural by-product of the interaction between the attorneys as they begin work on a case. Letters and e-mails are exchanged, phone calls are made, and each lawyer becomes oriented to the basic approach and style of the other. In most cases negotiators are not aware of the orientation dynamics. When opposing attorneys are law students participating in clinical courses or new law graduates, the operation of the orientation phase becomes obvious, and most attorneys become very aware of the nature of the relationships that are being established. The importance of the orientation phase is not limited to such special situations, however. In every case, even between experienced lawyers, the negotiating relationships that emerge will decide whether the participants will approach each other as cooperative/problem-solving, competitive/problem-solving, or competitive/adversarial negotiators, and will determine what strategies and tactics will be used by the attorneys involved

2. Positioning

The second aspect of Stage Two is closely related to the first, but it has a dynamic of its own. The lawyers articulate their opening positions. At this early stage in the dispute, that exchange not as simple as it appears. The facts are not all in, the legal questions are not fully researched, and unforeseen developments loom on the horizon. In the face of these uncertainties, the negotiators must leave themselves a certain amount of latitude, yet they must develop credible opening demands and offers.

As noted in the outline, there are essentially three strategies that can be used in framing an opening position. Negotiators may adopt the *maximalist strategy* of asking for more than they expect to obtain, they may adopt the *equitable strategy* of taking positions that are fair to both sides, or they may adopt the *integrative strategy* of searching for alternative solutions that would generate the most attractive combination for all concerned. Each strategy has its own strengths and weaknesses.

a.   Maximalist Positioning

Arguments for maximalist positioning begin with the assumption that opening offers constitute bargaining positions, and, no matter how long bargainers may deny it, they expect to come down from them to find agreements. Maximalist positioning has several advantages. These position statements effectively hide the bargainer's real or minimum expectations, they eliminate the danger of committing to overly modest case evaluations, they provide covers for them while they seeks to learn real opponent positions, and they will very likely induce opponents to reduce their expectations. They also provide negotiators with something to give up, with concessions they can make to come to terms with opponents. This last factor may be especially important when opponents also open high, and negotiators are required to trade concessions as they move toward mutually agreeable terms. These advantages lead many to believe that negotiators who make high opening demands, have high expectations, make relatively small and infrequent concessions, and are perceptive and unyielding fare better in the long run than their opponents.

The potential benefits of the maximalist approach need to be weighed against its potential demerits, which are those associated with competitive/adversarial strategies discussed at some length in Chapter Three. The most important weakness is the increased risk of bargaining stalemates. Competent opponents will prefer their non-settlement alternatives to the unreasonable demands and supporting tactics of maximalist negotiators, unless the opponents themselves can devise effective strategies to counter such maximalist behavior.

We observe in the data that competitive/adversarial attorneys at all levels of effectiveness are rated as making high opening demands. Yet, by definition, effective competitive/adversarials use the strategy proficiently, while ineffective competitive/adversarials do not. We are forced to conclude that in the legal context the maximalist strategy does not consistently bring high returns for those who use it—only for those who employ it effectively.

How high demands can be without losing their effectiveness depends on several considerations. One is the nature of the remedies being sought. By their nature, contract damages are less inflatable than personal injury damages, for example, and negotiators who multiply their contract damages as they do their personal injury claims will undermine their own credibility. Another consideration is local custom. Specialized groups within the bar develop norms and customs that provide measures against which the reasonableness or extremism of demands can be evaluated. Not all high demands are the same. Some demands lack credibility on their face by their inappropriateness and lack of congruity in the context in which they are made. But the level of demands is not the sole factor. The data suggest that effective competitive/adversarial negotiators are able to establish the credibility and plausibility of high demands by relying on convincing legal argumentation. Ineffective competitive/adversarials lack the skills to do this, and, in the absence of convincing support, their high demands lack credibility.

Finally, it should be noted that the effectiveness of high demands will depend upon the opponents against whom the high demands are made. In cases where opponents are unsure of the actual case values, high opening demands by maximizing negotiators have the desired effect. The opponents, unsure of case values, use the maximizer's high opening demands as standards against which to set their own goals. However, when the opponents have evaluated their cases and arrived at appropriate value judgments, the opponents interpreted maximizer high opening demands as evidence of unreasonableness. This causes maximizer credibility to be diminished, and the likelihood of bargaining breakdowns increases.

b. Equitable Positioning

Equitable positions are calculated to be fair to both sides. Their most notable proponent, O. Bartos,[2] challenged the assumption of maximalist theorists that both sides to negotiations are trying to maximize their own payoffs or benefits. He argued that a competing value is also operative—that negotiators feel a cooperative desire to arrive at solutions fair to both sides. In support of this argument, he cited not only humanistic literature defending equality as an essential ingredient of justice, but also anthropological and sociological studies confirming the widespread existence and operation in society of an egalitarian norm of reciprocity. Bartos conducted numerous theoretical and experimental negotiation studies which lead him to believe that the human desire to deal fairly with others is preferable to a more competitive strategy.

This equitable approach is considered as the most economical and efficient method of conflict resolution. It minimizes the risk of deadlock and avoids the costs of delay occasioned by extreme bargaining positions. Bartos recommended that negotiators be scrupulously fair and that they avoid the temptation to take advantage of naive opponents. He cautioned

2. O. Bartos, "Simple Model of Negotiation," in I.W. Zartman, *The Negotiation Process* 13 (1978).

that the equitable approach requires trust, which allows both sides to believe they are being treated fairly. Nonetheless, trust must be tempered with realism. It is out of trust that negotiators make concessions, but if their trust is not rewarded or returned in fair fashion, further concessions should be withheld until their opponents reciprocate.

Equitable negotiators do not always open negotiations with statements specifying their desires to achieve mutually beneficial solutions. Rather, they open with positions that show they are serious about finding fair agreement, and they trustingly work toward mid-points between their reasonable opening position and the reasonable opening positions of their opponents. Unless both sides come forward with reasonable opening positions, it will be difficult for one side to compel the other to move toward an equitable resolution.

Referring back to the data on cooperative/problem-solving and competitive/adversarial negotiators, we intuitively suspect that Bartos' equitable negotiators are cooperative/problem-solvers. This observation is borne out by the extremely high ratings received by cooperative/problem-solving attorneys on characteristics such as trustworthy, ethical, honest, and fair. Just as with our analysis of maximalist positioning by competitive/adversarial attorneys, it must be pointed out that the use of equitable positioning by cooperative/problem-solving attorneys does not always generate satisfactory results. It is obviously satisfactory as used by effective cooperative/problem-solvers, but it is likely to be deficient when used by ineffective cooperative/problem-solverss. We must conclude that the positioning strategy, whether maximalist or equitable, does not guarantee success. Whichever approach is used, it must be employed with care and acumen or it will not be effective.

c.   Integrative Positioning

Integrative Positioning involves more than opening demands and offers. It describes an attitude or approach that carries through the other stages of the negotiation, and is an alternative to pure positional bargaining. The most effective advocates of this method have been Roger Fisher and William Ury who advise negotiators to avoid positioning completely.[3] Among business people, the method is seen as the art of problem solving.

Integrative negotiators view cases as presenting alternative solutions, and they believe that chances for reaching agreements are enhanced by discovering innovative alternatives reflecting the underlying interests of the parties, and seeking to arrange the alternatives in packages that yield maximum benefit to both parties. This strategy is often identified with exchange transactions involving many variables, and is generally seen as having limited utility in personal injury actions, for example, where the fundamental issue is how much money defendants are going to pay plaintiffs—a classic distributive problem.

3.   *Getting to Yes* (2d ed. 1991).

Even personal injury cases may have important integrative elements that should not be dismissed. Where significant injuries are involved that will cause future medical difficulties, a one-time payment may not be as beneficial—personally and from a possible tax perspective—as a structured arrangement that provides for specified payments made over a number of years. Defendants may alternatively promise to cover all future claimant medical expenses, in exchange for a lower monetary payment. This satisfies plaintiff concerns about affording such future medical costs, and it allows defendants to spread their costs over many years.

We conclude that even in the domain of actionable disputes, there is substantial opportunity for use of an integrative approach. In reference to the data on negotiator types in Part I, it appears likely that integrative bargaining can be used by effective negotiators of all three styles, even though it is more likely to be employed by cooperative/problem-solvers and competitive/problem-solvers than competitive/adversarials.

3. Inalterable Commitments to Opening Positions

The next element of Stage Two relating to positioning is that both sides seek to establish the illusion that they are inalterably committed to their opening positions. The purposes served by this tactic are several. It lends credibility to opening demands and offers, and, particularly in the case of high opening demands, it provides time for such demands to influence the hopes and expectations of the other side. It gives negotiators time to make further evaluations of their situations and to gain information about what their opponents are willing to accept. When the negotiators wish to begin more serious discussions, they have to be prepared to move from their extreme opening positions. If they are overly enamored of their significant demands or parsimonious offers, subsequent movement may be difficult and negotiation breakdowns may result.

4. Duration of Stage Two

An important aspect of Stage Two is the fact that it generally consumes a longer period of time than all of the other stages combined. One reason for this is that in many actionable cases the attorneys do not begin serious settlement discussions until trial deadlines make themselves felt. This observation is supported by Professor Williams' finding that over 70% of cases in his study were resolved within thirty days of trial, with a hefty 13% being resolved on the day of trial. Court calendars are sometimes so crowded that these deadlines may not approach for two years or more. Few cases require this amount of time to become ripe for settlement, so clients may endure long delays attributed to court congestion even though their cases will ultimately be settled.

The solution to this problem was also suggested by Professor Williams' Phoenix data. The major problem giving rise to congested trial courts was not inefficient administration of cases by judicial personnel; it was the disproportionately high percentage of cases brought to trial by an identifiable subsection of the practicing bar. He found in 300 cases studied that the percentage of cases brought to trial was directly related to the negotiating skills of the attorneys involved. The less skilled they were at negotiation, the more cases they brought to the trial court for resolution. Effective negotiators as a group constituted half of the practicing bar (49%), yet, with their high settlement rate, they accounted for only 31% of the cases that went trial. Average negotiators constituted 37% of the bar, yet they accounted for 46% of the cases that went to trial. Ineffective negotiators constituted 14% of the Bar, but they accounted for 23% of the cases that went to trial. Together, average and ineffective negotiators constituted roughly half of the bar (51%), yet they accounted for over two thirds (69%) of the cases that went to trial.

The probability of pre-trail resolutions was also reflective of the trial effectiveness of the lawyers studied. Effective negotiators of both types were rated as highly effective *trial* attorneys. Unfortunately for the quality of trial court proceedings, these effective trial attorneys settled 80% of their cases. Although they made up 49% of the bar, they accounted for a disproportionately low 31% of all cases that went to trial. By comparison, less effective negotiators (except for the average/cooperative group) were rated as decidedly ineffective trial attorneys. Although they made up only 51% of the bar, they accounted for 69% of the cases that went to trial. The remarkable statistic is that if these less effective negotiators could have improved their negotiating skills sufficiently to bring their settlement rates into line with those of effective negotiators, their increased settlement rate would have reduced the trial burden of Phoenix courts by a full 37%.

The suggestion that less effective negotiators can develop their negotiation skills and thereby significantly reduce the number of cases they must take to trial is not one to be dismissed. Our state of knowledge about negotiation has vastly increased over the past thirty years. Properly organized and taught courses dramatically increase lawyer negotiating effectiveness, and less effective negotiators would benefit the most from these developments. To be sure, the objective is not merely a higher settlement rate, but improved procedures for the fair resolution of disputes.

C. STAGE THREE: ARGUMENTATION

---

1. Overview

It is axiomatic that the opening positions established by negotiations in Stage Two will be some distance apart. If not, there would be no controversy and the case would be resolved immediately. Given the distance between the opening positions, some procedure is necessary whereby claims may be explored and evaluated, and positions may be moderated. These dynamics come into play in Stage Three. Both sides begin to gather information about the real or hidden expectations of the other, while simultaneously trying to avoid disclosing information about their own minimum expectations and utilities. A great deal of information may be exchanged, but it is presented in a favorable light. Through this process, the legal and factual issues become better defined and the strengths and weaknesses of both sides become more apparent.

2. The Problem of Making Concessions

It is usually in Stage Three that the first concessions are made. Concessions are important devices because they are the primary means by which agreement is approached. They also have importance as instruments of strategy. The task of cooperative/problem-solving attorneys is to establish cooperative, trusting atmospheres where just and equitable outcomes can be sought. One of the primary means for doing this is through the selective granting of concessions. By comparison, the task of competitive/adversarial or maximalist negotiators is to obtain the maximum number of concessions from their opponents while making the fewest and smallest concessions possible. This is consistent with their goal of obtaining the maximum possible outcomes for themselves. Competitive/problem-solvers tend to move more cautiously than cooperative/problem-solvers, but more quickly than competitive/adversarials.

These conflicting approaches illustrate why the issue of concession-making assumes such importance in economic models of bargaining, and why it calls for more respectful treatment within the legal context. I.W. Zartman[4] described four sets of theories about concession rates that are relevant here. The theories concern predictions about what effect concessions will have on opponents. The first prediction is that concession rates will be reciprocal, in the sense that concessions by one negotiator will be matched by concessions of comparable value by the opponent. A second and inconsistent prediction is that concession rates will be exploitive, meaning that concessions by one negotiator will be met by smaller concessions from the opposite side. By this view, negotiators who make large concessions will find their opponents making minimal concessions in exchange, while negotiators who make small concessions hope to induce their opponents to make large concessions in return. The third prediction is that concession-making by one negotiator is unresponsive to the concession-making behavior of the other in the ways suggested above, but responds instead to deadline pressures. As trial dates approach, both sides use this time pressure to induce the other to make favorable final concessions. The fourth prediction is the projective view, which argues that parties mutually aim at a target point falling between

4. I.W. Zartman, *The Negotiation Process: Theories and Applications* 81 (Sage Publications 1978).

their opening positions ["bracketing"], and they consciously or unconsciously adjust their concession patterns to arrive at that mid-point.

The crucial task for effective negotiators is to determine which prediction accurately describes the way concessions will operate in specific negotiating situations with particular opponents, and then to adjust their own negotiating strategies according to that knowledge. As we see in videotaped examples of attorney negotiations, not all attorneys take this task adequately into account.

D. STAGE FOUR: EMERGENCE AND CRISIS

1. Effect of Deadlines

As a deadline approaches, a crisis is reached. Concessions have been made, neither side wishes to give anything more, both sides are wary of being exploited, and both sides know that they must stop somewhere. At this point, one party suggests a final offer and says, in effect, that's the best I can do. Take it or else we go to trial. As Ikle has emphasized, this kind of demand actually presents a threefold choice: take it, leave it, or come up with something else.[5] This acute observation suggests that attorneys who lack imagination may see only a two-fold choice: take it or leave it. They may decide that since they cannot take it, impasse has been reached, and the negotiation is over. It is important to remember the third alternative, to come up with something else. Furthermore, what negotiators come up with does not have to involve significant concessions. It can be an integrative proposal, suggesting other alternatives or new combinations of alternatives that increase the utility of settlement to the parties without decreasing their total payoffs.

The Phoenix data suggest that deadline pressures are perceived differently in each specialized area of law. In criminal law, deadline pressures are not extreme until a few days before trial; it is the same in personal injury cases. In commercial and real property disputes, however, the mere threat of filing a case may be considered heavy handed, and if the case is filed, the deadline pressures begin to mount two months or more before trial.[6] Attorneys should adjust their own expectations and

---

5. F. Ikle, *How Nations Negotiate* (Harper & Row 1964).

6. In his study, Professor Williams found that fully 35% of the real property disputes and 29% of the commercial disputes settled without filings. This compares with only 7.5% of personal injury cases and 13.8% of divorce cases. At the other end of the scale were criminal cases. None were considered' to have settled without formal charges being made, and a telling 32.3% were not resolved until the day of trial. An additional 35.5% were settled from 2 to 20 days before trial, with the remainder settling from 11 to 90 days before trial. By contrast, in personal injury cases only 2.5% held out until the day of trial, with a surprisingly high 42.5% being settled from 2 to 10 days before trial. That is clearly the crucial period for personal injury attorneys and clients. Commercial and real property cases are more strung out, indicating that attorneys prefer not to allow the trial dates to get so close as in criminal and personal injury cases. In commercial cases, for exam-

sensitivities accordingly. Personal injury lawyers who feel an intense need to settle two months before trial are likely to do their clients and themselves a disservice if they overreact to the slowly approaching trial date.

2.   The Client, the Opposing Party, and the Negotiation Process

We have said little in our analysis of bargaining stages about clients, preferring to focus exclusively on dynamics between the attorneys. However, the attorneys are not negotiating on behalf of their own immediate interests, but rather on behalf of clients. The clients come with their own sets of expectations about what their case outcomes should be—expectations that derive from a wide variety of sources, many of which are outside attorney cognizance and control. These include general expectations about how cases are processed through the American legal system, about the importance of trials as a standard of fairness and a forum for the vindication of wrongs, about the anticipated monetary values of their cases, and so on. Attorneys also have an input in creating client expectations. Their greatest influence is probably during the first few consultations with their clients, perhaps even before the clients accept the attorneys as their representatives. Attorneys may estimate for clients probable case values, often based on an assumption of 100% liability or clear breach of contract. As cases unfold, the attorneys mentally subtract value to reflect the degree of factual or legal weakness in the claims, while the clients continue to focus on the 100% liability figure. For whatever reason, the expectations of clients are commonly some distance from those of their attorneys, and it is in this context that the relationship of clients to the negotiation process becomes obvious and determinative. Professor Williams observed this, for example, in the Phoenix data, where attorneys judged that client refusals to accept deals was the primary reason for the failure to settle in over 50% of the cases that went to trial.

Lawyers are expressly commissioned to represent the interests of their clients, and the task includes helping their clients to form realistic expectations of how and on what terms their cases should be resolved. However, because of the high level of uncertainty inherent in the valuation of cases and prediction of court outcomes, lawyers cannot make unfailingly accurate judgments during the early stages of disputes. Arriving at these judgments involves a process that can only occur over time. In the largest number of instances, lawyer evaluations substantially change during that process as the full dimensions of both sides of cases become revealed. The task for lawyers is to create realistic expectations in their clients at the outset, and keep them abreast of their own evolving case evaluations.

ple, 4.5% settled the day of the trial, only 12.5% settled 2 to 10 days before trial, and the bulk of these cases settled from 11 to 60 days before trial.

Attorneys have a duty to develop case solutions that are acceptable not only to themselves and their clients, but also to the opposing attorneys and their clients. However, once solutions are achieved, psychological reinforcement may be required by all concerned. Effective negotiators will not only seek to reinforce themselves, but also will take great pains to provide adequate reinforcement to the opposing parties. If negotiators fail to provide such reinforcement, they may be faced with subsequent repudiations of agreements by disgruntled opponents. For these reasons, negotiators must make a point to include, as integral parts of Stages Four and Five, procedures that will reassure opposing parties, as well as their own clients.

E. STAGE FIVE: AGREEMENT OR FINAL BREAKDOWN

1. Agreement

If the parties come to an agreement, the work is not over. There are important steps yet to be taken. The first of these is to work out the details of the agreement. Some attorneys negotiate in a way that keeps the details alive and active in the ongoing discussion. This is a common feature of integrative bargaining, where alternative solutions to each issue are explored and mutually beneficial trades are discovered.

Other attorneys prefer to negotiate only the most basic issues, such as money, leaving the other terms to be wrapped up after general agreement has been reached. One variation of this strategy is to separate the issues according to how difficult they are to resolve, then to resolve them working from the easiest to the most difficult. Whatever variation or combination is used, the attorneys at some point have an agreement, yet important details may remain to be worked out. These are sometimes known as "Oh, by the way's." These details must be considered important to the overall quality and favorability of the agreement and should be given the attention they deserve.

The need for attention to detail becomes apparent as negotiators undertake the process of formalizing the agreement. This process is covered in Chapter 5, Section V(c) below. Treatment may also be found under the somewhat obscure heading of "Compromise and Settlement" in *Am.Jur.2d* and *Corpus Juris Secundum*. Both encyclopedias also provide extensive forms and other supporting documents.

2. Final Breakdown

If the parties are unable to arrive at a settlement and the negotiations are not revived, a final breakdown occurs and the case goes to trial for resolution. The term "final breakdown" is used because not all negotiation breakdowns are final. Breakdowns can occur as negotiating ploys designed to put pressure on opponents. As a simple example, insurance defense counsel effectively use this tactic to bring increased pressure to bear on their opponents by refusing to enter into serious negotiations until a few days (sometimes a few hours) before trial. They would be robbed of this tactic if plaintiff lawyers adopted a firm policy, and held to it, of never negotiating once cases are within a week of trial. The effect would be to move the operative deadline to a week before trial. It might yield advantages to one or both sides, but it might also increase the number of cases going to trial.

III. THE INTERPLAY BETWEEN LEGAL PROCEEDINGS AND THE NEGOTIATION PROCESS

To this point, we have been preoccupied with the dynamics of negotiation as a dispute resolution process. In the legal context, however, it cannot be analyzed independently. It is operating concurrently with a competing process having a force and dynamic of its own: litigation. In our discussion, we noted the pressures for settlement occasioned by trial deadlines. In reality, however, the arrival of the trial date is the culmination of a series of preparatory actions that begins before the case is filed and proceeds step by step through the complex procedures of choosing a forum, pleading, discovery, preparation of witnesses, preparation of evidence (documentary and demonstrative), pretrial conferences, motions and all related work. These aspects of legal procedures are undertaken (or have the potential of being undertaken) by the attorneys concurrently as the case moves, psychologically, through stages one to five of the negotiation process. Some procedures, such as pleading, coincide with basic elements of the negotiation process, including preparation and the articulation of (extreme) opening positions. The utilization and timing of other procedural steps are matters open to the discretion of the attorneys and can be used either to help or to hinder the psychology and dynamics of each successive stage in the negotiation process.

Effective negotiators will take full cognizance of the relationship between pre-trial procedures and the stages identified in the negotiation process. They will calculate their moves within the legal sphere to further their objectives of arriving, if possible, at settlements more favorable to their clients than trial would be likely to produce.

For example, in a contract dispute between two reputable businesses, it is commonly feasible and desirable to negotiate and arrive at a suitable agreement without ever filing an action. On the other hand, if one or both parties refuse to negotiate seriously, and other efforts fail, a forum is selected and a complaint is filed. In a business context, this is a serious step, and it may be enough to provoke serious attempts to resolve the case without trial. If it is not, further pre-trial procedures are undertaken step by step, always in ways that have the greatest strategic value for an advantageous settlement as well as maximum value in the event of trial.

The business dispute example just mentioned suggests the essential tension that exists between negotiation and formal legal processes; the former requiring a conciliatory approach and the latter a more adversarial approach. In Stewart Macaulay's pioneering study (1963), the typical sequence of escalation from conciliation to adversariness was as follows. First, relevant employees of the two businesses, usually production or purchasing people, would try to work out their differences informally. If this failed, the production or purchasing people would talk with house counsel or outside counsel concerning possible approaches to the other party, and they would again attempt to arrive at a resolution with their counterparts in the other business. If this was not fruitful, legal counsel would be asked to write a letter to the other business on letterhead stationery, so that they could see that lawyers were now involved. If this level of legal involvement was not sufficient, the attorneys were authorized to file an action. This sequence represents a gradual shift from a conciliatory approach to an adversarial one, and it has important implications for the outcome of the dispute and the future relations between the parties involved. In an adversarial relationship, there are not only the publicity, expenses, and delays of legal proceedings, but positions are hardened, relationships strained, and ill feelings bred. These are obviously detrimental and even fatal to the on-going business relationships involved.

The importance of restrained, conciliatory approaches to dispute resolution in the business context is often overlooked by attorneys. They become accustomed to using the legal process as a means of putting direct and unmistakable pressure to bear on opposing parties. They come to accept this level of tension as normal and desirable. While this attitude is obviously highly functional in many kinds of cases, it does not fit them all, least of all in the business context.

IV. PRE–BARGAINING DYNAMICS

Negotiations may include as many as five different dynamics. First, negotiators may consciously seek to develop their reputations as negotiators, and, in view of what the data say about reputations as trial attorneys, as proficient litigators. Common examples include the attorneys in every bar who are known and feared for their prowess at the negotiating table and/or in the courtroom. In many instances, even judges stand in awe and reverence of these advocates.

Second, one may begin an inventory and collection of resources that may prove useful once negotiations are underway. Taking a course in negotiation in law school or through a continuing legal education provider is an obvious example, as is the development of a negotiation notebook. A third dynamic is to exercise control over the timing of the bargaining: when it will begin, how long will sessions last, how long the whole process will take, and when will it finally terminate. It is likewise possible to have some influence over the location of the bargaining (my office, your office, a neutral third place) and the means of communication (telephone, e-mail, letter, face to face meeting, etc.) Advantage here is to plaintiffs, who have the burden of moving forward and who should see this as an opportunity, not a curse.

Fourth, there is sometimes a possibility of influencing the rules under which bargaining will take place. While legal negotiation presupposes legal rules, lawyers can influence the tenor and style of the negotiations—the informal etiquette that will or will not prevail. Finally, there is usually the chance to influence, and perhaps unilaterally determine, the definition of the issues at stake in the bargaining. Advantage here, again, is to plaintiffs, who can move forward on terms defined by their own preferences and strategies.

CHAPTER NOTE

1. Effects of Pretrial Conferences on Case Settlements

With the emergence of mediation as a frequent precursor to trial, pretrial conferences with a judge are becoming less important in the *settlement* process. The pretrial conference was originally conceived in large part as a device for reducing court congestion by helping attorneys settle their cases without trial. It has been widely adopted, nearly always with the hope it would help relieve court congestion. However, empirical studies of pretrial conferences have shown that the same percentage of cases tend to settle before trial, regardless of whether pretrial conferences are held. Pretrial conferences do not increase the likelihood of settlements (although they do appear to clarify factual and legal issues and thus reduce the burden of trial to some degree). Negotiators should not be misled into assuming that, if negotiations break down, pretrial conferences will induce opponents to accept reasonable settlements.

The insertion of judges into the negotiation process significantly complicates the dynamics. Judges are the symbol and embodiment of power in the legal system. They are expected to exercise this power. Their function is to encourage stipulations of fact and law, and to make express rulings regarding discovery and other matters basic to the interests of the attorneys. Attorneys face a genuine conflict between cooperative and adversarial demands made upon them in this context.

This conflict is compounded by the formality of many pretrial conference situations: a stenographer is often present, a record is being preserved, and the attorneys are naturally moved by this formality to adopt an adversarial approach for the record. This tendency to argumentation is encouraged by the fact that pretrial judges offer an important testing ground on which attorneys can try the theories and arguments they have developed. Inspection of videotapes of pretrial conferences demonstrates the validity of these observations. It can be seen that attorneys become preoccupied with persuading judges of the reasonableness and compelling nature of their positions and the unreasonableness of opponent positions. Attorneys also employ adversarial advocacy to influence judges to make favorable rulings and to apply pressure upon their opponents to settle.

Because of these factors, it is probably naive of attorneys to expect meaningful help from most judges in settling their cases. They must instead pay increased attention to their own skills and knowledge of the negotiation process to obtain favorable settlements.

On the other hand, in most jurisdictions there are "settling judges" who work more actively, if not aggressively, to encourage attorneys to settle. Some judicial training programs encourage judges to take more active approaches. When they perform this facilitative role effectively, they induce settlements in cases that would otherwise have gone to trial. Such judges are known by reputation in each locality and attorneys assigned to such judges should plan their cases with this additional factor in mind.

Except when appearing before true "settling judges," however, attorneys are best advised to harbor no illusions about pretrial conferences. Since statistics show they do not measurably improve the probability of settlements, the wisest course is for lawyers to rely on their own negotiating skills for settlement discussions and to use pretrial conferences as leverage toward this end. Objectives would obviously include: obtaining favorable rulings on discovery matters; formulating stipulations to reduce the factual and legal issues to their simplest terms; showing opponents the strength of their positions and their ability to argue them convincingly; and obtaining judicial and opponent reactions to their legal theories. In addition, if the judges conducting the conferences are settling judges, one goal should be to develop skills that enable advocates to diplomatically fend off or avoid unwarranted pressure on them and their clients to accept unfavorable settlement terms.

Chapter Five

THE LAW OF NEGOTIATION
AND SETTLEMENT

I. INTRODUCTION: IS THERE A LAW OF NEGOTIATION AND SETTLEMENT

It has been generally assumed that there was no body of law specifically applicable to the bargaining process. Negotiation has been perceived as an adjunct of the litigation process, which is governed by extensive collections of procedural, substantive, and ethical rules. The Code of Professional Responsibility and Model Rules have standards regulating trial conduct, trial publicity, communications with jurors, contacts with witnesses and courtroom officials, relationships with clients, relationships with opposing counsel, and relationships with judges. The law of evidence and the law of remedies govern substantive aspects of the litigation process. Since negotiation was perceived as incidental to litigation, there has been no apparent need for rules focusing specifically on the negotiation process.

The legal profession has become aware that negotiation is quantitatively more than an adjunct of litigation. It is the primary means of formal dispute resolution in the United States. It is time to recognize and contribute to the developing body of law governing the negotiated settlement of disputes.

II. THE GENERAL POLICY OF THE LAW TOWARD COMPROMISE AND SETTLEMENT

When the validity of settlement agreements is challenged, courts routinely assert a general policy in favor of negotiated settlements. Courts consistently acknowledge an important public interest in settling litigation. In support of this policy, courts often enforce settlement agreements despite minor errors in their formation and expansively interpret legal rules to preserve settlements. This policy is based on the perceived benefits of settlement compared with litigation. Settlements reduce legal expenses, save time for the parties and the court, and are more conducive to amicable outcomes and future relations between the parties. Nonetheless, the judicial policy favoring settlement agreements is weighed against other policy considerations. Courts will overturn settlement agreements found to be contrary to such other public interests.

III. CONTRACT LAW AS A SOURCE OF NEGOTIATION LAW

Settlement agreements are contracts. They are subject to the rules governing the formation, performance, and enforcement of contracts. Most of this law is unexceptional and need not be discussed here. This section discusses developments in contract law relating specifically, though not uniquely, to settlement agreements.

A. THE NOTION OF GOOD FAITH IN BARGAINING

Several developments in negotiation law are advanced in the *Restatement, Second, of Contracts* (1981). Section 205, articulates "a duty of good faith and fair dealing" in the performance and enforcement of contracts, defining good faith as, "honesty in fact in the conduct or transaction concerned." *See also* UCC Section 1–201(10). Professor Robert Summers has observed that the American good faith standard operates primarily as an "excluder" of "bad faith" conduct.[1] *Restatement* Section 205 adopts the excluding strategy by proscribing conduct that violates community standards of decency, fairness, or reasonableness.

How is a contractual duty of good faith relevant to legal negotiators? The *Restatement* defines the duty of good faith and fair dealing to apply to the assertion, settlement, and litigation of contract claims and defenses, all of which lawyers are frequently involved in. Comments to Section 205 specifically condemn such acts as:

1. Conjuring up a pretended dispute,

2. Asserting an interpretation contrary to one's own understanding,

3. Falsification of facts,

4. Taking unfair advantage of the necessitous circumstances of the other party to extort a modification of a contract,

5. Harassing demands for assurances of performance,

6. Rejection of performance for unstated reasons,

7. Willful failure to mitigate damages,

---

1. Robert Summers, *"Good Faith" in General Contract Law and the Sales Provi-* sions of the Uniform Commercial Code, 54 Va. L. Rev. 195, 199–207 (1968).

8. Abuse of a power to determine compliance or to terminate a contract.

The rather laissez faire American approach to good faith negotiating should be contrasted with Article 2–301(3) of the *Principles of European Contract Law* (Ole Lando & Hugh Beale, eds. 2000) which specifically recognizes: "It is contrary to good faith and fair dealing ... for a party to enter into or continue negotiations with no real intention to reach an agreement with the other party." Comment C indicates that a party entering into such sham negotiations may be held liable to the other party for the costs that party has incurred. Similar liability may be imposed on a party that breaks off on-going negotiations in bad faith to the detriment of the other side. Should U.S. courts or legislatures impose liability on such "bad faith" negotiators?

B. THE USE OF THREATS IN BARGAINING

Sections 175 and 176 of the *Restatement, Second, Contracts* limit the use of threats as negotiating tactics. Section 175 states: "If a party's manifestation of assent is induced by an improper threat by the other party that leaves the victim no reasonable alternative, the contract is voidable by the victim."

The meaning of improper threat is elaborated in Section 176, which establishes two categories of improper threats:

(1) A threat is improper if

    (a) what is threatened is a crime or a tort, or the threat itself would be a crime or a tort if it resulted in obtaining property,

    (b) what is threatened is a criminal prosecution,

    (c) what is threatened is the use of civil process and the threat is made in bad faith, or

    (d) the threat is a breach of the duty of good faith and fair dealing under a contract with the recipient.

(2) A threat is improper if the resulting exchange is not on fair terms, and

    (a) the threatened act would harm the recipient and would not significantly benefit the party making the threat,

    (b) the effectiveness of the threat in inducing the manifestation of assent is significantly increased by prior unfair dealing by the party making the threat, or

    (c) what is threatened is otherwise a use of power for illegitimate ends.

The drafters of section 176 recognize that the proper limits of bargaining cannot be defined with precision. In a phrase that seems addressed specifically to lawyers, they admit that "[h]ard bargaining between experienced adversaries of relatively equal power ought not to be discouraged." On the other hand, they recognize that threats can be so improper as to amount to an abuse of the bargaining process. Threats of physical violence, wrongful seizure or detention of property, tortious interference with contractual rights, or serious economic harm may amount to this. Comment (a) prompts courts to look at the fairness of the resulting agreement as evidence of whether a particular threat was improper.

Comment (b) to Section 175 affirms that threats to commence civil litigation are not ordinarily improper because defense of a civil action is considered, as a matter of policy, a reasonable alternative to acceding to the threat. However, if a threat involves "the seizure of property, the use of oppressive tactics, or the possibility of emotional consequences," defense in a civil action is not a reasonable alternative and the threat is improper. Illustration 2 gives an example of an improper threat:

> A makes an improper threat to commence a civil action and to file a lis pendens against a tract of land owned by B, unless B agrees to discharge a claim that B has against A. Because B is about to make a contract with C for the sale of the land and C refuses to make the contract if the levy is made, B agrees to discharge the claim. B has no reasonable alternative, A's threat is duress, and the contract is voidable by B.

Comment (d) to Section 176 follows by confirming there is no impropriety in good faith threats to commence civil litigation, even if the claim should later be shown to be without foundation. However, a threat may be deemed improper and in bad faith if "the person making the threat did not believe there was a reasonable basis for the threatened process, that he knew the threat would involve misuse of the process, or that he realized the demand he made was exorbitant."

The reporter's notes to Comment (f) cite the case of *Jamestown Farmers Elevator, Inc. v. General Mills*, 552 F.2d 1285 (8th Cir. 1977), in which the court held that "it was an improper threat for a large corporation to threaten extensive litigation before regulatory bodies that would put a smaller company out of business." In *Jamestown Farmers Elevator,* the threatening telephone conversation, as reported by an agent of a grain seller, who had previously contracted to sell grain to General Mills, went as follows:

> We're General Mills; and if you don't deliver this grain to us, why we'll have a battery of lawyers in there tomorrow morning to visit you, and then we are going to the North Dakota Public Service [Commission]; we're going to the Minneapolis Grain Exchange and we're going to the people in Montana and there will be no more Muschler Grain Company. We're going to take your license. (552 F.2d at 1289).

The Court of Appeals held that if this threat was made, it could "make out a claim of duress against General Mills." (552 F.2d. at 1291).

The court recognized that good faith insistence upon one's legal rights does not constitute duress, even if it should be found that the claim was not recognized at law. But to threaten to put a person out of business, or to deprive a person of his livelihood, or a threat of criminal or regulatory proceedings "made in order to secure another's consent to an undeserved bargain for one's own private benefit, may be sufficiently wrongful to constitute duress." (552 F.2d at 1291).

IV. ETHICAL CONSTRAINTS ON LEGAL NEGOTIATORS

The ABA Model Rules of Professional Conduct only incidentally regulate bargaining interactions between attorneys. Rule 1.4 requires lawyers to keep clients reasonably informed regarding the status of their legal matters. Comment 2 indicates that "a lawyer who receives from opposing counsel an offer of settlement ... must promptly inform the client of its substance unless the client has previously indicated that the proposal will be acceptable or unacceptable or has authorized the lawyer to accept or reject the offer." Nonetheless, when on-going negotiations are involved, attorneys are not obliged to contact their clients to tell them about every offer discussed. During such sessions, a number of position changes are likely to be made by both sides. Following such bargaining exchanges, however, attorneys should communicate outstanding offers to their clients within a reasonable period of time.

Rule 1.2 makes it clear that "a lawyer shall abide by a client's decisions concerning the objectives of representation ... [and] shall abide by a client's decision whether to settle a matter." Clients frequently ask their attorneys what they think of particular offers, and most legal representatives provide these clients with direct or indirect feedback in this regard. Whether they counsel in favor or against particular offers, they must always remember that their clients have the final say in this decision.

Probably the most substantive regulation of attorney conduct during bargaining interactions is set forth in Rule 4.1 which states that "a lawyer shall not knowingly make a false statement of material fact or law to a third person ..."* When Rule 4.1 was being drafted, individuals noted that negotiators frequently engage in "puffing" and "embellishment" which might be considered improper under this proscription. To take care of this concern, Comment 2 was added which provides:

> Whether a particular statement should be regarded as one of fact can depend on the circumstances. Under generally accepted conventions in negotiation, certain types of statements ordinarily are not taken as statements of material fact. Estimates of price or value

---

* See also Rule 8.4 which says that it is professional misconduct "for a lawyer to ... (c) engage in conduct involving dishonesty, fraud, deceit or misrepresentation."

placed on the subject of a transaction and a party's intentions as to an acceptable settlement of a claim are ordinarily in this category ...

Most legal negotiators thus expect opponents to over- or under-state the value of items being discussed for strategic purposes. They also accept the fact that opposing lawyers may tell them that particular offers are inadequate, even when they believe their clients would be receptive to such offers. The ironic aspect of Comment 2 concerns the fact that the most pertinent information lawyers must seek to ascertain during bargaining interactions concerns opponent values and settlement intentions, yet legal negotiators may ethically misrepresent that information. On the other hand, most lawyers expect opponents to "puff" and "embellish," and they do not consider such conduct to be improper—so long as it does not go beyond the bounds of propriety.

We always admonish our students to be scrupulously honest, however, when they communicate about material fact or material law. Not only would it be unethical to misrepresent such information, but such conduct could create credibility problems that would undermine these negotiations and their future interactions with these attorneys. When persons realize that opponents have misrepresented material fact or law, they have to recognize the fact they are dealing with dishonest parties. They should not trust such persons with respect to other questionable representations. As a result, they must verify everything they are told, and reduce to writing everything agreed upon. This causes the negotiation process to become cumbersome and inefficient. Mutually beneficial trades may be lost, due to a lack of trust. In addition, lawyers who have been lied to with respect to material information are likely to tell others about the dishonest individuals they have encountered, causing those persons future difficulties when they interact with other lawyers.

When we are asked by students whether we think certain statements would be considered acceptable "puffing" or unacceptable mendacity, we usually ask them to put themselves in the shoes of their opponents. Would they consider such statements to be acceptable if made by their adversaries? If they believe it would be acceptable for their opponents to engage in such "puffing," it would probably be all right for them to do so. On the other hand, if they would consider such statements to go beyond the bounds of propriety if done by others to them, they should refrain from such deceptive actions.

Robert Bordone has recently asserted that the "win-win" negotiation principles articulated in *Getting to Yes* by Roger Fisher and William Ury are so universally accepted by effective legal negotiators that we should no longer permit bargainers to engage in "puffing," "bluffing," or "embellishment." "If we have come to a point where the vast majority of those who study negotiation across a range of disciplines would prescribe collaboration and problem-solving over haggling and contention because it produces *better results for clients*, why would the legal profession continue to allow lawyers to choose an outdated, less effective approach to negotiation?"[2] He urges bar associations to impose new ethical codes that require negotiating lawyers to share information, be completely forthright, and work collaboratively with others. He recommends that attorneys who fail to follow these prescriptions be subject to discipline. When you work on negotiation exercises in negotiation courses or on behalf of real clients, are you willing to disclose most, if not all, of your side's confidential information to your opponents and to articulate opening positions close to where you hope to end up—or do you emphasize positive information over negative information, over- or under-state the value of items to be exchanged for strategic purposes, or begin with demands or offers that reflect where you really wish to settle or ask for more or offer less than you hope to achieve to test the other side's resolve?

We encourage our students to be scrupulously honest when disclosing material fact or law during negotiations not only based upon moral considerations, but also because of very practical considerations. Attorneys who misrepresent material factual or legal issues to opposing counsel during negotiations may expose their own clients to legal liability. Their clients may be sued for fraud if opposing parties rely upon their material misrepresentations and suffer economic harm.[3] Section 525 of the Restatement (Second) of Torts (1977) provides: "One who fraudulently makes a misrepresentation of fact, opinion, intention or law for the purpose of inducing another to act or to refrain from action in reliance upon it, is subject to liability to the other in deceit for pecuniary loss caused to him by his justifiable reliance upon the misrepresentation." Although mere statements of opinion are generally not actionable, Section 539 of the Restatement (Second) of Torts provides that "a statement of opinion as to facts not disclosed and not otherwise known to the recipient may, if it is reasonable to do so, be interpreted by him as an implied statement (a) that the facts known to the maker are not incompatible with his opinion; or (b) that he knows facts sufficient to justify him in forming it ..." It thus behooves negotiators stating opinions regarding the value of items being exchanged to be careful not to suggest that their opinions are based upon material facts not known by the persons with whom they are communicating but are known by themselves.[4]

---

2. Robert C. Bordone, *Fitting the Ethics to the Forum: A Proposal for Process–Enabling Ethical Codes*, 21 Ohio St. J. Disp. Res. 1, 33 (2005) (emphasis in original). Compare Charles B. Craver, *Negotiation Ethics: How to Be Deceptive Without Being Dishonest/How to Be Assertive Without Being Offensive*, 38 S. Tex. L. Rev. 713 (1997); Gerald B. Wetlaufer, *The Ethics of Lying in Negotiations*, 75 Iowa L. Rev. 1219 (1990). See generally *Dispute Resolution Ethics* (P. Bernard & B. Garth, eds.) (ABA Section of Dispute Resolution 2002).

3. See generally Rex Perschbacher, *Regulating Lawyers' Negotiations*, 27 Ariz. L. Rev. 75 (1985).

4. See, e.g., Kabatchnick v. Hanover–Elm Building Corp., 328 Mass. 341, 103 N.E.2d 692 (1952) (holding that false statements concerning competing offers allegedly received by sellers may subject the sellers to fraud liability where prospective buyers reasonably rely upon the special knowledge implicitly possessed by sellers making such misrepresentations).

Their clients may be exposed to liability under other statutes as well. For example, in *NLRB v. Waymouth Farms, Inc.*, 172 F.3d 598 (8th Cir. 1999), the court held that an employer that misrepresented its actual intent to relocate its business a few miles from its existing facility and induced the representative labor organization to believe that it was relocating to another state violated its bargaining duty under the National Labor Relations Act. The court found that the duty to bargain in good faith requires negotiating parties to provide each other with truthful information they can rely upon when making strategic bargaining decisions.

V. FORMATION, INTERPRETATION AND ENFORCEMENT OF SETTLEMENT AGREEMENTS

In general, the principles of contract law apply to settlement agreements and releases. Offer, acceptance and consideration rules apply and the defenses and remedies applicable in contract law generally apply to compromise agreements. However, because compromise agreements involve the relinquishment of a person's right to sue (a highly protected right in our society), certain problems peculiar to compromise and settlement have received special treatment by the courts.

A. OFFER AND ACCEPTANCE

Like other contracts, compromise agreements are formed by valid offers and acceptances.[5] Acceptance must usually occur within a reasonable time, on the terms offered. Acceptance may be implied, such as through retention of an amount tendered in full settlement of an obligation,[6] or the retention of a check or draft.[7] However, forbearance from bringing suit does not in itself constitute an offer or an acceptance of compromise, unless it is communicated to the other party as such.[8]

B. CONSIDERATION

In general, the rules regarding consideration apply unchanged to settlement agreements. Consideration for such agreements is found in the compromise of amounts demanded and in the relinquishment of claims in a dispute. A subsequent finding that no legal claim was present does not invalidate a compromise—if the parties believed in good faith that a valid claim existed.[9]

5. Wicker v. Board of Public Instruction of Dade County, 182 F.2d 764 (5th Cir. 1950).

6. Little Rock Packing Co. v. Massachusetts Bonding & Insurance Co., 262 F.2d 327 (8th Cir. 1959).

7. See 42 A.L.R.4th 12 (2006).

8. Stoddard v. Mix, 14 Conn. 12 (1840), and Gregg v. Weathersfield, 55 Vt. 385 (1883).

9. City Street Improvement Co. v. Pearson, 181 Cal. 640, 185 P. 962 (1919), and Posey v. Lambert–Grisham Hardware Co., 197 Ky. 373, 247 S.W. 30 (1923).

C. WRITINGS AND FORMALITIES

Once the terms of settlement are agreed upon, the lawyer's task focuses on formalizing and carrying out the agreement. As a general rule, compromise agreements are not required to be in writing to be valid. However, there are two exceptions: First, local rules and court procedures may require a writing to evidence the agreement. In these jurisdictions, settlement documents must be signed and in writing. When writings are required, courts are likely to hold the parties strictly to that requirement.[10]

Second, a writing is required if the subject matter of the compromise falls within the statute of frauds. The statute, however, applies only to the subject matter of the compromise agreement and not to the antecedent claim. For example, a compromise agreement requiring one party to convey real estate to another would fall under the statute. On the other hand, the compromise of a dispute involving ownership of land, requiring one party to pay money to the other, but involving no transfer of land, would not fall under the statute of frauds, because the subject matter of the compromise agreement is payment of money, not the conveyance of land.

It is generally good practice to make the agreement part of the record of the case. Most court requirements are satisfied by orally announcing the agreement in court as the court reporter takes it down as part of the court record. However, if the agreement is in the form of a stipulation and court rules require stipulations to be written, an oral stipulation for the record will not be binding even though settlements need not otherwise be written.[11]

Some courts require attorneys to promptly notify the court when pending actions are settled. While settlements are still binding if the attorneys fail to notify the court, sanctions may be imposed against the attorneys for interfering with court proceedings. Even when formal notice to the court is not required, documenting the agreement on the record by means of a consent judgment, a nonsuit, or a dismissal with prejudice renders the settlement more conclusive than a simple release and may therefore be desirable. Parties may usually obtain a consent judgment by appearing before the judge in chambers and having the judge sign a judgment order they have prepared for this purpose. State statutes generally define the exact procedures to be followed. Once filed, consent judgments will appear in the same manner as judgments rendered after full trials. Consent judgments bind the parties both as judgments of the court and as contractual agreements.

A dismissal with prejudice to any further suit may be used in place of a consent judgment to add finality to a settlement. State procedures

---

10. See, *e.g.*, *Davies v. Canco Enterprises*, 350 So.2d 23 (Fla.App.1977) (settlement agreement which had been incorporated into the transcript of a deposition but which had been signed by neither party was "of no force and effect").

11. *Moore v. Gunning*, 328 So.2d 462 (Fla.App.1976).

may vary, but the procedure is illustrated in Fed. Rules Civ. Proc. Rule 41(a), requiring a stipulation signed by all the parties to be filed with the court. The stipulation must state that the action is dismissed with prejudice, or it is assumed to be without prejudice.

D. INTERPRETATION OF THE AGREEMENT

Under general rules of contract law, interpretation of settlement agreements is generally limited to the terms of the agreement itself. Extrinsic evidence is generally admissible to show that the agreement is not integrated, that the recital of facts is not accurate, that conditions precedent have not been fulfilled or that conditions subsequent have or have not occurred, that the agreement was intended to affect third parties, or that the stated consideration was never received. Extrinsic evidence may also be used to show that the agreement purports to release the claims of a minor or in some other way violates public policy.[12]

The intent of the parties generally determines which claims are released when the agreement contains general language. That intent may be judged from both the language of the agreement and the circumstances surrounding its making. Usually, general language is limited by specific language; however, if the general language indicates that the dominant purpose was a general release, it may control. All claims may be released if there is no mention of specific claims. Claims arising from a single cause of action cannot be made the subject of separate suits, and when the suit as a unit is released all related claims are usually implicitly included. A party may wish to release only the claim for personal injury and not property damage. If this is their intention, the property damage claim should be specifically excluded from the settlement agreement. If separate consideration is specified for the release of general and specific claims, effect will be given to the general release.

Joint tortfeasor problems begin with the common law rule that the release of one joint tortfeasor releases all of the tortfeasors. This was based on the rationale that a person is entitled to only one satisfaction on a claim, and satisfaction by one tortfeasor releases all others. It was because of this problem that the covenant not to sue was developed. In covenants not to sue, injured parties make contracts with tortfeasors not to bring actions against them in return for the settlement payments. Since there is no formal release, courts often hold that covenants not to sue do not operate to release other tortfeasors not expressly mentioned in the covenants.

The Uniform Contribution Among Tortfeasors Act abolished the common law rule of releases and allows contribution among tortfeasors.

---

12. See generally Clark Havighurst, *Principles of Construction and the Parol Evidence Rule Applied to Releases*, 60 Nw. U.L.Rev. 599 (1958). See also Robert Lindsey, *Documentation of Settlements*, 27 Ark. L.Rev. 27 (1973).

In states adopting this act, a release of one tortfeasor does not release the other common tortfeasors. The amount recoverable from the remaining defendants is, however, reduced by the settling defendant's pro rata share of liability so that only one actual satisfaction is received.

E. CONFLICT OF LAWS—GOVERNING LAW

Normally the same conflict of laws principles are applied to settlements as are applied to contracts generally: the law of the state in which the compromise agreement was made generally governs questions of validity and construction of the compromise. Questions of authority may be governed by the law of the state in which a party was domiciled or the agency contract created, and matters relating to the breach of a compromise agreement are generally governed by the law of the state in which the agreement was to be performed.

Sometimes a compromise will have a significant effect on the antecedent obligations of the parties, and certain aspects may be governed by the law of the state where those obligations were created. This is especially true in the settlement of tort claims which may be governed by the law of the place where the tort occurred.

F. FEDERAL RULES OF CIVIL PROCEDURE: RULE 68 OFFERS OF COMPROMISE

FRCP 68 and similar state statutes provide procedural incentives to settle. These rules were not used frequently in the past but there is a trend towards their greater use and a greater awareness of their potential impact.

FRCP 68 Provides:

> At any time more than 10 days before the trial begins, a party defending against a claim may serve upon the adverse party an offer to allow judgment to be taken against the defending party for the money or property or to the effect specified in the offer, with costs then accrued. If within 10 days after the service of the offer the adverse party serves written notice that the offer is accepted, either party may then file the offer and notice of acceptance together with proof of service thereof and thereupon the clerk shall enter judgment. An offer not accepted shall be deemed withdrawn and evidence thereof is not admissible except in a proceeding to determine costs. If the judgment finally obtained by the offeree is not more favorable than the offer, the offeree must pay the costs incurred after the making of the offer. The fact that an offer is made but not accepted does not preclude a subsequent offer. When the liability of one party to another has been determined by verdict or order or judgment, but the amount or extent of the liability remains to be determined by further proceedings, the party adjudged liable may make an offer of judgment, which shall have the same effect as an offer made before trial if it is served within a reasonable time not

less than 10 days prior to the commencement of hearings to determine the amount or extent of liability.

It is unclear how substantial the offer must be for Rule 68 to apply. The Seventh Circuit held that an offer of $450 in a case claimed to be worth $20,000 was not enough to invoke the statute. The court held the rule applies only to "good faith" offers.[13] On appeal, the Supreme Court declined to decide this question, since it held that Rule 68 only applies to situations in which offerees prevail at trial, but obtain judgments less generous than written offers previously tendered.[14]

The most important issue surrounding Rule 68 is whether the costs to be paid by the losing party should include attorney fees, which usually make up the greatest part of litigation costs. Contrary to English practice, attorney fees in the U.S. have not generally been assessed against losing parties unless there is express statutory authorization for them. When special circumstances favor such awards, exceptions have been made to the "American rule," and there is a strong policy argument in favor of including attorney fees in the "costs incurred" provision of Rule 68. As of now, however, attorney fees are generally not available under Rule 68—*unless* authorized under the specific statutes involved.

> [G]iven the importance of "costs" to the Rule, it is very unlikely that this omission [the failure to specifically include attorney fees] was mere oversight; on the contrary, the most reasonable inference is that the term "costs" in Rule 68 was intended to refer to all costs properly awardable under the relevant substantive statute or other authority. In other words, all costs properly awardable in an action are to be considered within the scope of Rule 68 "costs." Thus, absent congressional expressions to the contrary, where the underlying statute defines "costs" to include attorney's fees, we are satisfied such fees are to be included as costs for purposes of Rule 68.[15]

Chesny had brought a wrongful death action under 42 U.S.C. § 1983 against police officers who had shot and killed his son. Under § 1988, prevailing § 1983 plaintiffs are entitled to attorney fee awards. Nonetheless, since Chesny had rejected a settlement offer more generous than the award he obtained at trial, the Supreme Court held that he could not obtain attorney fees for the period following the Rule 68 offer he had rejected, because Rule 68 was intended to shift costs from defendants who make reasonable settlement offers to claimants who reject those offers and fail to obtain more generous awards at trial. Since § 1988 authorized attorney fee awards, attorney fees constituted "costs" within the meaning of Rule 68.

13. August v. Delta Air Lines, Inc., 600 F.2d 699 (7th Cir. 1979).

14. Delta Air Lines v. August, 450 U.S. 346, 101 S.Ct. 1146, 67 L.Ed.2d 287 (1981).

15. *Marek v. Chesny*, 473 U.S. 1, 9, 105 S.Ct. 3012, 87 L.Ed.2d 1 (1985).

G. COURT SUPERVISION AND APPROVAL OF SETTLEMENTS

Courts may be involved in settlements in two ways. First, through actual participation in the settlement process, and, second, in reviewing those settlements generated without court supervision. Court participation in the settlement process often begins in pretrial and settlement conferences. Federal court rules set up the framework for pretrial procedures, which may vary from a requirement of settlement discussions, to encouraging settlement by allowing consideration of any matters which may aid in the disposition of cases including the use of special procedures such as mediation or non-binding arbitration "when authorized by state or local rule." (FRCP 16). Most states also provide separate procedures for settlement conferences.

Class action settlements must be judicially approved to prevent legalized blackmail and protect absent class members.[16] The court must examine the terms of the agreement, not the underlying issues of the case, and determine that there was no fraud or collusion in reaching the settlement and that the compromise is fair and adequate. Factors which the court should consider include: (1) the relative strength of the parties, (2) mutual sacrifice to avoid unprofitable litigation, (3) existence of vindictive motives or pressures, (4) the recommendation of counsel, (5) the number of parties which object to the agreement, (6) the ability of the defendant to pay a judgment greater than the settlement, and (7) the business judgment of the parties, which should not be replaced by the court's unless the settlement is unfair on its face.

H. EFFECT OF NEGOTIATIONS ON STATUTES OF LIMITATIONS

One of the choices plaintiffs must make is whether to file suit before commencing settlement negotiations. Particularly in business settings, there is great reluctance to sue fellow merchants. However, there is always a danger that negotiations may continue until the statute of limitations has run, thereby providing the other party with a defense against suit.

Absent a showing of wrongful conduct by the potential defendant, courts uniformly hold that the mere fact that settlement negotiations are underway does not of itself prevent the statute of limitations from running. This is true where it seems clear that the defendant in fact intended to settle but did not.

Even when the defendant's actions would create justifiable reliance at one point in time, the defendant may be allowed to plead the statute of limitations as a defense if his conduct was broken off leaving the plaintiff sufficient time to file her complaint.

---

16. See F.R.C.P. 23(e). See generally K. Forde, *Settlement of the Class Action*, 5 Litigation 23 (Fall, 1978).

VI.   DEFECTS IN COMPROMISE AND SETTLEMENT AGREEMENTS

A.   INTRODUCTION

Despite the policy favoring settlements, settlement agreements are considered contracts and their validity may be challenged based on traditional contract defenses, including: illegality, duress, undue influence, mistake, misrepresentation, fraud, uncertainty or vagueness, lack of capacity or authority, and public policy. When the challenge is to the settlement agreement itself, the defect must relate to the compromise agreement, not to the antecedent claim.

B.   FRAUD, MISREPRESENTATION, AND MISTAKE

Fraud, misrepresentation, and mistake are the most common grounds for invalidating settlement agreements, especially those made by insurance carriers in settlement of tort claims. When injured parties are wrongly induced to settle for much less than the actual damages incurred, public policy demands that the settlements be reviewed and, where unreasonably one-sided, rescinded.

C.   MARY CARTER AGREEMENTS

A particularly troublesome problem is presented in cases involving a single plaintiff and multiple defendants, where one (or more) of the defendants agrees to settle with the plaintiff for a guaranteed amount, which decreases in an inverse relation to the amount the plaintiff recovers from the remaining defendants. There are many variations of this standard arrangement, but the plaintiff is always guaranteed a specific amount (often given to the plaintiff as an advance), and the defendant's liability is expressly limited. An example of such an agreement is *General Motors Corporation v. Lahocki*, 286 Md. 714, 410 A.2d 1039 (1980). The plaintiff broke his back when the GM van in which he was riding hit unlit wooden barricades placed in the roadway by defendant Contee Sand and Gravel, Inc. Lahocki was thrown onto the street and suffered a fractured spine. Lahocki sued Contee and GM for negligence, alleging against GM that the vehicle was "uncrashworthy". Before trial Contee and Lahocki made an agreement which provided that, "Contee would pay to Lahocki $150,000 except in three circumstances: (1) If Contee's pro rata share of a judgment against it was in excess of $150,000 then Contee would pay this up to $250,000, (2) if final judgment was entered against GM alone, Contee would pay nothing to the Lahockis, even if the Lahockis and GM thereafter settled the case, or (3) if the Lahockis settled with GM, then the sum to be paid by Contee to the Lahockis was to be but $100,000." (410 A.2d at 1041). This agreement limited Contee's liability to a maximum of $250,000. If GM were found solely liable or if GM settled with Lahocki, Contee would owe nothing, making it to Contee's advantage to prove GM solely liable. If GM were found not to have been liable, Contee would owe $150,000.

The judge was informed of the agreement but the jury was not. Because of this agreement the position of Contee in the adversarial proceeding was reversed; he was financially encouraged to assist the plaintiff, unknown to the jury. Contee assisted Lahocki in paying the fee of an expert testifying against GM. Since Contee was still appearing as a defendant, his attorney was allowed to cross-examine Lahocki's witnesses. In doing so, Contee's attorney merely had the witnesses repeat damaging information against GM and cure defects that Lahocki's attorney had left. Not realizing Contee's change in position, the jury found GM solely liable and awarded Lahocki $1.2 million (plus $300,000 to his wife). The court of appeals reversed. Following the trend in some states, it held that these agreements are not against public policy per se, but that they must be revealed to the jury so it can evaluate the circumstances before it. These settlements are known variously as Guaranteed Verdict Agreements, Mary Carter Agreements (after *Booth v. Mary Carter Paint Co.*, 202 So.2d 8 (Fla.App.1967)) or Gallagher Covenants, (after *City of Tucson v. Gallagher*, 108 Ariz. 140, 493 P.2d 1197 (1972)). They are problematic because the defendants often remain part of the action until the case is over, while their interests have shifted from limiting the plaintiff's recovery to increasing it against the other defendants.

Because of the potential for abuse, many scholars have strongly opposed these agreements and many states have declared them void as against public policy. Courts have generally required some degree of disclosure to the jury of such agreements. Some courts, however, have limited the usefulness of the disclosure requirement by allowing information damaging to the remaining defendants to be included in the agreement itself, allowing it to come to the attention of the jury if the pact is revealed.

VII. SPECIAL RULES APPLICABLE TO INSURERS

Insurers play a major role in the settlement of most tort cases. Because of the frequency with which insurers settle and the frequent imbalance of power between the insurance companies and injured plaintiffs, special rules have been developed in many states and courts which regulate insurer conduct in negotiations. The general rule is that the insurer must weigh the insured's interest equally with its own in deciding whether to accept an offer of settlement or to commence negotiations.[17] This has been interpreted to impose an obligation either to bargain in good faith—or to not bargain in bad faith—or just to not act negligently. Failure to properly protect insured interests may result in punitive damage awards.

---

17. Young v. American Casualty Co. of Reading, Pennsylvania, 416 F.2d 906 (2d   Cir. 1969) certiorari dismissed 396 U.S. 997, 90 S.Ct. 580, 24 L.Ed.2d 490 (1970).

Good faith has been defined in general contract terms to involve "fair dealing [so] that neither party will do anything which will injure the right of the other to receive the benefits of the agreement."[18] Similarly, bad faith refusal to settle has been defined as the intentional disregard of the insured's financial interests, or placing its own interest above that of the insured.[19] Allegedly negligent behavior is evaluated by employing the standard of a reasonable insurer in the same or similar circumstances. In California there is a statutory duty on the insurance company to negotiate in good faith in an effort to reach a settlement.[20]

The general conflict of interest situation occurs where a plaintiff in an insurance case offers to settle for less than the insurance policy coverage. Many states impose on the insurer a duty to settle within the policy limits. However, the more difficult situation is where the claimant wants more than the insurance policy limits.

Factors the courts have considered as affecting the liability of a company where there is a conflict of interest are: (a) the strength of the claimant's case, (b) attempts by the insurer to induce the insured to contribute to the settlement, (c) failure by the insurer to properly investigate the case, (d) the rejection of attorney's advice by the insurer, (e) failure to inform the insured of an offer, (f) amount for which insured may be liable, and (g) the extent to which the insured induced the insurer's rejection of offers.[21]

VIII.   RULES OF EVIDENCE

The rules of evidence can have a great effect on encouraging or discouraging settlement negotiations. These rules not only help determine the strength of each party's position, but also govern how openly the parties may communicate during actual negotiations.

Under the common law, the general rule is that evidence of offers to compromise disputes is not admissible to prove offeror liability in trial. Three reasons have been given as justification for this rule. The "English" or "contract" theory is based on the view that offers are assumed to be made without prejudice and, unless the offer is accepted and a contract actually formed, the offer has no evidentiary force. Another basis given is that of relevancy. The offer to compromise is viewed under this theory as demonstrating a desire for peace and not an admission of any wrong done, therefore evidence of this sort has no relevance to actual liability and is excluded. The rule has also been rationalized as a privileged exception to the evidence rules, based on the policy of the courts to encourage settlements. None of these theories generally ex-

18. Crisci v. Security Insurance Co., 66 Cal.2d 425, 429, 58 Cal.Rptr. 13, 17, 426 P.2d 173, 176 (1967).

19. Kricar, Inc. v. General Accident Fire and Life Assurance Corp., Ltd., 542 F.2d 1135 (9th Cir. 1976).

20. Cal.Stat., Ins. § 790.03(h).

21. See Cochran, *The Obligation To Settle Within Policy Limits*, 41 Miss.L.J. 398, 402–406 (1970). See generally Sykes, "Bad Faith" Refusal to Settle by Liability Insures, 23 J. Leg. St. 77 (1994).

cludes from evidence admitted statements of fact or collateral statements and conduct not forming the actual compromise offer.

Most U.S. courts follow the relevancy theory, but the effect is almost the same regardless of the theory being applied: courts have the difficult job of separating statements making up the actual compromise offer from those merely surrounding it. For example, at common law, if liability were conceded in the compromise and negotiations were held merely to establish the amount of the damage or loss, the offer of compromise was admissible to establish liability—though not as proof of the amount of the loss. The statement "O.K., I'll agree I was negligent, let's talk about damages" is admissible, while the statement, "Let's assume, just for the purposes of these negotiations, that I was negligent, what would you think the damages ought to be?" is not.

Attorneys have developed various methods for dealing with admissibility problems. One solution is to refuse to negotiate until the other side agrees in writing that anything said is without prejudice to their client's rights. Absent such agreements, attorneys can avoid admissions by phrasing all factual statements hypothetically and by including disclaimers in all writings so that the statements will be of no value as evidence. For example, "We admit, for the sake of these negotiations only,...." This approach has resulted in less open negotiations and formed a trap for unwary or unsophisticated lawyers who might not be careful enough in their choice of terms.

To correct this problem, Rule 408 of the Federal Rules of Evidence was enacted by congress in 1975. The rule is specifically based on the public policy favoring the compromise and settlement of disputes (see 56 F.R.D. 183, 227–228, (1972)). It provides:

> Evidence of (1) furnishing or offering or promising to furnish, or (2) accepting or offering or promising to accept, a valuable consideration in compromising or attempting to compromise a claim which was disputed as to either validity or amount, is not admissible to prove liability for or invalidity of the claim or its amount. Evidence of conduct or statements made in compromise negotiations is likewise not admissible. This rule does not require the exclusion of any evidence otherwise discoverable merely because it is presented in the course of compromise negotiations. This rule also does not require exclusion when the evidence is offered for another purpose, such as proving bias or prejudice of a witness, negativing a contention of undue delay, or proving an effort to obstruct a criminal investigation or prosecution.

Notable in the rule is the use of the term "a valuable consideration," intended to do away with so-called, "nuisance offers"—offers of only minimal value in relation to the size of the injury. This addition has been criticized for creating unnecessary ambiguity in the rule, and it is not clear how valuable the consideration must be. Rule 408 also departs from the common law by including disputes as to either "validity or amount". Under rule 408, a compromise offer is inadmissible to prove either liability or the amount of liability.

The rule contains two explicit exceptions: evidence "otherwise discoverable" and a provision for "collateral use" of the evidence. The first exception was added to make sure that litigants could not avoid the admission of relevant and discoverable facts into trial by admitting them in compromise negotiations. In other words, admissions in compromise negotiations are not inadmissible if they are also discovered through independent proper means.

The second exception allows evidence gained during compromise negotiations to be used, "when the evidence is offered for another purpose [other than proving liability]". The rule goes on to list examples of other proper purposes, such as the need for a jury to ascertain a witness's bias or prejudice. This exception arises most often in multiple party cases and is properly used where the statements made will be used to impeach the credibility of a person not a party to the compromise agreement. A question still exists whether courts should allow statements made during compromise negotiations to be admitted to impeach the parties to the compromise. Such use would seem to violate the policy upon which the rule is based. It is important to note that neither the common law nor rule 408 applies until there is an attempt to compromise a disputed claim. Both elements must be present, or statements made will be held admissible.

A number of states have passed rules of evidence the same as or similar to rule 408. Other states have attempted to codify the common law rules. The main difference between these rules is whether factual statements made during settlement discussions are admissible or not.

Two other federal rules of evidence bearing on settlement agreements are rules 409 and 410. Rule 409 states simply, "Evidence of furnishing or offering or promising to pay medical, hospital, or similar expenses occasioned by an injury is not admissible to prove liability for the injury." This rule is based not only on the policy of encouraging settlement, but also on the policy of encouraging the prompt assistance to injured persons by defendants or their insurance companies. It should be noted, however, that the rule does not cover conduct or statements made which are not an integral part of this payment.

The Federal Rule is consistent with the common law rule in most states that evidence of medical assistance is inadmissible to establish liability of parties rendering such assistance. The states have based this on the policy encouraging such help and on the rationale that such assistance is made primarily out of humane motives and not as admissions of guilt.

Rule 410 deals specifically with the use of evidence gained from plea bargain discussions pertaining to criminal cases. This rule is much stricter than rule 408 and specifically excludes plea negotiation evidence from subsequent trial proceedings.

Chapter Six

THE IMPACT OF ECONOMIC AND PSYCHOLOGICAL FACTORS ON THE DECISION–MAKING PROCESS

I. INTRODUCTION

Actual law practice is quite different from hypothetical law school discussions and theoretical appellate court arguments. In law practice,

> [f]acts may be unavailable, obscure, disputed, or distorted. The law may be unclear, or in flux. The goals of other persons—clients, adversaries, and decision-makers, to name a few—may be cloudy or may conflict with those of the lawyer. The lawyer may be caught in a bind between two or more conflicting ethical values, or between an ethical value and a very important practical goal. Choice of the best strategy may require him to estimate and weigh probabilities. The lawyer rarely feels that he has enough time in which to do the most thorough job that he could.[1]

II. ECONOMIC ANALYSIS OF CASES: THE MISSING LAWYER SKILL

We are conditioned by legal method to define the lawyer's functions as those of weighing facts, recognizing the issues, and applying relevant legal principles ("preventive law" when drafting contracts and wills or "remedial law" when suing for personal injuries or breach of contract). This conception is reflected in studies of lawyer competency. For exam-

---

1. Michael Meltsner and Philip Schrag, *Report from a CLEPR Colony*, 76 Colum. L.Rev. 581, 584 (1976). See generally Stefan H.H. Krieger & Richard K. Neumann, Es-

ple, an American Bar Association Task Force on Lawyer Competency defined it as the ability to:[2]

1. analyze legal problems;

2. perform legal research;

3. collect and sort facts;

4. write effectively . . . ;

5. communicate orally with effectiveness in a variety of settings;

6. perform important lawyer tasks calling on both communication and interpersonal skills:

   (i) interviewing,

   (ii) counseling,

   (iii) negotiation; and

7. organize and manage legal work.

Curiously, the ability to determine the economic value of cases is not included in definitions of lawyer competency. For attorneys, analyzing factual and legal aspects of cases unfortunately means something less than the application of financial analysis, and decision making routinely used in business and accounting professions.

Trial lawyers know from experience that "facts are everything". Very few cases lawyers at the trial level turn on questions of law. This is true for civil and criminal cases, but is more apparent in the criminal setting. There is rarely an issue whether a crime has been committed; the issue is whether the accused is the person who committed it. In this setting (as in the great majority of civil cases) facts are determinative. The relative skills and diligence in fact gathering of investigators and attorneys on both sides largely determine case outcomes, both in terms of liability or guilt and in terms of remedy.[3]

Lawyers are, in a sense, lulled by the legal culture into relatively unsophisticated financial methods of evaluating cases. The legal culture assumes that the lawyer's task is to present the facts and law in their

sential Lawyering Skills: Interviewing, Counseling, Negotiation, and Persuasive Fact Analysis (2d ed. 2003).

2. ABA Section on Legal Education and Admission to the Bar, *Report and Recommendations of the Task Force on Lawyer Competency* 9 & 10 (1979).

3. An excellent guide to fact gathering is Robert L. Simmons, *Winning Before Trial: How to Prepare Cases for the Best Settlement or Trial Result* (Executive Reports Corp. 1974) (2 vols.). Simmons gives excellent and exhaustive treatment to inter-

viewing witnesses (friendly, unfriendly, disinterested), investigative techniques (investigative techniques for attorneys, and knowing when and how to hire investigators), checklists of kinds of facts to search for in the most common types of cases, and use of interrogatories and other discovery techniques. For an interesting view of the fact gathering process in criminal cases, see *Special Project: A Study of the Fact Investigation Practices of Criminal Lawyers in Phoenix, Arizona*, 1981 Arizona State Law Journal 447–626 (1981).

strategically most favorable light to a judge and jury, who will determine what is truth and who will award dollar damages commensurate with the wrong. This conception of "value" shifts the ultimate responsibility for calculating damages to judge and jury, inducing attorneys to think of case values primarily in terms of probable jury verdicts.

One example of the difficulty lawyers have in calculating case values is given in Douglas Rosenthal's study of personal injury cases in New York.[4] Rosenthal picked 61 personal injury cases that had been settled, then selected 5 experts to independently review the actual case files and give their assessments of the settlement values of those cases. The first two experts were experienced plaintiffs' personal injury lawyers, the third had been a plaintiff's lawyer for about 25 years but had recently begun doing insurance defense work, and the last two experts were insurance people (one an insurance defense lawyer and the other an experienced claims adjuster). This method provided 6 different settlement figures for each case, all taken from the files upon which actual settlements were based: the actual settlement amounts, plus predicted settlement values independently arrived at by each of the five experts. As illustrated by the numbers in Table 6–1, the variation among these six figures is dramatic.

4. Douglas E. Rosenthal, *Lawyer and Client: Who's In Charge* (Russell Sage Foundation 1974).

ANALYSIS OF CASES

Table 6–1*

Activity and Recovery Scores for the Sample Clients

Client Number	Activity Score	Actual Recovery[a]	Panel Mean[b]	Panelist Evaluations[c]					Coefficient of Variability
				#1	#2	#3	#4	#5	
1	2	$ 5,900	$ 7,600	$ 6,000	$ 7,500	$ 8,500	$ 8,500	$ 7,500	0.1348
2	0	3,500	21,500	22,500	17,500	40,000	20,000	7,500	0.5490
3	8	42,500	34,000	45,000	40,000	45,000	25,000	15,000	0.3945
4	3	2,000	8,800	8,500	8,500	9,500	8,500	8,500	0.0508
5	3	4,250	3,200	1,800	4,000	4,000	3,500	2,500	0.3102
6	3	3,500	4,300	7,500	5,000	3,500	3,500	2,000	0.4836
7	4	2,000	2,200	2,300	2,000	750	4,500	1,500	0.6370
8	8	5,000	6,600	6,500	5,000	7,500	12,500	1,500	0.6078
9	1	3,000	6,900	11,000	5,800	6,000	8,500	3,000	0.4409
10	2	5,000	11,600	7,500	12,500	20,000	15,000	3,000	0.5680
11	6	3,500	2,800	1,500	4,300	2,000	4,500	1,500	0.5480
12	2	12,000	21,000	17,500	17,500	35,000	20,000	15,000	0.3820
13	3	3,500	2,600	2,000	2,750	2,500	4,500	1,000	0.5010
14	2	6,300	6,700	12,500	5,500	4,000	8,500	2,800	0.5854
15	0	3,250	4,200	2,500	3,000	7,500	4,500	3,300	0.4824
16	2	2,000	3,400	4,500	3,000	3,500	5,000	1,000	0.4580
17	1	2,900	4,800	4,700	4,500	6,000	5,500	3,000	0.2418
18	2	7,500	11,900	17,500	8,500	20,000	10,000	3,500	0.5679
19	3	2,250	10,100	15,000	13,500	8,000	10,000	4,000	0.4349
20	2	5,250	12,600	6,000	30,000	17,500	7,500	2,000	0.8950
21	4	9,000	7,400	3,500	7,500	10,000	8,500	7,500	0.3254
22	6	35,000	37,000	35,000	45,000	40,000	50,000	15,000	0.3651
23	2	14,250	15,800	17,500	11,500	25,000	10,000	15,000	0.3748
24	1	13,500	10,800	15,000	7,500	15,000	7,500	8,800	0.3630
25	4	2,250	3,400	2,100	3,250	3,000	4,500	2,500	0.2979
26	2	2,000	3,500	3,500	3,800	3,500	4,000	2,000	0.2349
27	0	2,000	3,500	3,000	3,750	3,500	3,500	3,500	0.0793
28	1	3,000	3,400	2,800	3,750	5,000	4,500	1,800	0.4639
29	5	7,000	5,000	2,500	5,500	6,000	7,500	3,500	0.4000
30	2	3,150	12,000	3,000	9,500	10,000	22,500	15,000	0.6045
31	7	8,000	9,800	12,500	10,000	12,500	10,000	4,000	0.3545
32	3	5,600	20,000	30,000	25,000	30,000	10,000	5,000	0.5063
33	6	$ 4,000	$ 7,200	$ 8,500	$ 4,500	$ 7,500	$ 7,500	$ 7,500	0.1939
34	6	2,150	2,900	2,500	3,000	2,500	4,500	1,500	0.3952
35	4	2,900	12,000	22,500	5,500	12,500	12,000	7,500	0.5480
36	8	4,500	9,300	6,500	10,000	15,000	10,000	5,000	0.4157
37	2	5,000	24,200	30,000	16,000	25,000	35,000	15,000	0.3999
38	0	8,000	4,800	6,000	6,000	7,500	3,000	1,500	0.5134
39	4	5,200	2,600	1,000	3,750	2,500	3,000	2,500	0.3946
40	0	6,500	10,900	7,000	12,500	15,000	15,000	5,000	0.4258
41	no personal injury								
42	2	3,250	4,500	3,300	4,400	7,500	5,000	2,500	0.3777
43	5	22,500	29,500	15,000	50,000	35,000	30,000	17,500	0.4809
44	2	2,300	3,000	2,000	3,500	5,000	3,000	1,500	0.4564
45	3	13,500	20,000	15,000	15,000	30,000	20,000	20,000	0.3062
46	4	23,200	21,000	20,000	27,500	17,500	20,000	20,000	0.1805
47	2	4,500	8,500	4,000	11,500	10,000	13,500	3,500	0.5310
48	3	17,000	18,000	11,000	20,000	30,000	25,000	4,000	0.5839
49	0	3,000	4,800	8,500	3,500	6,500	2,500	3,000	0.5398
50	2	4,000	3,600	6,000	3,500	6,000	3,000	2,000	0.4099
51	2	2,900	4,100	3,500	6,500	5,000	3,500	2,000	0.4171
52	1	2,200	3,200	3,300	3,500	3,500	3,500	2,000	0.2070
53	3	25,000	10,000	3,000	12,000	25,000	2,500	7,500	0.9226
54	3	2,000	4,600	6,500	3,500	7,500	4,000	1,500	0.5219
55	1	3,400	2,500	1,800	3,700	2,500	2,800	1,500	0.3527
56[d]	–	3,800	1,300	1,500	800	1,500	2,000	750	0.4042
57	7	6,950	5,800	7,500	7,500	7,500	5,000	1,500	0.4545
58	0	2,250	3,500	6,500	3,300	2,500	4,000	1,000	0.5875
59	3	3,250	4,000	4,500	3,500	5,000	4,250	2,500	0.2467
60	6	20,000	22,500	22,500	22,500	22,500	25,000	20,000	0.0785
61	3	5,500	6,000	10,000	4,750	7,500	5,000	2,500	0.4831

* *Lawyer and Client: Who's in Charge?* Douglas Rosenthal; Russell Sage Foundation: New York (1974), pp. 204–205. Reprinted by permission.
[a] Rounded to nearest 50.00
[b] Rounded to nearest 100.00
[c] The two insurance adjusters are panelist #4 and #5.
[d] Lawyer handling own claim.

For example, the case involving Client Number 1 is one of the few in which the panel members are comfortably close to each other in their evaluations. Compare Case Number Two, which settled for $3,500 and was evaluated at $22,500, $17,500, $40,000, $20,000, and $7,500 by the experts. Most of the cases show differences approaching this extreme.

The Des Moines study described in Chapter One gives further evidence of dramatic disparities in lawyer case evaluations. In that study we asked attorneys who were conducting settlement discussions pertaining to the same hypothetical personal injury case to report their opening positions and final settlement.

Results of Des Moines Experiment

Attorneys	Plaintiff's Opening Demand	Defendant's Opening Offer	Settlement
Attorneys 1A and 1B	$32,000	$10,000	$18,000
Attorneys 2A and 2B	$50,000	$25,000	Impasse
Attorneys 3A and 3B	$675,000	$32,150	$95,000
Attorneys 4A and 4B	$110,000	$3,000	$25,120
Attorneys 5A and 5B	Unreported	Unreported	$15,000
Attorneys 6A and 6B	$100,000	$5,000	$25,000
Attorneys 7A and 7B	$475,000	$15,000	Impasse
Attorneys 8A and 8B	$180,000	$40,000	$80,000
Attorneys 9A and 9B	$210,000	$17,000	$57,000
Attorneys 10A and 10B	$350,000	$48,500	$61,000
Attorneys 11A and 11B	$87,500	$15,000	$30,000
Attorneys 12A and 12B	$175,000	$50,000	Impasse
Attorneys 13A and 13B	$97,000	$10,000	$57,500
Attorneys 14A and 14B	$100,000	Unreported	$56,875

Average Settlement $47,318

Notice that plaintiffs' opening demands varied from a low of $32,000 to a high of $675,000, and that the *lowest* demand by a plaintiff ($32,000) was substantially *less than* the average settlement amount ($47,318). Likewise, the range between high and low offers by defense counsel is dramatic; with the highest offer by a defendant ($50,000) *above* the average settlement amount.

The alternative to such diverse results is for attorneys to move toward more objective methods of determining case values, adding to their legal expertise knowledge of the financial and quantitative decision making tools used by business and financial experts. They must also understand psychological phenomena that influence decision-making and often induce individuals to make suboptimal decisions.

III. METHODS FOR ECONOMIC CASE EVALUATIONS

Lawyers use a variety of methods to formulate case values for negotiation and settlement purposes. Most are based on estimates of what cases would bring if they were decided by juries. Despite the volumes of research on juries, however, lawyers still have no reliable method for predicting what particular juries will do. As a result, one of the most difficult—yet crucial—professional functions of lawyers is to make educated estimates about case "values."

When they evaluate routine personal injury cases, attorneys and insurance claims adjusters often rely on formulas or rules of convenience that produce values based on some multiple of "special damages" or actual medical and other costs of the injury. They rely upon an arbitrary multiplier that may be as low as two or three or as high as ten. For example, the formula of "three times special damages" has been described as allocating "one third to the lawyer, one third to the physician, and one third to the claimant."[5] In cases involving more complex damages such as continued pain and suffering, evaluators often propose arbitrary fixed dollar amounts per week for general pain and suffering; i.e., $2000–$5000 per week for the period of total disability and $500–$2000 per week for the period of partial disability. These formulas provide "ballpark" figures, but they obviously ignore individual differences between cases and severely simplify issues of actual harm done.

Since predicted trial outcomes constitute the most common measure of case values, attorneys typically refer to various jury verdict report services for case evaluation assistance. These reports generally describe the basic case facts and plaintiff's injuries. They list the actual settlement amounts for cases disposed of prior to trial. For cases that went to trial, they list the final offers or demands reported by the parties and the actual jury verdicts obtained.

Rather than looking exclusively at past jury awards, attorneys may calculate case values by more direct methods. The following examples provide a format for itemizing damages for personal injury cases. These methods are improvements over "rules of convenience" and professional guesses, because they are more structured and objective. However, they do not fully account for such major considerations as the timing of payments and methods of evaluating subjective harm such as pain and suffering.

---

5. H. Lawrence Ross, *Settled Out of Court* 108 (Aldine Publishing Co. 2nd ed.1980).

One widely recognized formula, developed by Robert L. Simmons, invites attorneys to subdivide cases into six categories and estimate values for each.[6] These categories include:

PPV —The probability of a plaintiff's verdict.
PAV —The probable average verdict.
UV —The uncollectible portion of the verdict.
PC —The plaintiff's estimated cost of obtaining verdict.
DC —The defendant's estimated cost of defense.
I —The value of the intangible factors.
FSV —The fair settlement value.

Expressed algebraically, the formula looks like this:

$$(PPV \times PAV) - UV - PC + DC \pm I = FSV$$

This formula includes some time value of money concepts and seeks to arrive at net valuation figures for clients. Such methods are useful to the extent they help attorneys arrive at objective valuations and be aware of the components of those valuations.

A more detailed listing of variables can be compiled by reading the case evaluation literature and keeping track of items thought to be important by different commentators. Relevant factors include:

A. COMBINED FORMULA COMPONENTS

    1. Expenses

        A. Medical

            (1) Hospital expenses

                a. Surgery

                b. Nursing care

                c. Cost of braces, prostheses, or other special devices

            (2) Medication expenses

            (3) Physician expenses

                a. Treatment at hospital or nursing home

                b. Treatment as outpatient or at home

        B. Legal

            (1) Fees

                a. Hours for attorneys

                b. Hours for legal assistants

                c. Hours for non-legals

                d. Percentage of award on contingent fee basis

            (2) Expenses

6. Robert L. Simmons, *Winning Before Trial: How to Prepare Cases for the Best*   *Settlement or Trial Result,* 708–715 (Executive Reports Corp.1974).

        a. Discovery. This would include costs incurred in seeking factual and legal evidence and documentation, depositions, witness costs, etc.

        b. Closing. These would include costs to collect the judgment, costs to transfer property, etc.

        c. Court costs

        d. Other

    C. Personal

      (1) Travel

      (2) Loss of time to parties

2. Lost Earnings

    A. Past

      (1) From total disability = wage x time not able to work at all

      (2) From partial disability = (earnings before accident—earnings after accident) x time partially disabled

    B. Future

      (1) Totally disabled = wage x future time not able to work

      (2) Partially disabled = decrease in wage (and/or earning capacity) x time partially disabled

3. Other damages

    A. Property

4. Intangibles

    A. Pain and Suffering. This is calculated by assessing the compensatory value to the plaintiff, either as a lump sum or as a multiple of damages, with regard to specific occurrences of pain and suffering:

      (1) Due to the injury

      (2) Due to surgery or other medical treatment

      (3) Due to wearing braces, prostheses, etc.

    B. Loss of Life's Pleasures. Calculated similarly to pain and suffering

      (1) Resulting from disfigurement

      (2) Resulting from disability, loss of limb, etc.

    C. Subjective jury factors

    Add or subtract some percentage (*e.g.* 10%) from the value or add or subtract a lump sum (*e.g.* $5000 each) for each factor below depending on whether it benefits or hurts plaintiff

     (1) Counsel advantage based on skill or experience

     (2) Target defendant, such as a large corporation or one with a bad public image

     (3) Plaintiff needs the money

     (4) Defendant's financial resources

     (5) Plaintiff's personal profile, such as a strong sympathetic or negative image

     (6) Defendant's personal profile

5. Probabilities. Some attorneys attempt to describe estimated outcomes in terms of probabilities. These may be calculated on the basis of a systematic assessment of individual variables, or as a more intuitive, global "feeling" for what the jury is likely to do. Entering probabilities into the calculation can be done using the following three variables:

   A. What is the likelihood of a favorable verdict;

   B. Assuming a plaintiff's verdict, what amount of damages is likely to be awarded. Note that this may be expressed in probabilities too. For example, an attorney may estimate that if plaintiff wins, there is a 20% chance of $20,000 in damages, a 60% chance of $40,000, and a 20% chance of $60,000;

   C. Assuming a plaintiff's verdict, what is the likelihood of collecting the full amount of damages from the defendant.

Contemporary plaintiff and defendant attorneys frequently create decision trees to factor in the relevant considerations and to calculate case values. They estimate the probability that their cases would move through each stage of the litigation process and the likely outcomes for each such stage. By adding the probable outcomes for each stage together, attorneys can develop overall case values. The following decision tree provides a representative sample.[7]

---

7. See Jeffrey M. Senger, *Decision Analysis in Negotiation*, 87 Marquette L. Rev. 723, 729–732 (2004). See generally Howard Raiffa, *Negotiation Analysis* (Harvard University Press 2003).

TABLE 6-2   PLAINTIFF DECISION TREE
MEDICAL MALPRACTICE CASE

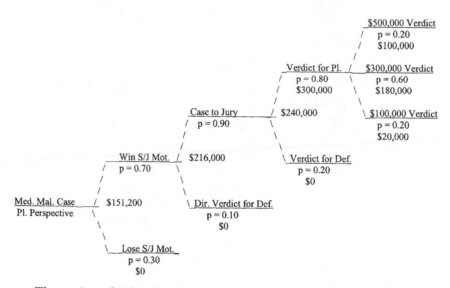

The projected value for this case to the plaintiff would be $151,200—the sum of the various branches of the decision tree. Due to an "egocentric bias," plaintiff lawyers tend to over-estimate likely jury outcomes, while defense lawyers tend to under-estimate such outcomes. Two important considerations bring the two sides closer together. First, the fact that plaintiffs tend to focus on their *downside risks* (losing or obtaining lower verdicts), while defendants focus on their *upside risks* (losing large awards). Second are the anticipated litigation costs. Plaintiff attorneys have to *subtract* such costs from their projected trial results, while defendant attorneys must add such costs to their anticipated jury results.

IV. AN OBJECTIVE ECONOMIC METHOD FOR CASE EVALUATION

A. INTRODUCTION

Some lawyers—and law professors—seem to believe that cases can be evaluated in purely objective terms. They fail to appreciate the fact that cases involve human beings and have unique, non-quantifiable aspects to them. Juries are also composed of human beings, and their responses to the facts of individual cases cannot be understood in purely objective terms. However, the presence of subjective or non-quantifiable factors, such as pain and suffering, mental anguish, or the likeable or dislikeable characteristics of the parties, should not prevent lawyers from evaluating the probable impact of the objective factors. Once the objective value is established, however, the subjective factors must be considered.

There are several items to be considered in an objective model: (1) actual costs or losses to the plaintiff; (2) future losses to the plaintiff that are certain; (3) future losses to the plaintiff that are contingent or variable; (4) relevant costs or losses to the defendant; (5) economic effects of time/money relationships; and (6) tax effects. Items 1 through 4 are detailed above, so the discussion will now turn to items 5 and 6.

B.   TIME VALUE OF MONEY

A dollar now is worth more than a dollar a year from now due to the impact of inflation. This is the basic concept behind time value calculations of money. Several factors enter into time value calculations (inflation, the risk of non-payment, and uncertain future conditions), but the basic idea is that when you consider money, the *timing* of the receipts or payments ranks second only to *amount* in importance. Suppose a beneficiary under a trust has an absolute right to receive $50,000 five years from today; a financial analyst can quickly calculate the *present value* of that right based on the value of money over time. Assuming, for illustration, an interest rate of 6% compounded annually, the value today of that sum would be $37,363 [$50,000 ÷ (1.06)^5].

This same principle is true when money is compounded over periods of time other than one-year intervals. It is very important to think of *periods* and not *years* when considering time value. For example, the $50,000 could have been compounded quarterly instead of annually. If this were the case, it would be necessary to consider the total number of periods (and not years), and the interest rate per period (instead of the annual interest rate). The quarterly interest rate would be 1.50% (6% divided by 4) and the money would be taken over a time frame of 20 periods (5 years times 4). The present value using this method would be $37,124—compared with $37,363 if the money were compounded on an annual basis. When using an interest rate, it is therefore important to consider how often the interest is compounded. Using the interest rate to calculate the present value of a future sum is called *discounting* the amount; using the interest rate to determine the future value of a present sum is called *compounding* the amount.

A second method of computing the time value of money involves the use of electronic calculators. Calculators equipped with basic financial functions have keys that can be used to enter any three of the four basic variables—present value, future value, rate of interest per period, and number of periods—and the calculators will compute the value of the fourth variable.

Present and future values can also be calculated by using tables—readily available on the Internet—or through the use of mathematical formulas. Formulas are more versatile than the tables, and attorneys must be able to use them if they are to competently represent clients in any matters involving an interplay between time and money. There are four basic variables used in time-value formulas:

PV —Used to represent the PRESENT VALUE.
FV —Used to represent the FUTURE VALUE.
i   —Used to represent the rate of INTEREST per period.
n   —Used to represent the number of PERIODS for which interest will be paid.

The relationship between time and money (i.e. the present value of a future sum or the future value of a present sum) is expressed in two standard formulas which can likewise be solved with a calculator:

$$FV = PV \times (1 + i)^n$$

$$PV = FV \div (1 + i)^n$$

If you do not have a calculator on hand, tables may be used to make the time-value calculations. A quick Google search (e.g., "present value + future payments") can enable you to find detailed tables that will let you determine the present value of future payments or the future value of present payments based upon different interest rates. When significant sums are involved, many attorneys retain the services of actuaries who can calculate these values for them.

Using the methods just described, attorneys can figure the present value or the future value of any one payment or receipt, or of a schedule of many payments and receipts by figuring each amount separately. There are cases, however, where even these relatively easy methods would prove to be tedious. For example, using a 6% annual interest rate, what is the present value of the stream of lost wages of a worker who has been injured and will not be able to work for 5 years if her monthly wage was $3,348.00? This problem would require multiple individual calculations if done by the single payment method. This kind of a problem, however, is a special case—where the stream of payments is called an *annuity*. An annuity is a series of payments of a fixed amount for a specified number of periods.

The easiest way to calculate the present or future value of annuities is to use financial calculators. Most such calculators provide keys for entering values of the known variables, and the calculators give you the values of the unknown variables. Annuity tables can also be used, or actuaries can be employed.

C. THE APPROPRIATE RATE OF INTEREST FOR TIME–VALUE CALCULATION USE

The interest rate used in the time value calculations greatly affects the ultimate outcomes, and thus a key factor in the reliability of the calculations is the appropriateness of the interest rate variable. The rate used should usually reflect the value of money to your client. The rate may be based on the saving or borrowing rates of the individuals involved, or an established rate may be used, such as a fixed amount above or below the current prime rate. The key "ingredients" in an interest rate figure include the inflation factor and the risk factor. For example, in a scenario with no risk of non-payment and with no inflation, an individual might be willing to lend money at a rate of 2%. This would be a base amount to which would be added an amount representing expected inflation—say 4%, and an amount for risk coverage, which for this example might be 2%. Under these circumstances, a rate of 8% would be appropriate.

D.   THE TAX ASPECTS OF SETTLEMENT

The day is past when lawyers could ignore the tax implications of settlements. At present levels of taxation, the economic value of a settlement for the plaintiff or the defendant can routinely vary by as much as 40%, depending upon the tax treatment of the money or property involved.

The tax effects of settlement agreements depend upon two primary factors: (1) the characterization of the values exchanged for tax purposes, and (2) the timing of payments.

To the defendant, there is a large saving if the payment is deductible from gross income (i.e. if the payment qualifies as an income tax deduction) rather than being payable with after-tax dollars. The cost of a payment by the defendant is also conditioned by the timing of taxation. If the payment is deductible, can it all be deducted in this tax year, or must it be amortized or depreciated over a number of years?

For the plaintiff, the question is whether money received will constitute taxable income, and, if so, at what rate. If it is tax exempt, there is no tax to be paid. If it is characterized as ordinary income, it will be subject to the plaintiff's regular tax rate. If it is characterized as capital gain, it will be subject to tax, but at a more favorable rate than ordinary income.

Compensation for lost wages and punitive damages generally constitutes taxable income. Under Section 104(a)(2) of the Tax Code, however, compensatory damages do not constitute taxable gross income if received "on account of personal physical injuries or physical illness." It is thus beneficial to characterize as much of settlement payments as reasonably supportable as compensation for physical injuries or physical illness to allow claimants to exclude this portion of their compensation from their gross income. Such an arrangement tends to help defendants by allowing them to make less generous payments due to the tax savings enjoyed by the recipients of those payments.

If claimants receive large lump sum payments, they will probably have to pay taxes on those amounts at the highest tax rate. On the other hand, if the payments are spread out over a number of years, the annual payments may be taxable at lower rates for persons without other significant taxable income. The use of periodic payments over a number of years can thus reduce the taxes claimants will have to pay on the overall sums they receive.

V. DECISION-MAKING INFLUENCES

When lawyers negotiate, it is generally assumed that they and their respective clients evaluate settlement offers in a rational and unemotional manner. They carefully assess the probability they will prevail at trial and the likely jury awards if defendant liability is found. No matter how hard human beings work to make such determinations in a wholly logical fashion, certain empirically established psychological factors are likely to influence their decisions in ways that are not completely rational.

A. FIXED PIE ASSUMPTION

Many legal negotiators—especially in the litigation context—assume that the parties are fighting over a fixed amount of money and that each dollar obtained by the plaintiff results in an equal loss for the defendant. Rarely do both sides value money identically. Claimants who have outstanding medical bills and who have suffered lost earnings may truly have to obtain sufficient amounts of money to cover these critical losses. If less is offered by defendants, they will opt for trial outcomes they hope will exceed their basic needs. Nonetheless, once they receive offers that cover these amounts, they tend to view the extra dollars as beneficial, but not essential. They are likely to accept offers that exceed these minimal amounts over the uncertainty of trials.

Defendants who have exposed themselves to liability due to negligent conduct or other wrongful conduct usually recognize the need to offer sufficient amounts to compensate the injured parties for the damages they have sustained. Nonetheless, when plaintiffs demand sums in excess of these compensatory amounts, defendants are likely to become difficult and uncompromising. They view claimant demands for more money as beyond the pale.

Plaintiffs need to carefully articulate rationales supporting their damage claims. To the extent they can demonstrate their right to what they are seeking, defendants are likely to view the amounts they request as reasonable compensation. These amounts thus seem less significant to the defendants, who recognize their liability for these damages, than to the plaintiffs, who consider these sums essential to their complete restitution. On the other hand, defendants must similarly indicate why plaintiffs are not entitled to amounts that would make them more than "whole" for the injuries they have sustained, since these dollars would become more significant to the defendants, who view them as excessive, than to the plaintiffs, who recognize that they are not essential to their recovery.

How else can seemingly zero-sum money disputes be converted into non-zero-sum negotiations? If the negotiators explore the underlying needs and interests of the parties, they may discover issues that may be used to expand the overall pie and improve the positions of both sides. Why are the claimants demanding large sums to settle their law suits? Are they primarily concerned about the fact they may spend all of the money they receive and still require future medical treatment? If so, defendants can assuage these concerns by offering less substantial amounts immediately and promising to take care of future claimant medical needs. They may alternatively offer to provide claimants with structured settlements that will provide them with guaranteed payments for each of the next ten or fifteen years, or for the rest of their lives. Such arrangements can take care of plaintiff concerns regarding their future needs, and turn zero-sum negotiations into win-win undertakings.

How can plaintiffs offset the seemingly zero-sum impact of demands for specific amounts that have to be paid immediately? They can recognize that defendants may have other interests the claimants may be able to satisfy. For example, defendants may wish to obtain agreements with non-admission clauses, so they can maintain that they really did nothing wrong. Defendants may also wish to obtain confidentiality clauses that will prevent claimants from disclosing any information which might embarrass the defendants. Most plaintiffs do not mind agreeing to such provisions, but defendants frequently consider these terms essential. They will thus increase the monetary amounts they are willing to pay in exchange for these items. Defendants should similarly appreciate the fact that claimants may reduce their monetary demands if they obtain other forms of relief. For example, individuals who believe they were treated badly may wish to obtain an apology from the responsible parties, and they may reduce their monetary desires if defendants demonstrate appropriate contrition. These apologies need not include admissions of responsibility. Sometimes it is sufficient for defendants to merely apologize for the harm claimants have suffered or to apologize for the negative feelings expressed by claimants. These acts of "recognition" can often diminish claimant desires for retribution.

Whenever negotiators think they are involved in fixed-pie interactions, they should step back and assess the underlying interests of the different participants. Would claimants be willing to accept future payments or in-kind compensation (e.g., hospitals promising to take care of future claimant medical needs)? Would defendants be willing to pay more if they could obtain non-admission or confidentiality provisions? By exploring these types of issues, negotiators may be able to expand the overall pie and simultaneously enhance the interests of both sides.

B. EGOCENTRIC/SELF–SERVING BIAS

When lawyers and clients evaluate cases, they tend to see things from their own side's perspective.[9] As a result, plaintiffs tend to over-estimate the likelihood of success and the size of the resulting awards, while defendants tend to under-estimate the likelihood of claimant success and the size of the resulting verdicts. Some people may think that this phenomenon is due to the fact that lawyers sympathetic to claimants are likely to represent plaintiffs, while attorneys sympathetic to defendants are likely to represent defendant insurance firms. This assumption is not necessarily correct. If we ask the students in our class to evaluate a typical personal injury case, but designate half of the students as plaintiff representatives and the other half as defendant representatives, the plaintiff representatives over-estimate the case value and the defendant representatives under-estimate the case value.

To limit the influence of the egocentric bias, lawyers should appreciate its impact and try to assess the values of their cases as objectively as possible. In larger value cases, attorneys often employ focus groups who are likely to reflect jury pool members if the cases have to be tried. Attorneys summarize the evidence and applicable legal principles in a neutral manner and ask the focus group members how they would rule if they were the actual jurors. These independent groups tend to provide fairly accurate assessments of the critical factors: (1) the probability the claimants would prevail at trial and (2) the likely verdicts if the plaintiffs did win. Even with focus groups, however, three of ten participants may indicate that they favor the defendants, while the other seven favor the plaintiffs. When asked about the size of the awards they would support, the range may be from $100,000 to $750,000 or from $1.5 million to $10 million. It thus makes it difficult for attorneys to predict with accuracy the likely verdicts if the claimants did prevail. Nonetheless, this factor actually militates in favor of negotiated settlements, due to an important consideration. Plaintiff attorneys tend to focus on their down-side potential (*i.e.*, the fact they might lose entirely or the lower verdicts they might obtain), while defendant lawyers tend to focus on their up-side risk (*i.e.*, how much might they lose if the claimants did prevail).

C. ANCHORING IMPACT OF INITIAL OFFERS

When attorneys begin negotiations, they are not certain about the true values of the cases they are discussing. No matter how thoroughly prepared they are, they only have a general range of likely results in mind. Empirical studies indicate that their ultimate value determinations may be significantly affected by the opening positions articulated by their opponents.[10] When opponents begin with offers or demands that are more favorable to the recipients than they anticipated, the offerees

---

9. See Russell Korobkin, *Psychological Impediments to Mediation Success: Theory and Practice*, 21 Ohio St. J. Disp. Res. 281, 284–88 (2006); George Loewenstein, Samuel Issacharoff, Colin Camerer & Linda Babcock, *Self-Serving Assessments of Fairness and Pretrial Bargaining*, 22 J. Legal Stud.

135 (1993). This phenomenon may also be referred to as "optimistic overconfidence."

10. See Russell Korobkin & Chris Guthrie, *Psychological Barriers to Litigation Settlement: An Experimental Approach*, 93 Mich. L. Rev. 107, 138–42 (1994).

begin to think they will achieve better results than they initially thought they could. The offerees move psychologically away from the offerors and work to obtain better deals for themselves. On the other hand, when opponents begin with offers or demands that are less generous to the recipients than they expected, the offerees begin to think they will not do as well as they hoped, and they lower their expectations. They tend to reduce their aspiration levels, and may even articulate initial offers of their own that are less generous to their own sides than they originally planned to announce.

Attorneys preparing for bargaining interactions should appreciate the potential anchoring impact of their opening position statements. They should not plan to announce wholly one-sided positions favoring their clients, because such unsupportable offers would undermine their own credibility. On the other hand, they should not be too generous to their opponents to avoid increasing offeree aspirations. They should instead formulate opening positions that are a reasonable distance from where they expect to come out *and* which they can rationally defend to their opponents.

The most effective way to counteract the anchoring impact of opponent opening offers is through careful preparation. Individuals who have thoroughly evaluated case values and formulated realistic opening positions, aspiration levels, and bottom lines are less influenced by this factor than their less well prepared cohorts. Fully prepared negotiators tend to focus on their own preliminary assessments, and do not let opponent opening offers change their focus. If they can ignore the initial positions of their opponents and articulate reasonably defensible positions favoring their own clients, they may be able to reverse the tables and use their own opening offers to anchor the subsequent discussions with their adversaries.

D. GAIN–LOSS FRAMING

Suppose you have to choose between the following two options:

If you select Option 1, you will receive $1000.

If you select Option 2, there is a 20 percent chance you will receive $5000 and an 80 percent chance you will receive nothing.

Most persons accept the certain $1000 gain offered by Option 1 over the higher, but less likely, reward offered by Option 2.[11] Suppose the options were framed in the following way:

If you select Option 1, you will lose $1000.

If you select Option 2, there is a 20 percent chance you will lose $5000 and an 80 percent chance you will lose nothing.

11. See Russell Korobkin, *Psychological Impediments to Mediation Success: Theory and Practice*, 21 Ohio St. J. Disp. Res. 281, 308–314 (2006); Jeffrey J. Rachlinski, *Gains, Losses, and the Psychology of Litigation*, 70 S. Cal. L. Rev. 113 (1996).

When facing the second set of options, most people select Option 2. They are unwilling to accept the certain loss of $1000 and prefer Option 2 that may enable them to avoid any loss despite the 20 percent chance of losing $5000.

Individuals facing a certain *gain* and the possibility of a greater gain or no gain tend to be risk averse. They accept the sure gain. On the other hand, persons facing a certain *loss* or the possibility of a greater loss or no loss tend to be risk-takers. They accept the option that may enable them to avoid any loss.

The impact of *gain-loss framing* can significantly influence dispute resolution negotiations. Plaintiffs—and plaintiff attorneys who are usually employed on a contingent fee basis—tend to be risk averse. When they receive defendant settlement offers, they are facing certain gains and the possibility of greater gains or no gains if they reject those offers. On the other hand, defendants facing sure losses in the form of plaintiff demands and the possibility of greater losses or no losses if they reject those demands tend to be risk takers. They are more likely to opt for trials than plaintiffs or their counsel.

How can plaintiff lawyers counteract this gain-loss bias? They can try to articulate positions that seem like "gains" to the defendants. Instead of demanding $X to cover claimant losses, plaintiff attorneys should indicate that for this amount the defendant problems will be solved. If defendants can be induced to view such plaintiff position statements as "gains," they would be more likely to accept the sure gains over their trial alternatives.

E. REACTIVE DEVALUATION

When negotiating parties receive offers from their opponents, they tend to assume that those offers favor the offerors at the expense of the offerees. As a result, they often reject them, even when they fall within their own settlement ranges. This "reactive devaluation" causes parties to reject positions they might have accepted had they been suggested by neutral third persons—such as judges or mediators.[12]

How can reactive devaluation be minimized? Advocates who are contemplating position changes should not make them too quickly, lest they make opponents suspicious of their true value. If the offerors take a little longer before they articulate new positions and make their opponents work harder to elicit them, their offers may be attributed to the tenacity of the offerees and be treated more favorably. Another way to counteract reactive devaluation is through resort to third-party neutrals. Judges conducting settlement conferences or mediators conducting for-

---

12. See Russell Korobkin, *Psychological Impediments to Mediation Success: Theory and Practice*, 21 Ohio St. J. Disp. Res. 281, 316–319 (2006); Lee Ross, *Reactive Devaluation in Negotiation and Conflict Resolution* in *Barriers to Conflict Resolution* 26–42 (Kenneth Arrow, Robert Mnookin, Lee Ross, Amos Tversky & Robert Wilson, eds. 1995).

mal mediation sessions can be asked in separate caucus meetings to propose solutions they would like both sides to consider. Since these offers would emanate from dispassionate neutrals instead of from interested parties, they would be received more openly by both sides.

F. REGRET AVERSION

Human beings hate to make decisions that subsequent developments may prove to have been suboptimal. For example, people often hesitate to make significant purchases at one store for fear they may discover the same items on sale for less at other stores. As a result, they hesitate to make final purchase decisions at any store.[13]

How does such "regret aversion" influence settlement negotiations? It actually militates in favor of bargained resolutions. Both plaintiffs and defendants are hesitant to reject definitive settlement offers, when their subsequent trial results may turn out to be less beneficial than the offers they rejected. When litigants are discussing possible settlement arrangements, they should suggest that their opponents may fare worse if the cases have to be tried. If they can instill in opponent minds the fear they may make incorrect decisions now if they reject the outstanding settlement offers, they would be more likely to accept those offers to avoid subsequent developments that would prove they made the wrong decision in this regard.

CHAPTER NOTES

1. Actuarial and Tax Implications of Settlement Offers

As we have discussed, most litigators are neither mathematically adept nor tax experts. As a result, they don't know how to calculate the present value of future payments or the tax advantages of future payments or payments characterized in particular ways. If they are to provide their clients with optimal advice, they should consult actuaries who can easily determine the present value of future payments, and tax specialists who can help them formulate settlements that minimize tax liabilities for claimants receiving substantial payments.

2. Overcoming Decision–Making Influences

We have seen that both plaintiff and defendant lawyers should learn to use decision trees and focus groups to develop accurate case evaluations. What is the probability the claimants would prevail at trial and what are the likely trial outcomes if they do prevail? Advocates concerned about the impact of the egocentric bias can ask colleagues or friends how they think their cases would be resolved. In large value cases, they may employ focus groups to obtain this information. These neutral evaluations can provide claimant and defendant representatives with detached assessments they may have difficulty generating on their own. Such neutral evaluations should also

---

13. See Chris Guthrie, *Better Settle than Sorry: The Regret Aversion Theory of Liti-* gation Behavior, 1999 Univ. of Ill. L. Rev. 43 (1999).

minimize the anchoring impact of opponent opening offers that are not reflective of the objective assessments already made by this side.

Chapter Seven

PERSONAL FACTORS THAT MAY INFLUENCE NEGOTIATOR PERFORMANCE

In the three decades we have both taught legal negotiation courses, we have had many gifted negotiators and many less proficient negotiators in our classes. We have often wondered about the personal characteristics of individuals that might contribute to their negotiation performance. Are students with higher GPAs likely to be more proficient negotiators than other students? Are men or women likely to achieve different results when they are involved in bargaining interactions? Would different results be found between Caucasian–American and African–American negotiators? In this chapter, we will explore these areas in an effort to determine which personal attributes, if any, predict negotiator performance.

A. ABSTRACT REASONING ABILITY (IQ) vs. EMOTIONAL INTELLIGENCE (EI)

Several years ago, Professor Craver decided to determine whether high achieving students—represented by higher law school grade point averages (GPAs)—achieved better results on course negotiation exercises than lower GPA students. In his course, he explores negotiator styles, the negotiation process, verbal and nonverbal communication, negotiation techniques, telephone and e-mail interactions, international negotiations, mediation, negotiation ethics, and other relevant issues. He also has the students engage in a series of eight or nine negotiation exercises. The first three or four are practice exercises designed to acquaint the students with the negotiation process. The last five exercises, however, affect student course grades. The results of each of these exercises are rank-ordered from high to low with respect to the representatives on each side of the matter being negotiated, and the total rank-order scores for the students account for two–thirds of their final grades. He also encourages bargaining efficiency by demonstrating how in multiple item negotiations, the parties on both sides can achieve results that place each above average if they maximize their joint returns, while less efficient opponents may both end up below average by failing to divide the items optimally. The remaining one-third of their grade is based upon a ten to fifteen page paper evaluating student negotiating experiences in light of the concepts explored during the semester. Students have an option to take the class on a credit/no-credit basis and are guaranteed "credits" if they participate in the assigned exercises–no matter how well or poorly they do—and prepare acceptable course papers.[1]

THE IMPACT OF STUDENT GPAs AND A PASS/FAIL OPTION ON CLINICAL NEGOTIA-TION COURSE PERFORMANCE

By Charles B. Craver
15 Ohio State Journal on Dispute Resolution 373, 374, 379–80, 381–84 (2000)[2]

I. INTRODUCTION

* * *

I frequently have wondered whether the fundamental skills developed in that legal skills class are related to those developed in traditional law school courses. Would students who perform well in other law school courses achieve better results in my Legal Negotiating class than colleagues who do not perform as well in traditional courses?

Students who maintain consistently high grade point averages (GPAs) usually are considered—by both academics and practicing attorneys deciding which recent graduates to hire as associates—intelligent, industrious, organized, and articulate. Would these personal attributes carry over to skills courses and positively influence student performance on negotiation class exercises or course papers? If so, there should be a statistically significant positive correlation between student GPAs and Legal Negotiating class achievement.

* * *

III. STATISTICAL FINDINGS

When we attempt to determine whether there may be a relationship between different factors, it is appropriate to establish Null and Alternative Hypotheses. The Null Hypothesis assumes the absence of any correlation, while the Alternative Hypothesis assumes that some rela-

---

1. The students who take the course on a credit/no-credit basis do substantially less well on the negotiation exercises than the students who take the class for regular grades. See Charles B. Craver, *The Impact of a Pass/Fail Option on Negotiation Course Performance*, 48 J. Legal Educ. 176, 182–83 (1998). To obtain optimal negotiation results, students have to devote more time to their pre-interaction preparation and work harder during their interactions to further their side's interests. If students are debat-

ing whether to spend an extra half hour in preparation or an extra hour negotiating and they are guaranteed "credit" grades, they decide that the extra effort required to achieve better results should be spent on coursework for which they will receive regular grades.

2. Copyright © 2000 Ohio State Journal on Dispute Resolution. Reprinted by permission.

tionship in fact exists. The relevant data then are analyzed to determine whether there appears to be a correlation between the factors being compared.

Statistical tests calculate the probability that any observed differences between compared factors are due to random considerations rather than some alternative explanation. The probability that any observed difference is due to chance is referred to as the "p-value." Social scientists traditionally reject the Null Hypothesis when the p-value pertaining to a discerned difference is less than 0.05, which indicates a probability of less than one in twenty that the observed difference is due to chance rather than the assumed alternative explanation. When, on the other hand, the probability is high that the observed difference is due to chance—a p-value of above 0.05—social scientists traditionally do not reject the Null Hypothesis.

* * *

[Null Hypothesis I: There is no correlation between student GPAs and the results achieved on Legal Negotiation course exercises.

Alternative Hypothesis I: There is a positive correlation between student GPAs and the results achieved on Legal Negotiation course exercises.

Null Hypothesis II: There is no correlation between student GPAs and student performance on Legal Negotiation course papers.

Alternative Hypothesis II: There is a positive correlation between student GPAs and the results achieved on Legal Negotiation course papers.]

... To test these two hypotheses, Spearman rank-order coefficients (Rs) were calculated for each of the thirteen years I have taught Legal Negotiating at George Washington University. The first Rs column compares student GPAs with negotiation exercise results; the second Rs column compares student GPAs with course paper scores; and the third Rs column provides the Rs coefficients needed for a statistically significant correlation (positive $(+)$ or negative $(-)$) for the stated sample sizes (N) at the 0.05 level of significance. Because both Alternative Hypotheses are based on the premise that if correlations between student GPAs and negotiation exercise results or course paper scores are discerned, they would be positive rather than negative, I have used one-tailed—rather than two-tailed—probability values. The results are set forth in Table 2.

Table 2. Spearman Rank Order Coefficients Comparing Student GPAs with Negotiation Exercise Results and Course Paper Scores

Semester	N	Rs Negotiation Exercises	Rs Paper Scores	Rs 0.05 Level of Significance
Fall 1986	45	+0.213	+0.217	0.248
Spring 1988	55	+0.212	+0.007	0.224

Semester	N	Rs Negotiation Exercises	Rs Paper Scores	Rs 0.05 Level of Significance
Spring 1989	58	+0.072	+0.002	0.218
Spring 1990	58	−0.206	−0.047	0.218
Spring 1991	61	−0.021	+0.153	0.213
Spring 1992	48	+0.120	+0.005	0.240
Fall 1992	59	+0.169	+0.164	0.216
Fall 1993	59	−0.034	+0.075	0.216
Fall 1994	62	−0.106	+0.060	0.211
Fall 1995	56	+0.002	−0.047	0.222
Fall 1996	51	−0.093	+0.346	0.233
Fall 1997	40	−0.052	−0.114	0.264
Fall 1998	46	+0.027	−0.062	0.246

The Spearman rank order coefficients comparing student GPAs with negotiation exercise results were slightly positive for seven of the thirteen years and slightly negative for the other six years. There is not a single year, however, for which the Spearman coefficient established a correlation at the 0.05 level of significance. These findings warrant rejection of the Alternative Hypothesis suggesting a possible positive correlation between student GPAs and negotiation exercise performance and acceptance of the Null Hypothesis suggesting the absence of any such correlation.

One possible explanation for the unanticipated absence of any statistically significant correlation between law school grades and negotiation exercise results might involve the relatively homogeneous nature of law school matriculants. Typical students at George Washington University Law School have undergraduate grade point averages in excess of 3.5 on a 4.0 scale and LSAT scores above the 90th percentile. If the academic capabilities of the students in my Legal Negotiating class were relatively indistinguishable, one might expect to find no meaningful differences between negotiation exercise results and overall law school performance. However, this explanation cannot be sustained. Professors teaching traditional law school courses generally have found that examinations normally generate an expansive range of student responses that permit reasonable demarcations among the various class members. Few would suggest that student homogeneity has precluded the drawing of meaningful distinctions with respect to performance in regular courses. There is no reason to suspect that student homogeneity would account for the absence of any perceived correlation between student GPAs and negotiation exercise results.

What else might account for the absence of any perceived correlation between student GPAs and negotiation exercise results? A critical factor might be the different capabilities being measured by traditional law school examinations and by simulation exercises. Students who perform well on examinations generally possess high abstract reasoning skills. They are able to memorize legal doctrines and know how to apply those principles to hypothetical fact patterns in an abstract manner. Good negotiators, on the other hand, possess good interpersonal skills. They know how to "read" other people and persuade those persons to give them what they prefer to have. These personal attributes concern what Daniel Goleman has characterized as *Emotional Intelligence* (1995).

There does not appear to be any correlation between abstract reasoning skills—most often measured by IQ tests—and emotional intelligence. While a few gifted individuals may possess both capabilities, most people are fortunate if they have an abundance of either. As a result, there is no reason to suspect that students who have the high abstract reasoning skills needed to achieve elevated GPAs would be among the finite number of persons who also possess the enhanced emotional intelligence that would be most relevant with respect to performance on negotiation exercises.

It is also interesting to note the absence of any statistically significant correlation between student GPAs and course paper scores. Slight positive Spearman coefficients were obtained for nine of the thirteen years, with slight negative coefficients being found for the other four years. For three of the years for which positive coefficients were obtained—1988, 1989, and spring of 1992—the coefficients were below 0.01. The year 1996 was the sole year for which a coefficient was found that was statistically significant at the 0.05 level. These findings would warrant rejection of the Alternative Hypothesis suggesting a positive correlation between student GPAs and course paper scores and acceptance of the Null Hypothesis suggesting the absence of any such correlation.

Some observers might be more surprised by the absence of any observable relationship between student GPAs and course paper scores than they were with respect to the results obtained comparing student GPAs with negotiation exercise performance. While they may appreciate the difference between the abstract reasoning skills that contribute to success on traditional law school examinations and the emotional intelligence relevant to successful negotiation performance, they might reasonably wonder why the same abstract reasoning capabilities measured by student GPAs are not relevant to the preparation of course papers.

... [M]y Legal Negotiating course papers are not like conventional seminar papers. I do not require students to engage in scholarly research. I instead require them to analyze their negotiation exercise experiences in light of the various concepts we have explored throughout the term. While I do require the use of analytical skills, much of what students write concerns interpersonal capabilities or the lack thereof. They are forced to evaluate their bargaining interactions with fellow students in an effort to appreciate the factors that may have accounted for the results they have achieved on their exercises. More of their analysis focuses on emotional intelligence factors than on abstract reasoning capabilities.

The finding of no correlation between abstract reasoning skills and negotiation performance has led Professor Craver to explore the possible relationship between emotional intelligence and negotiation performance. What is "emotional intelligence"? Professors John Mayer and Peter Salovey have been among the pioneers in this developing area. They suggest that "emotional intelligence involves the ability to perceive accurately, appraise, and express emotion; the ability to access and/or generate feelings when they facilitate thought; the ability to understand emotion and emotional knowledge; and the ability to regulate emotions to promote emotional and intellectual growth."[3]

What personal characteristics are indicative of high emotional intelligence? First, the ability to reflectively monitor emotional feelings in oneself and others; second, the ability to manage or control emotional feelings in oneself and in others; third, the ability to interpret and understand complex emotional feelings in oneself and in others; and fourth, the ability to adapt to different emotional situations, and to express one's own emotions in appropriate ways.[4]

During 2005 and 2006, Professor Craver has been working with Psychology Professor Allison Abbe to measure the emotional intelligence levels of his Legal Negotiation class students and to correlate those scores with their performance on negotiation exercises. Their preliminary results have found a statistically significant correlation between overall emotional intelligence and negotiation exercise performance. They hope to complete this work during 2007. This is a remarkable finding, due to the lack of any correlation between negotiation performance and any other personal characteristics previously studied.

As they complete their study, Professors Abbe and Craver plan to break down overall emotional intelligence into discreet components in an effort to determine which aspects of emotional intelligence are most predictive of negotiator proficiency. They also hope to explore ways to teach emotional intelligence to law students who are generally oblivious to such psychological considerations.[5]

B. IMPACT OF GENDER

GENDER AND NEGOTIATION PERFORMANCE
By Charles B. Craver
4 *Sociological Practice* 183–87; 190–92 (2002).[6]

INTRODUCTION

When men and women negotiate with people of the opposite gender–and even the same gender–stereotypical beliefs influence their interac-

---

3. John D. Mayer & Peter Salovey, *What Is Emotional Intelligence?* in *Emotional Intelligence* 29,35 (Peter Salovey, Marc A. Brackett & John D. Mayer, eds.) (Dude Publishing 2004).

4. See *id.* at 35–43. See generally *Emotional Intelligence* (Peter Salovey, Marc A. Brackett & John D. Mayer, eds.) (Dude Publishing 2004); Reuven Bar–On & James D.A. Parker, eds., *The Handbook of Emotional Intelligence* (Jossey–Bass 2000).

5. See Peter Reilly, *Teaching Law students How to Feel: Using Negotiations Training to Increase Emotional Intelligence*, 21 Neg. J. 301 (2005).

6. Copyright © 2002 by Springer Science and Business Media. Reprinted with kind permission from Springer Science and Business Media.

tions. Many men and women assume that males are more likely to be highly competitive, manipulative, win-lose negotiators who want to defeat their opponents. Females are expected to be more accommodating, win-win negotiators who seek to preserve existing relationships by maximizing the joint return achieved by negotiating parties. If these stereotypical assumptions are correct, we might reasonably expect male lawyers and business persons to achieve better results when they negotiate than female attorneys and business persons.

* * *

REAL AND PERCEIVED GENDER–BASED DIFFERENCES

Many persons think that men and women behave in stereotypically different ways when the interact (Burrell, et al., 1988, at 453). Various traits are attributed to males, while other characteristics are attributed to females. While some of these gender-based beliefs may reflect real–*i.e.*, empirically established–behavioral traits, others have no scientifically established bases. Whether or not these distinctions are real or imagined, they may influence the way men and women interact when they negotiate, because the participants *expect* these factors to affect their dealings.

Men are thought to be rational and logical, while women are considered emotional and intuitive (Deaux, 1976, at 13). Men are expected to emphasize objective fact, while women focus more on the maintenance of relationships (Gilligan, 1982). As a result, men are expected to define issues in abstract terms and try to resolve them through the application of abstract reasoning (Project, 1988, at 1227).

Men are expected to be dominant and authoritative, while women are supposed to be passive and submissive (Maccoby & Jacklin, 1974, at 228, 234). When men and women interact, males tend to speak for longer periods of time and to interrupt more often than women (Project, 1988, at 1220; Tannen, 1994, at 53–77). Men usually exert more influence over the topics being discussed. They employ more direct language, while women tend to exhibit tentative and deferential speech patterns (Smith–Lovin & Robinson, 1992, at 124–26). This male tendency to dominate male-female interactions could provide men with an advantage during bargaining encounters, by allowing them to control the agenda and direct the substantive discussions.

During personal interactions, men are more likely than women to employ "highly intensive language" to persuade others, and they tend to be more effective using this approach (Burgoon, et al., 1983, at 284, 292). Women, on the other hand, are more likely to use less intense language during persuasive encounters, and they are inclined to be more effective behaving this way. Females tend to employ language containing more disclaimers ("I think"; "you know") than their male cohorts (Smeltzer

& Watson, 1986, at 78), which may cause women to be perceived as less forceful.

Formal education diminishes the presence of gender-based communication differences (Burrell, et al., 1988, at 453). This factor explains why male and female lawyers tend to employ similar language when they endeavor to persuade others. Nonetheless, even when women use the same language as men, they may be perceived as being less persuasive (Burrell, et al., 1988, at 463). This gender-based factor is counterbalanced, however, by the fact that women continue to be more sensitive to nonverbal signals than their male cohorts (Hall, 1984, at 15–17).

Gender-based stereotypes cause many people difficulty when they interact with attorneys and business people of the opposite gender (Kolb & Williams, 2000; Kolb, 2000). Men often expect women to behave like "ladies" during their negotiation interactions. Overt aggressiveness that would be considered vigorous advocacy if employed by men may be characterized as offensive and threatening when used by women. This is especially true when females employ foul language and loud voices. Male negotiators who would immediately counter these tactics by other men with quid pro quo responses frequently find it difficult to adopt retaliatory approaches against "ladies." When men permit such an irrelevant factor to influence and restrict their use of responsive tactics, they provide their female opponents with an inherent bargaining advantage. Some men also find it difficult to act as competitively against female opponents as they would against male opponents. Male negotiators who are afraid to behave as competitively toward female opponents as they would against male adversaries give further leverage to their female opponents.

* * *

Male attorneys and business people occasionally make the mistake of assuming that their female opponents will not engage in as many negotiating "games" as their male adversaries. Even many women erroneously assume that other females are unlikely to employ the Machiavellian tactics stereotypically associated with members of the competitive male culture. Men and women who expect their female adversaries to behave less competitively and more cooperatively often ignore the realities of their negotiation encounters and give a significant bargaining advantage to women who are actually willing to employ manipulative tactics.

Some male negotiators attempt to obtain a psychological advantage against aggressive female bargainers by casting aspersions on the femininity of those individuals. They hope to embarrass those participants and make them feel self-conscious with respect to the approach they are using. Female negotiators should never allow adversaries to employ this tactic. They have the right to use any techniques they think appropriate, regardless of the stereotypes those tactics may contradict. To male opponents who raise specious objections to their otherwise proper conduct, they should reply that they do not wish to be viewed as "ladies," but merely as participants in bargaining encounters in which their gender should be irrelevant.

Female negotiators who discover that gender-based stereotypes are negatively affecting their bargaining interactions may wish to directly raise the issue to diminish the impact of negative stereotyping (Schneider, 1994, at 112–13). They may ask opponents if they find it difficult to negotiate against female adversaries. While most male opponents will immediately deny any such beliefs, they are likely to internally reevaluate their treatment of female opponents. Once both parties acknowledge, internally or externally, the possible impact of stereotypical beliefs, they can try to avoid group generalizations and focus on the particular individuals with whom they must currently interact.

Empirical studies indicate that men and women do not behave identically in competitive situations. Females tend to be initially more trusting and trustworthy than their male cohorts, but they are usually less willing to forgive violations of their trust than are men (Rubin & Brown, 1975, at 171–73). People interacting with female negotiators who exhibit verbal and nonverbal signals consistent with such female expectations may be able to establish trusting and cooperative relationships with them so long as they do not engage in conduct of an untrusting nature.

When men and women interact in different settings, they both engage in some untruthful behavior. Males tend to lie on a self-oriented basis to enhance their own images ("braggadocio"), while women tend to engage in other-oriented deception intended to make others feel better ("I love that new outfit"; "you made a great presentation") (DePaulo, et al., 1996, at 986–87). This difference would probably cause males to feel more comfortable than women when they employ deceptive behavior during bargaining encounters to advance their own interests, because such conduct would be of a self-oriented nature.

One observer has suggested that "women are more likely [than men] to avoid competitive wishes, and not likely to do as well in competition." (Stiver, 1983, at 5) Many women are apprehensive regarding the negative consequences they associate with competitive achievement, fearing that competitive success will alienate them from others (Gilligan, 1982, at 14–15). Males in my Legal Negotiation course tend to be more accepting of extreme results obtained by other men than by such results achieved by women. Even female students tend to be more critical of women who attain exceptional results than they are of men who do so.

Males tend to exude more confidence than women in performance-oriented settings. Even when minimally prepared, men think they can "wing it" and get through successfully (Goleman, 1998, at 7). On the other hand, no matter how thoroughly prepared women are, they tend to feel unprepared (Evans, 2000, at 84–85; McIntosh, 1985). I have often observed this difference among my Legal Negotiation students. Successful males think they can achieve beneficial results in future settings, while successful females continue to express doubts about their own capabilities. I find this frustrating, because the accomplished women are as proficient as their accomplished male cohorts.

Male and female self-confidence is influenced by the stereotypical ways in which others evaluate their performances. Men who perform masculine tasks no more proficiently than women tend to be given higher evaluations than their equally performing female cohorts (Foschi, 1991, at 185). When men are successful, their performance tends to be attributed to intrinsic factors such as hard work and intelligence; when women are successful, their performance is likely to be attributed to extrinsic factors such as luck or the assistance of others (Deaux, 1976, at 30–32). This phenomenon enhances male self-confidence by enabling them to receive credit for their accomplishments, while it undermines the self-confidence of successful women by diminishing the personal credit they deserve for their efforts.

Men and women often differ with respect to their view of appropriate bargaining outcomes. Women tend to believe in "equal" exchanges, while men tend to expect "equitable" distributions (Lewicki, et al., 1994, at 330). These predispositions may induce female negotiators to accept equal results despite their possession of greater bargaining strength, while male bargainers seek equitable exchanges that reflect relevant power imbalances.

Gender-based competitive differences may be attributable to the different acculturation process for boys and girls (Menkel–Meadow, 2000, at 362–64). Parents tend to be more protective of their daughters than their sons (Marone, 1992, at 42–45). Most boys are exposed to competitive situations at an early age (Evans, 2000, at 12–13; Tannen, 1990, at 43–47). They have been encouraged to participate in little league baseball, basketball, football, soccer, and other competitive athletic endeavors. These activities introduce boys to the "thrill of victory and the agony of defeat" during their formative years (Harragan, 1977, at 75–78). "Traditional girls' games like jump rope and hopscotch are turntaking games, where competition is indirect since one person's success does not necessarily signify another's failure." (Gilligan, 1982, at 10). By adulthood, men are more likely to have become accustomed to the rigors of overt competition than women. While it is true that little league and interscholastic sports for women have become more competitive in recent years, most continue to be less overtly competitive than corresponding male athletic endeavors (Evans, 2000, at 80).

* * *

STATISTICAL RESULTS

Since I have not observed any differences in the negotiation results achieved by male and female students, my Null Hypothesis is that there is no difference between men and women with respect to performance on the negotiation exercises. My Alternative Hypothesis is that there is a gender-based difference between men and women with respect to performance on the negotiation exercises. My database included negotiation results from sixteen Legal Negotiation classes at George Washington University.... The mean negotiation scores were calculated for males and females in each of the sixteen classes. A t-test was then performed for each class to determine if there was a statistically significant difference between the male and female means for any class. T-test probability values of 0.10 or lower would establish statistical significance at the 0.10 level, while t-test probability values of 0.05 or lower would demonstrate significance at the 0.05 level (Barnes & Conley, 1986, at 306–08). Since I hypothesized that no statistically significant differences would be found and had no reason to suspect that if any difference was found it would favor males or females, two-tailed t-test probability values were calculated. The relevant data are set forth in Table 1.

Table 1

T–Test Comparisons of Gender–Based Means

Year	N	Male Negot. Mean	Female Negot. Mean	Difference Means	p-value
1986	45	29.67	30.39	−0.71	.76
1988	55	38.67	38.79	−0.12	.96
1989	58	41.23	40.40	0.83	.77
1990	58	42.30	37.96	4.33	.14
1991	61	41.29	39.90	1.39	.61
1992	48	35.15	37.64	−2.49	.37
1992.5	59	40.15	40.32	−0.17	.95
1993	59	39.85	40.52	−0.67	.84
1994	62	40.75	37.50	3.26	.31
1995	56	32.23	26.14	6.09	.01
1996	51	34.53	36.47	−1.94	.49
1997	40	28.14	25.37	2.77	.19
1998	46	34.64	31.60	3.04	.19
1999	48	32.26	30.77	1.49	.60
2000	41	28.09	25.57	2.52	.31
2001	35	24.67	26.19	−1.52	.52

A review of the data set forth in Table 1 suggests the absence of any correlation between gender and negotiation performance. For only a single year (1995) was a statistically significant correlation discerned.

For the other fifteen years, not a single statistically significant correlation was obtained at even the 0.10 level. For nine of the sixteen years (1989, 1990, 1991, 1994, 1995, 1997, 1998, 1999 & 2000) the male mean was slightly higher than the female mean, while for the other seven years (1986, 1988, 1992, 1992.5, 1993, 1996 & 2001) the female mean was slightly higher than the male mean. These findings clearly support acceptance of the Null Hypothesis suggesting the absence of any statistically significant correlation between gender and negotiation performance.

FINDING IMPLICATIONS

Over the past sixteen years, I have discovered that both practicing attorneys and law students of both genders permit gender-based stereotypes to influence their negotiating interactions with persons of the opposite gender–and even people of the same gender. Many individuals assume that men are highly competitive and manipulative negotiators who always seek to obtain maximum results for themselves. Female negotiators, on the other hand, are expected to be more accommodating and less competitive interactants who try to maximize the joint return achieved by the parties.

On those occasions in my Legal Negotiation class when two women have been paired against two other women, they have often allowed stereotypical beliefs to influence their interaction. They have regularly expressed the preliminary view that their interaction will be more pleasant due to the absence of the overt win-lose competitiveness they attribute to their male cohorts. Once their bargaining encounters have commenced, however, they have generally behaved as competitively as their male classmates.

* * *

Legal practitioners and business firm officials should acknowledge the impact that gender-based stereotypes may have upon negotiation interactions. Male attorneys who think that female opponents will not be as competitive or manipulative as their male colleagues will provide women adversaries with an inherent advantage. They will let their guards down and behave less competitively against female opponents than they would toward male opponents. Female negotiators must also reject gender-based stereotypical beliefs with respect to both male and female opponents. Women who conclude that adversaries are treating them less seriously because of their gender should not hesitate to take advantage of the situation. The favorable bargaining outcomes achieved by these women should teach chauvinistic opponents a crucial lesson.

REFERENCES

Barnes, David W. & John M. Conley. 1986. *Statistical Evidence in Litigation*. Boston: Little, Brown & Co.

Burgoon, Michael, et al. 1983. "Friendly or Unfriendly Persuasion—The Effects of Violations of Expectations by Males and Females." *Human Communications Research* 10: 283–294.

Burrell, Nancy, A., et al. 1988 "Gender–Based Perceptual Biases in Mediation." *Communication Research* 15:447–469.

Craver, Charles B. 4th ed. 2001. *Effective Legal Negotiation and Settlement*. New York: Lexis.

Deaux, Kay, 1976. *The Behavior of Women and Men*. Monterey, CA: Brooks/Cole Pub.

DePaulo, Bela, et al. 1996. "Lying in Everyday Life." *Journal of Personality and Social Psychology* 70: 979–995.

Evans, Gail. 2000. *Play Like a Man, Win Like a Woman*. New York: Broadway Books.

Foschi, Martha. 1991. "Gender and Double Standards for Competence" in *Gender, Interaction, and Inequality* 181–207 (Cecilia L. Ridgeway ed.). New York: Springer–Verlag.

Gilligan, Carol. 1982. *In a Different Voice*. Cambridge, MA: Harvard University Press.

Goleman, Daniel. 1998. *Working with Emotional Intelligence*. New York: Bantam.

Hall, Judith A. 1984. *Nonverbal Sex Differences: Communication, Accuracy and Expressive Style*. Baltimore: Johns Hopkins University Press.

Harragan, Barbara. 1977. *Games Mother Never Taught You*. New York: Warner Books.

Kolb, Deborah. 2000. "More Than Just a Footnote: Constructing a Theoretical Framework for Teaching About Gender in Negotiation." *Negotiation Journal*. 16: 47–356.

Kolb, Deborah & Judith Williams. 2000. *The Shadow Negotiation*. New York: Simon & Schuster.

Lewicki, Roy J., et al. 2nd ed.1994. *Negotiation*. Burr Ridge. IL: Irwin.

Maccoby, Eleanor Emmons & Carol Nagy Jacklin. 1974. *The Psychology of Sex Differences*. Stanford, CA: Stanford University Press.

Marone, Nicky. 1992. *Women and Risk*. New York: St. Martin's Press.

McIntosh, Peggy. 1985. *Feeling Like a Fraud*. (Paper Published by Wellesley College Stone Center for Developmental Services and Studies Works in Progress Series).

Menkel–Meadow, Carrie. 2000. "Teaching About Gender and Negotiation: Sex, Truths, and Videotape." *Negotiation Journal* 16: 357–375.

Project, "Gender, Legal Education, and the Legal Profession: An Empirical Study of Stanford Law Students and Graduates." *Stanford Law Review* 40: 1209–1259.

Rubin, Jeffrey & Bert Brown. 1975. *The Social Psychology of Bargaining and Negotiation*. New York: Academic Press.

Schneider, Andrea Kupfer, 1994. "Effective Responses to Offensive Comments." *Negotiation Journal* (April 1994) 107–115.

Schneider, Andrea Kupfer. 2000. "Perception, Reputation and Reality." 10 *Dispute Resolution Magazine*. (Summer 2000) 24–28.

Smeltzer, Larry R. & Kittie W. Watson. 1986. "Gender Differences in Verbal Communications During Negotiations." *Communications Research Report* 3: 74–79.

Smith–Lovin, Lynn & Dawn T. Robinson. 1992. "Gender and Conversational Dynamics" in *Gender, Interaction, and Inequality* 122–156 (Cecilia L. Ridgeway, ed.). New York: Springer–Verlag.

Stiver, Irene P. 1983. *Work Inhibitions in Women*. (Paper Published by Wellesley College Stone Center for Developmental Services and Studies Works in Progress Series).

Tannen, Deborah. 1994. *Talking From 9 to 5*. New York: William Morrow.

Tannen, Deborah. 1990. *You Just Don't Understand*. New York: William Morrow.

C.   IMPACT OF RACE

RACE AND NEGOTIATION PERFORMANCE

By Charles B. Craver
8 Dispute Resolution Magazine 22–26 (Fall 2001).[7]

In major league baseball, nineteen percent of the players are black. As of 1992, 150 of the 200 agents registered with Major League Baseball Players Association had active clientele; black agents accounted for a mere three percent of this 150. In professional football, sixty-nine percent of the players are black, but black agents comprise only fourteen percent of the registered agents with active files. Worse yet, more than eighty percent of the NBA's players are black, but less than ten percent of them have black agents.[1]

I. INTRODUCTION

Why are many prominent black athletes reluctant to retain black agents to represent them? One factor undoubtedly concerns the high profile success of white agents such as David Falk in basketball and Leigh Steinberg in football, and the ability of these super-agents to

---

7. Copyright © 2001 by Charles B. Craver. Subsequent reprint by permission from the Dispute Resolution Section of the American Bar Association.

1. James G. Sammataro, *Business and Brotherhood, Can They Coincide? A Search Into Why Black Athletes Do Not Hire Black Agents*, 42 HOW. L.J. 535, 546–47 (1999).

attract draft eligible black athletes. Another may involve the fact that "many black players have internalized racial stereotypes about blacks and thus, discriminate against their own people."[2] These athletes may privately believe that white agents can negotiate better contracts than black agents.

... James Sammataro reasonably asks "whether there are in fact any meaningful differences in the manner in which white and black agents negotiate and, more important, whether these differences significantly affect the resulting contracts."[3] ...

In this article, I will empirically compare the results achieved by black and white students on the exercises conducted in my Legal Negotiating course. I will initially explore the perceived differences between black and white behavior. I will then examine statistically established distinctions relevant to negotiation interactions, discuss unsupportable stereotypes, and compare the manner in which blacks and whites deal with the stress of highly competitive situations.

I will then make a statistical comparison between the results achieved by black and white students during the past nine years on the negotiation exercises employed in my Legal Negotiating course. Despite the fact that some stereotypical beliefs might suggest that black students would not be as effective as their white cohorts in such competitive encounters, my anecdotal experiences have not discerned any apparent differences regarding the results attained by black and white students. I have thus hypothesized that I would find no statistically significant differences between the settlements achieved by the black and white students in my Legal Negotiating course.

II. REAL AND PERCEIVED RACIAL DIFFERENCES

Negotiations involving participants from diverse ethnic backgrounds frequently develop differently than bargaining interactions involving persons from similar backgrounds. People tend to negotiate more cooperatively with opponents of the same race and culture than with adversaries of different races and cultures.[4] Apparently, similarity induces trust and reduces the need for each interactor to maintain a particular "face" in the other's eyes.

Different meanings may be ascribed to identical speech and behavior by members of different races because of their different acculturation experiences.[5] For example, if a white hiring partner of a prestigious law firm were to ask white and black law student applicants about their

---

2. *Id.* at 548. *See also* Kenneth L. Shropshire, *Sports Agents, Role Models and Race–Consciousness*, 6 MARQ. SPORTS L.J. 267, 269–71 (1996).

3. *Id.* at 554.

4. *See* JEFFREY Z. RUBIN & BERT R. BROWN, THE SOCIAL PSYCHOLOGY OF BARGAINING AND NEGOTIATION 163 (1975).

5. *See* Martin N. Davidson & Leonard Greenhalgh, *The Role of Emotion in Negotiation: The Impact of Anger and Race*, 7 RESEARCH ON NEGOTIATION IN ORGANIZATIONS 3, 20–22 (1999).

LSAT scores and law school GPAs, the white students would probably provide the requested information without hesitancy, while the black students might wonder if the partner were asking only black students about such factors based upon the partner's biased belief that minority law students are less qualified than their non-minority cohorts.

Individuals from different ethnic backgrounds bring certain stereotypical baggage into their new interactions.[6] It is amazing how many common characteristics–positive, negative, and neutral—are attributed by many persons to all individuals of a particular race. Professor Andrea Rich's study of the perceptions of UCLA undergraduate students in the early 1970s graphically demonstrated the close similarities between Caucasian and Chicano stereotypes of African–Americans, between Caucasian and African–American stereotypes of Chicanos, and between African–American and Chicano stereotypes of Caucasians.[7] When people who harbor such stereotypical beliefs initially encounter individuals from other races, they tend to attribute their stereotypical preconceptions to those persons, and this phenomenon may influence the preliminary portion of their interaction.

Students I have taught at various law schools over the past twenty-five years have often allowed their stereotypical beliefs to influence their bargaining encounters. Many of my students—regardless of their ethnicity—think that Caucasian males are the most Machiavellian and competitive negotiators. They expect them to employ adversarial and manipulative tactics to obtain optimal results for themselves. On the other hand, numerous students expect African–American, Asian–American, and Latino–American negotiators to be more accommodating and less competitive. Even members of one race often stereotype other members of the same race. When opponents fail to behave in the anticipated manner, the bargaining process may be adversely affected.

Despite the unreliability of many stereotypical beliefs and the absence of more recent surveys, several empirical studies have found a few relevant differences between black and white interactants. Blacks tend to be high in terms of Interpersonal Orientation (IO).[8] High IO individuals are more sensitive and responsive to the interpersonal aspects of their relationships with others.[9] This tendency should make blacks more effective negotiators. Because bargaining outcomes are directly affected by the interpersonal skills of the participants, high IO individuals should be able to achieve better results than their low IO cohorts.

During verbal encounters, blacks tend to speak more forcefully and with greater verbal aggressiveness than whites.[10] In competitive settings,

---

6. *See* Sammataro, *supra* note 1, at 555; Shropshire, *supra* note 2, at 277.

7. *See* ANDREA L. RICH, INTERRACIAL COMMUNICATION 51–62 (1974).

8. *See* RUBIN & BROWN, *supra* note 4, at 164.

9. *See id.* at 158.

10. *See* Davidson & Greenhalgh, *supra* note 5, at 22.

this trait might enhance the bargaining effectiveness of individuals with these traits, while in cooperative situations it might undermine their ability to achieve mutual accords. When they interact with others, blacks tend to make less eye contact while listening to others than do whites, which may be perceived by speakers as an indication of indifference to what is being said or of disrespect toward the speaker.[11] Such behavior might undermine the ability of the persons with minimal eye contact to establish the kind of rapport that can advance bargaining discussions.

Most negotiators tend to employ a cooperative/problem-solving or a competitive/adversarial style when they bargain with others. Cooperative/problem-solvers tend to be open with their information, prefer to use objective criteria to guide their discussions, and endeavor to maximize the joint return achieved by interactants, while competitive/adversarials tend to be less open with information, focus more on stated positions than objective factors, are manipulative, and attempt to maximize their own side's return. White negotiators usually employ relatively consistent bargaining styles, while blacks tend to adopt styles that are reflective of the race of their opponents. Blacks tend to perform more effectively when they compete with whites and when they cooperate with other blacks.[12]

* * *

IV. STATISTICAL FINDINGS

* * *

This study evaluates the possible relationship between race and performance on negotiation exercises. The Null Hypothesis is that there is no correlation between race and the results students achieve on Legal Negotiating course exercises. The Alternative Hypothesis is that there is a relationship between race and the results students achieve on Legal Negotiating course exercises.

Although I have sixteen years of Legal Negotiation course data at George Washington University, I decided to focus on the data covering the past nine years, because the classes I taught from 1986 through the Spring of 1992 contained insufficient numbers of black students to permit meaningful statistical comparisons. . . .

To determine whether there are statistically significant differences between the negotiation exercise scores achieved by black and white students, I employed two separate procedures. I first computed the mean scores for black and white students for each of the past nine years, and

11. *See* ROBERT G. HARPER, ARTHUR N. WEINS & JOSEPH D. MATARAZZO, NONVERBAL COMMUNICATION: THE STATE OF THE ART 188 (1978).

12. *See* P.S. Fry & K.J. Coe, *Achievement Performance of Internally and Exter-* *nally Oriented Black and White High School Students Under Conditions of Competition and Co–Operation Expectancies*, 50 BR. J. EDUC. PSYCH. 162, 166 (1980). *See also* RUBIN & BROWN, *supra* note 4, at 164.

compared the mean differences using a t-test. The results are set forth in Table 1.

TABLE 1

t-Test Comparison of Student Race and Negotiation Score Means

Year	N Wht.	N Blk.	Mean Wht. Neg. Score	Mean Blk. Neg. Score	Mean Neg. Score Diff.	Wht. Std. Dev.	Blk. Std. Dev.	P–Value
1992	51	3	41.033	38.333	2.700	9.521	7.422	0.6325
1993	53	4	40.630	34.825	5.805	10.845	13.564	0.3137
1994	52	5	39.665	40.240	−0.575	11.833	11.358	0.9175
1995	44	4	28.941	36.200	−7.259	9.528	7.767	0.1470
1996	44	3	35.016	37.800	−2.784	10.137	9.987	0.6473
1997	34	5	26.797	28.160	−1.363	6.453	7.548	0.6679
1998	31	6	33.855	33.883	−0.028	7.987	8.452	0.9937
1999	41	6	31.661	32.200	−0.539	9.995	6.007	0.8987
2000	32	7	27.572	23.714	3.858	7.722	8.169	0.2432

The statistical data set forth in the Table provide strong support for the Null Hypothesis. There is not a single year for which the t-Test resulted in a mean difference based upon race at the 0.05—or even the 0.10—level of statistical significance. For three of the nine years the mean negotiation scores for white students were slightly above the mean scores for black students, while for the other six years, the mean negotiation scores for black students were slightly above the mean scores for white students.

In recognition of the fact that the total number of black students in some of the classes was relatively low, I also calculated a Pearson Correlation Coefficient for the aggregate data pertaining to all nine years. The correlation coefficient comparing race with mean negotiation exercise scores was a mere–0.0527, with a p-value of 0.2594. This p-value provides further statistical support for the Null Hypothesis.

The last factor to be evaluated concerns a comparison of the black and white student standard deviations. For five years, the standard deviations for white students were slightly above those for black students, while the reverse was true with respect to the other four years. These data indicate that the different negotiation results achieved by black and white students had a similar dispersion.

V.   IMPLICATIONS

Individuals who commence negotiations with people of different races should appreciate the need to establish trusting and cooperative relationships before the serious substantive discussions begin. This approach should significantly enhance the likelihood of mutually beneficial transactions. The preliminary stage of their interaction may be used to generate a modicum of rapport. Negotiators should try to minimize the counterproductive stereotypes they may consciously or subconsciously harbor toward persons of their opponent's ethnicity. If they anticipate difficult interactions as a result of such usually irrational preconceptions, they are likely to generate self-fulfilling prophecies. If they conversely expect their opponents to behave more cooperatively and less manipulatively because of their ethnicity, they may carelessly lower their guard and give their opponents an inherent bargaining advantage. Negotiators must also try to understand any seemingly illogical reactions their opponents may initially exhibit toward them as a result of those individuals' stereotyping of them.

If the first contact negotiators have with opponents indicates that those persons are expecting highly competitive transactions, they should not hesitate to employ "attitudinal bargaining" to disabuse their opponents of this preconception. They should create cooperative physical and psychological environments. Warm handshakes and open postures can initially diminish combative atmospheres. Cooperative negotiators can sit adjacent to, instead of directly across from, opponents. In a few instances, it may be necessary to directly broach the subject of negative stereotyping, since this may be the most efficacious way to negate the influence of these feelings.[13]

People who participate in bargaining transactions should recognize that the specific circumstances and unique personal traits of the individual negotiators—rather than generalized beliefs regarding ethnic characteristics—determine the way in which each interaction evolves. Each opponent has to be evaluated and dealt with differently. Is that individual a cooperative or a competitive bargainer? Does the other side possess greater, equal, or less bargaining power concerning the issues to be addressed? What bargaining techniques are likely to influence that person? What negotiating techniques has that individual decided to employ, and what are the most effective ways to counter those tactics? As the instant transaction unfolds, each negotiator will have to make strategic changes to respond to unanticipated disclosures or to changed circumstances.

When negotiators find themselves attributing certain characteristics to opponents, they must carefully determine whether those attributes are based on specific information pertaining to those particular opponents or to vague generalizations regarding people of their race. If people bargained only with individuals of the same race, they would quickly realize how different we all are. Some opponents would behave cooperatively, while others would act in a competitive manner. Some would exhibit win-lose tendencies, while others would evidence win-win attitudes. Techniques that would be effective against some opponents would be ineffective against others.

* * *

Athletes and other performers who have to retain the services of professional negotiators should not underestimate the bargaining abilities of black agents. There is no reason to believe that black negotiators would be less capable in this regard than white agents. Some black

---

13. *See* Andrea Kupfer Schneider, *Effective Responses to Offensive Comments*, 10 NEGOT. J. 107, 112–13 (April, 1994).

athletes and performers may think that black agents could not negotiate as effectively with white owners and managers as white agents. Because the black students in my Legal Negotiation course achieved results comparable to those attained by white students in situations in which they were generally interacting with white students (because of the small number of black classmates), there is no reason to believe that black agents could not deal effectively with white owners and managers. This is especially true today, given the increased number of black general managers and coaches who not only conduct many of the salary negotiations with sports agents, but also have to interact regularly with their white team owners.

The nine years of Legal Negotiation course data evaluated by me indicate the absence of any statistically significant correlation between student race and the results achieved on negotiation exercises. These findings would suggest that even if cultural and behavioral differences between black and white students exist, those differences have no impact on students' ability to achieve beneficial negotiation exercise results.

CHAPTER NOTES

1. Impact of Race, Gender, Ethnicity, or Similar Factors

Have you ever thought that a law school or professional interaction was influenced by your gender, ethnicity, or similar factor? If so, how was it affected? How did you deal—or could you have dealt—with the situation to lessen the impact? Regarding the subtle ways such hidden agendas can influence professional interactions, see Deborah Kolb & Judith Williams, *The Shadow Negotiation* (Simon & Schuster 2000) and *Everyday Negotiation* (Jossey–Bass 2003). If you are a white male, when was the last time you were reminded of–or even thought about–your race or your gender? Women and people of color are regularly reminded of their gender and/or ethnicity while walking down the street and interacting with others in personal or professional settings.

2. Hesitancy of Women to Initiate Salary Negotiations

In *Women Don't Ask* (Princeton University Press 2003), Linda Babcock and Sara Laschever indicated that while fifty-seven percent of male business graduates of Carnegie Mellon University bargained with prospective employers over their starting salaries, only seven percent of female graduates did so, resulting in a male salary advantage of almost $4000. Most employers expect new hires to bargain somewhat over the initial terms of their employment and respect those who try to do so politely. In some cases, the base salary may not be negotiable, but other terms may be. For example, many employers are willing to pay new employees for their relocation expenses, agree to reimburse them for professional development courses they may wish to take, extend health care coverage to spouses or significant others, etc. See generally Robin L. Pinkley & Gregory B. Northcraft, *Get Paid What You're Worth* (St. Martins Press 2000); Lee E. Miller & Jessica Miller, *A Women's Guide to Successful Negotiating* (McGraw–Hill 2002). See also Charles B. Craver, *If Women Don't Ask: Implications for Bargaining Encounters, the Equal Pay Act, and Title VII*, 102 Mich. L. Rev. 1104 (2004).

*

Appendix I

RESEARCH METHODOLOGY: THE BYU LEGAL NEGOTIATION PROJECT

The objective of this study was to obtain descriptions of attorneys engaged in negotiation within the context of the legal system. Prior to developing the research instruments, a survey of relevant literature in the social sciences and legal domains was conducted. We then selected metropolitan areas as test sites, and proceeded to make contact with leaders of the Bar in each area to obtain their permission and cooperation in the research. For our first test area, we also solicited from Bar leaders names of respected, experienced attorneys to serve as advisors to the project.

We then conducted a total of 47 structured, one-hour, tape recorded interviews with members of the Bar in our test area. In the course of these interviews, attorneys were asked to name traits of effective and ineffective attorney/negotiators. These interviews were subsequently transcribed as an aid to analysis. These interviews were used, along with the literature previously mentioned, to develop a set of hypotheses about negotiator effectiveness and to derive three sets of descriptive scales for use in mailed questionnaires. Our work during this time was reviewed and made more relevant to the legal context by the advisory committee.

The mailed questionnaire was designed not only to test hypotheses available from the literature and from attorney interviews, but also to provide raw material from which a valid empirical description of negotiators behavior could be drawn whether or not anticipated by our hypotheses. Section I of the questionnaire asked for basic demographic data about the respondent. It then directed the respondent to think of the last attorney with whom they had negotiated, and, without naming the attorney, to provide basic demographic information about the attorney and about the subject-matter involved in the negotiation. The respondent was then asked, in Section II of the questionnaire, to rate the behavior of that attorney according to three sets of scales. The first set was an adjective checklist of 77 items, including many of the items commonly used in adjective checklists (Gough and Heilbrun, 1965), supplemented by items derived from the attorney interviews. They were rated on scales of zero (not characteristic) to five (highly characteristic).

The second set of scales consisted of 43 bipolar adjective pairs selected in part from such scales as Sherwood's Self Concept Inventory (Sherwood, 1962) and in part from concepts obtained in the attorney interviews. These scales were rated from 1 (extremely characteristic on one pole of the scale) to 7 (extremely characteristic at other pole). The last set of scales in the questionnaire had twelve items concerning the apparent goals or objectives of the rated attorney.

Section III of the questionnaire asked for a fuller description of the subject-matter of the negotiation. Questions included whether the matter was a transaction (such as negotiation of a contract or business agreement) or a legal dispute (defined as a case which could be pursued through litigation); whether the case went to trial; how it was resolved if it did not go to trial; if it was settled by negotiated agreement, how many days before trial was it settled; if it went to trial, what were the primary reasons; and whether opposing counsel could have done more to promote a negotiated settlement.

Section IV asked the respondent to rate the reputation and performance of the rated attorney as a negotiator and, if the case went to trial, his or her effectiveness as a litigator.

The questionnaire was mailed to a random sample of one thousand licensed attorneys in the Phoenix, Arizona metropolitan area. Each attorney was mailed a copy of the questionnaire accompanied by a cover letter signed by the President of the County Bar Association. Follow-up letters were sent and telephone calls made to members of the sample who had not responded within two weeks. A total of 351 usable questionnaires were returned for a response rate of 35%.

Results were coded and analyzed according to standard statistical routines, including factor analysis, multiple regression analysis, and discriminant analysis. In addition, the data were analyzed according to Q methodology as conceived by Stephenson (1935) and Thomson (1935) and articulated by Brown (1980). Q methodology is a technique of factor analysis involving the transpose of the R matrix (where a single matrix of data are factored by columns and then again by rows) under the special condition that the measuring unit is the same both for rows and columns (Brown 1980, p. 13). Some statisticians use cluster analysis in lieu of Q methodology.

Q methodology was applied in response to our discontent with some of the limitations of R technique. We found that the standard factor analyses defined negotiator behavior in terms of its constituent parts, but it provided no information about the relative significance of the parts to negotiator effectiveness nor about the functional relationship of the parts to each other.

In our first application of Q methodology, we limited the analysis to an inverted factor analysis (SPSS, Nie et al., 1975:470n) of three groups of data: descriptions of negotiators rated as effective, average, or ineffective. The inverted analysis produced two principle factors for each group, with each factor representing negotiating characteristics operantly defined in terms of the behavior of the subjects. The behaviors were determined by the rankings of actual negotiator characteristics as reported by rating attorneys (Brown 1980 pp. 22–23). Thus, the factors represent actual patterns of reported negotiating behavior as contrasted to pre-determined categories developed by the researchers for testing or evaluation. (See Brown 1980 p. 28 for further justification and interpretation of the kind of data obtained by Q methodology).

*

Appendix II

TABLES

The tables present, in rank order, the mean rating for effective, average, and ineffective attorneys according to their classification as cooperative or competitive negotiators. Since all attorneys were described by identical questionnaire items, the interpretation of each negotiator type depends upon comparison of the *rank order* of the higher scoring items for each type. The rank order was determined by computing a mean (average) score for each group on each item, then ranking items for each group in order of the mean score.

THE ADJECTIVE CHECKLIST

The adjective checklist presented 75 adjectives and asked the responding attorney to rate the extent to which the adjective described the negotiator being rated regardless of whether it added to or detracted from her effectiveness as a negotiator. Six ratings were possible: zero, 1, 2, 3, 4, and 5. Thus for each adjective such as bluffer, rude, tough, etc. the responding attorney would indicate with a zero, 1, 2, 3, 4, or 5 the extent to which each adjective is characteristic of the attorney being rated. In analyzing the data, the scores of all attorneys in each type and level of effectiveness were averaged, giving a composite score on that item. With a zero to five range, the highest rating possible is 5.00. The items are presented in rank order on pages 158 and 159.

THE BIPOLAR ADJECTIVE SCALES

The bipolar adjective scales consisted of 43 items rated on a scale of 1 to 7. The 26 highest rated items were selected for analysis. These ratings are given on pages 160 and 161.

Effective Cooperative
Adjective Checklist
(Phoenix Q-Analysis)

1. Experienced
2. Realistic
3. Ethical
4. Rational
5. Perceptive
6. Trustworthy
7. Convincing
8. Analytical
9. Fair
10. Creative
11. Self-controlled
12. Versatile
13. Personable
14. Adaptable
15. Wise
16. Objective
17. Poised
18. Careful
19. Organizing
20. Legally astute
21. Helpful
22. Discreet
23. Loyal
24. Sociable
25. Warm
26. Deliberate
27. Dignified
28. Patient
29. Smooth
30. Forceful
31. Clever
32. Masculine
33. Ambitious
34. Moderate
35. Cautious
36. Obliging
37. Sympathetic
38. Tough
39. Forgiving
40. Dominant
41. Praising
42. Gentle
43. Conservative
44. Stern
45. Demanding
46. Manipulative
47. Suspicious
48. Idealistic
49. Bluffer
50. Picky
51. Argumentative
52. Egotistical
53. Sentimental
54. Impatient
55. Unpredictable
56. Headstrong
57. Rude
58. Selfish
59. Impulsive
60. Evasive
61. Hostile
62. Greedy
63. Staller
64. Sarcastic
65. Rebellious
66. Intolerant
67. Quarrelsome
68. Loud
69. Irritating
70. Conniving
71. Timid
72. Reckless
73. Complaining
74. Feminine
75. Spineless

Effective Aggressive
Adjective Checklist
(Phoenix Q-Analysis)

1. Convincing
2. Experienced
3. Perceptive
4. Rational
5. Analytical
6. Creative
7. Ambitious
8. Dominant
9. Forceful
10. Realistic
11. Tough
12. Self-controlled
13. Clever
14. Poised
15. Ethical
16. Legally astute
17. Adaptable
18. Versatile
19. Egotistical
20. Trustworthy
21. Personable
22. Smooth
23. Organizing
24. Sociable
25. Demanding
26. Wise
27. Masculine
28. Manipulative
29. Careful
30. Fair
31. Argumentative
32. Deliberate
33. Cautious
34. Stern
35. Bluffer
36. Helpful
37. Objective
38. Dignified
39. Suspicious
40. Discreet
41. Patient
42. Warm
43. Headstrong
44. Loyal
45. Picky
46. Impatient
47. Selfish
48. Obliging
49. Moderate
50. Evasive
51. Praising
52. Greedy
53. Conniving
54. Unpredictable
55. Quarrelsome
56. Loud
57. Sympathetic
58. Irritating
59. Intolerant
60. Sarcastic
61. Conservative
62. Hostile
63. Forgiving
64. Impulsive
65. Staller
66. Gentle
67. Rebellious
68. Complaining
69. Idealistic
70. Sentimental
71. Rude
72. Reckless
73. Spineless
74. Feminine
75. Timid

Average Cooperatives
Adjective Checklist
(Phoenix Q-Analysis)

1. Ethical
2. Trustworthy
3. Rational
4. Personable
5. Cautious
6. Realistic
7. Self-controlled
8. Careful
9. Discreet
10. Sociable
11. Objective
12. Legally astute
13. Analytical
14. Fair
15. Loyal
16. Perceptive
17. Helpful
18. Deliberate
19. Experienced
20. Organizing
21. Dignified
22. Warm
23. Conservative
24. Adaptable
25. Wise
26. Moderate
27. Poised
28. Ambitious
29. Forceful
30. Patient
31. Smooth
32. Clever
33. Convincing
34. Creative
35. Demanding
36. Versatile
37. Gentle
38. Masculine
39. Forgiving
40. Obliging
41. Argumentative
42. Dominant
43. Bluffer
44. Sympathetic
45. Praising
46. Suspicious
47. Picky
48. Tough
49. Evasive
50. Egotistical
51. Idealistic
52. Stern
53. Headstrong
54. Impatient
55. Complaining
56. Impulsive
57. Manipulative
58. Greedy
59. Staller
60. Quarrelsome
61. Unpredictable
62. Timid
63. Selfish
64. Sentimental
65. Intolerant
66. Irritating
67. Hostile
68. Conniving
69. Loud
70. Sarcastic
71. Reckless
72. Rebellious
73. Feminine
74. Rude
75. Spineless

Average Aggressive Adjective Checklist (Phoenix Q-Analysis)	Ineffective Cooperative Adjective Checklist (Phoenix Q-Analysis)	Ineffective Aggressive Adjective Checklist (Phoenix Q-Analysis)
1. Argumentative	1. Ethical	1. Irritating
2. Ambitious	2. Complaining	2. Egotistical
3. Demanding	3. Personable	3. Argumentative
4. Bluffer	4. Fair	4. Quarrelsome
5. Egotistical	5. Gentle	5. Headstrong
6. Sociable	6. Conservative	6. Impatient
7. Ethical	7. Trustworthy	7. Greedy
8. Evasive	8. Masculine	8. Demanding
9. Legally astute	9. Staller	9. Loud
10. Suspicious	10. Obliging	10. Intolerant
11. Greedy	11. Demanding	11. Complaining
12. Cautious	12. Cautious	12. Rude
13. Headstrong	13. Deliberate	13. Conniving
14. Impatient	14. Experienced	14. Sarcastic
15. Personable	15. Patient	15. Impulsive
16. Complaining	16. Moderate	16. Suspicious
17. Quarrelsome	17. Forgiving	17. Unpredictable
18. Unpredictable	18. Argumentative	18. Evasive
19. Trustworthy	19. Idealistic	19. Hostile
20. Rational	20. Sociable	20. Bluffer
21. Loyal	21. Suspicious	21. Manipulative
22. Masculine	22. Irritating	22. Ambitious
23. Forceful	23. Rational	23. Picky
24. Discreet	24. Bluffer	24. Selfish
25. Obliging	25. Timid	25. Rebellious
26. Impulsive	26. Discreet	26. Reckless
27. Intolerant	27. Warm	27. Tough
28. Irritating	28. Sympathetic	28. Dominant
29. Picky	29. Dignified	29. Stern
30. Staller	30. Poised	30. Staller
31. Analytical	31. Helpful	31. Forceful
32. Smooth	32. Self-controlled	32. Masculine
33. Moderate	33. Legally astute	33. Clever
34. Realistic	34. Unpredictable	34. Experienced
35. Manipulative	35. Egotistical	35. Loyal
36. Dominant	36. Headstrong	36. Spineless
37. Careful	37. Careful	37. Cautious
38. Fair	38. Impatient	38. Sociable
39. Adaptable	39. Impulsive	39. Careful
40. Self-controlled	40. Analytical	40. Legally astute
41. Conservative	41. Realistic	41. Self-controlled
42. Deliberate	42. Objective	42. Smooth
43. Clever	43. Picky	43. Deliberate
44. Dignified	44. Praising	44. Organizing
45. Experienced	45. Sentimental	45. Ethical
46. Tough	46. Evasive	46. Idealistic
47. Perceptive	47. Perceptive	47. Personable
48. Praising	48. Adaptable	48. Conservative
49. Patient	49. Ambitious	49. Versatile
50. Hostile	50. Quarrelsome	50. Dignified
51. Forgiving	51. Wise	51. Poised
52. Sarcastic	52. Organizing	52. Timid
53. Organizing	53. Convincing	53. Rational
54. Objective	54. Creative	54. Discreet
55. Creative	55. Intolerant	55. Moderate
56. Warm	56. Stern	56. Trustworthy
57. Selfish	57. Spineless	57. Analytical
58. Idealistic	58. Selfish	58. Perceptive
59. Poised	59. Greedy	59. Sentimental
60. Versatile	60. Sarcastic	60. Gentle
61. Conniving	61. Hostile	61. Fair
62. Sympathetic	62. Smooth	62. Creative
63. Helpful	63. Forceful	63. Sympathetic
64. Stern	64. Clever	64. Praising
65. Wise	65. Tough	65. Adaptable
66. Gentle	66. Conniving	66. Realistic
67. Loud	67. Reckless	67. Obliging
68. Convincing	68. Versatile	68. Wise
69. Rebellious	69. Manipulative	69. Forgiving
70. Rude	70. Loyal	70. Patient
71. Timid	71. Rebellious	71. Objective
72. Sentimental	72. Dominant	72. Helpful
73. Spineless	73. Rude	73. Convincing
74. Reckless	74. Loud	74. Warm
75. Feminine	75. Feminine	75. Feminine

[C5422]

159

Effective/Cooperatives
Bipolar Adjective Scales
(Phoenix Q-Analysis)

1. Dishonest
   Honest — 6.69
2. Discourteous
   Courteous — 6.56
3. Disregarded customs and courtesies of the bar
   Adhered to customs and courtesies of the bar — 6.46
4. Unintelligent
   Intelligent — 6.34
5. Disinterested in the needs of his clients
   Knew the needs of his clients — 6.22
6. Unfriendly
   Friendly — 6.18
7. Distrustful
   Trustful — 6.04
8. Unreasonable
   Reasonable — 6.02
9. Insincere
   Sincere — 6.00
10. Tactless
    Tactful — 5.96
11. Devious
    Forthright — 5.92
12. Min. prepared on factual elements of the case
    Thoroughly prepared on the factual elements — 5.89
13. Unwilling to share information
    Willing to share information — 5.79
14. Obstructed
    Facilitated — 5.71
15. Used threats
    Did not use threats — 5.64
16. Emotional
    Logical — 5.62
17. Unsure of the value of the case
    Accurately estimated the value of the case — 5.61
18. Min. prepared on legal elements of the case
    Thoroughly prepared on the legal elements of the case — 5.47
19. Disinterested in my position
    Probed my position — 5.45
20. Disinterested in the needs of my client
    Knew the needs of my client — 5.39
21. Took one position and refused to move from it
    Was willing to move from original position — 5.35
22. Ineffective trial attorney
    Effective trial attorney — 5.34
23. Unskillful in reading my cues
    Skillful in reading my cues — 5.33
24. Passive
    Active — 5.23
25. Uncooperative
    Cooperative — 5.23
26. Took an unrealistic initial position
    Took a realistic initial position — 5.14
27. Revealed information gradually
    Revealed information early — 5.12
28. Not careful about timing & sequence of actions
    Careful about timing & sequence of actions — 5.09
29. Emotionally involved
    Emotionally detached — 5.05
30. Disinterested in my personality
    Got to know my personality — 5.03
31. Formal
    Informal — 4.98
32. Used take it or leave it
    Did not use take it or leave it — 4.97
33. Rigid
    Flexible — 4.94
34. Did not consider my needs
    Considered my needs — 4.92
35. Passive
    Aggressive — 4.78
36. Arrogant
    Modest — 4.59
37. Willing to stretch the facts
    Unwilling to stretch the facts — 4.41
38. Unconcerned about how I would look in the eyes of my client
    Concerned about how I would look — 4.29
39. Unwilling to stretch the rules
    Willing to stretch the rules — 4.09
40. Narrow range of bargaining strategies
    Wide range of bargaining strategies — 3.76
41. Made a high opening demand
    Made a low opening demand — 3.72
42. Defended
    Attacked — 3.63
43. Did own factual investigation and preparation
    Hired an investigator for investigation — 3.27

Effective/Aggressives
Bipolar Adjective Scales
(Phoenix Q-Analysis)

1. Passive
   Aggressive — 6.05
2. Defended
   Attacked — 6.04
3. Ineffective trial attorney
   Effective trial attorney — 6.00
4. Unintelligent
   Intelligent — 6.00
5. Min. prepared on factual elements of the case
   Thoroughly prepared on the factual elements — 5.82
6. Passive
   Active — 5.73
7. Disinterested in the needs of his client
   Knew the needs of his client — 5.38
8. Dishonest
   Honest — 5.09
9. Disregarded customs & courtesies of the bar
   Adhered to the customs & courtesies of the bar — 5.05
10. Min. prepared on legal elements of the case
    Thoroughly prepared on the legal elements — 4.77
11. Not careful about timing & sequence of actions
    Careful about timing & sequence of actions — 4.73
12. Unskillful in reading my cues
    Skillful in reading my cues — 4.59
13. Tactless
    Tactful — 4.41
14. Disinterested in my position
    Probed my position — 4.41
15. Emotional
    Logical — 4.36
16. Narrow range of bargaining strategies
    Wide range of bargaining strategies — 4.36
17. Disinterested in my personality
    Got to know my personality — 4.32
18. Took one position and refused to move from it
    Was willing to move from original position — 4.32
19. Unsure of the value of the case
    Accurately estimated the value of the case — 4.29
20. Emotionally involved
    Emotionally detached — 4.23
21. Unfriendly
    Friendly — 4.14
22. Did own factual investigation & preparation
    Hired an investigator for investigation — 4.05
23. Unwilling to stretch the rules
    Willing to stretch the rules — 4.05
24. Discourteous
    Courteous — 4.00
25. Unreasonable
    Reasonable — 3.95
26. Formal
    Informal — 3.95
27. Distrustful
    Trustful — 3.91
28. Insincere
    Sincere — 3.86
29. Unwilling to share information
    Willing to share information — 3.61
30. Obstructed
    Facilitated — 3.55
31. Used take it or leave it
    Did not use take it or leave it — 3.55
32. Revealed information gradually
    Revealed information early — 3.55
33. Uncooperative
    Cooperative — 3.50
34. Willing to stretch the facts
    Unwilling to stretch the facts — 3.45
35. Unconcerned about how I would look in the eyes of my client
    Concerned about how I would look — 3.43
36. Did not consider my needs
    Considered my needs — 3.41
37. Disinterested in the needs of my client
    Knew the needs of my client — 3.28
38. Rigid
    Flexible — 2.91
39. Used threats
    Did not use threats — 2.91
40. Arrogant
    Modest — 2.27
41. Took an unrealistic initial position
    Took a realistic initial position — 2.18
42. Made a high opening demand
    Made a low opening demand — 2.14
43. Devious
    Forthright — 3.73

Average/Cooperatives
Bipolar Adjective Scales
(Phoenix Q-Analysis)

1. Dishonest
   Honest — 6.23
2. Unfriendly
   Friendly — 5.93
3. Disregarded customs and courtesies of the bar
   Adhered to customs and courtesies of the bar — 5.87
4. Disinterested in the needs of his client
   Knew the needs of his client — 5.85
5. Discourteous
   Courteous — 5.82
6. Devious
   Forthright — 5.57
7. Insincere
   Sincere — 5.55
8. Uncooperative
   Cooperative — 5.51
9. Distrustful
   Trustful — 5.39
10. Unintelligent
    Intelligent — 5.37
11. Min. prepared on factual elements of the case
    Thoroughly prepared on the factual elements — 5.37
12. Unreasonable
    Reasonable — 5.30
13. Used threats
    Did not use threats — 5.19
14. Tactless
    Tactful — 5.17
15. Formal
    Informal — 5.12
16. Took one position and refused to move from it
    Was willing to move from original position — 4.94
17. Unwilling to share information
    Willing to share information — 4.94
18. Obstructed
    Facilitated — 4.93
19. Emotional
    Logical — 4.70
20. Arrogant
    Modest — 4.67
21. Disinterested in my personality
    Got to know my personality — 4.66
22. Passive
    Active — 4.65
23. Ineffective trial attorney
    Effective trial attorney — 4.60
24. Disinterested in my position
    Probed my position — 4.60
25. Rigid
    Flexible — 4.55
26. Emotionally involved
    Emotionally detached — 4.55
27. Used take it or leave it
    Did not use take it or leave it — 4.49
28. Did not consider my needs
    Considered my needs — 4.48
29. Unwilling to stretch the rules
    Willing to stretch the rules — 4.46
30. Min. prepared on legal elements of the case
    Thoroughly prepared on the legal elements — 4.29
31. Passive
    Aggressive — 4.22
32. Not careful about timing & sequence of actions
    Careful about timing & sequence of actions — 4.23
33. Revealed information gradually
    Revealed information early — 4.20
34. Unskillful in reading my cues
    Skillful in reading my cues — 4.20
35. Disinterested in the needs of my client
    Knew the needs of my client — 4.20
36. Unconcerned about how I would look in the eyes of my client
    Concerned about how I would look — 3.87
37. Took an unrealistic initial position
    Took a realistic initial position — 3.80
38. Unsure of the value of the case
    Accurately estimated the value of the case — 3.76
39. Willing to stretch the facts
    Unwilling to stretch the facts — 3.68
40. Defended
    Attacked — 3.63
41. Did own factual investigation & preparation
    Hired an investigator for investigation — 3.35
42. Narrow range of bargaining strategies
    Wide range of bargaining strategies — 3.33
43. Made a high opening demand
    Made a low opening demand — 2.96

Average Aggressives
Bipolar Adjective Scales
(Phoenix Q-Analysis)

1. Disinterested in the needs of his clients / Knew the needs of his clients — 5.06
2. Passive / Aggressive — 5.34
3. Min. prepared on factual elements of the case / Thoroughly prepared on the factual elements — 5.03
4. Unintelligent / Intelligent — 4.97
5. Passive / Active — 4.91
6. Defended / Attacked — 4.83
7. Disregarded customs & courtesies of the bar / Adhered to customs & courtesies of the bar — 4.40
8. Ineffective trial attorney / Effective trial attorney — 4.35
9. Dishonest / Honest — 4.26
10. Unfriendly / Friendly — 4.23
11. Not careful about timing & sequence of actions / Careful about timing & sequence of actions — 4.00
12. Formal / Informal — 3.97
13. Min. prepared on legal elements of the case / Thoroughly prepared on the legal elements — 3.95
14. Unwilling to stretch the rules / Willing to stretch the rules — 3.94
15. Disinterested in my personality / Got to know my personality — 3.91
16. Disinterested in my position / Probed my position — 3.86
17. Insincere / Sincere — 3.71
18. distrustful / Trustful — 3.56
19. Discourteous / Courteous — 3.63
20. Emotional / Logical — 3.62
21. Emotionally involved / Emotionally detached — 3.60
22. Willing to stretch the facts / Unwilling to stretch the facts — 3.60
23. Tactless / Tactful — 3.57
24. Used threats / Did not use threats — 3.54
25. Unwilling to share information / Willing to share information — 3.54
26. Took one position and refused to move from it / Was willing to move from original position — 3.51
27. Unskilful in reading my cues / Skilful in reading my cues — 3.50
28. Used take it or leave it / Did not use take it or leave it — 3.34
29. Uncooperative / Cooperative — 3.26
30. Unsure of the value of the case / Accurately estimated the value of the case — 3.24
31. Obstructed / Facilitated — 3.23
32. Devious / Forthright — 3.20
33. Revealed information gradually / Revealed information early — 3.14
34. Unconcerned about how I would look in the eyes of my client / Concerned about how I would look — 3.14
35. Unreasonable / Reasonable — 3.11
36. Did own factual investigation & preparation / Hired an investigator for investigation — 3.06
37. Made a high opening demand / Made a low opening demand — 2.94
38. Disinterested in the needs of my client / Knew the needs of my client — 2.83
39. Narrow range of bargaining strategies / Wide range of bargaining strategies — 2.60
40. Rigid / Flexible — 2.60
41. Did not consider my needs / Considered my needs — 2.60
42. Took an unrealistic initial position / Took a realistic initial position — 2.57
43. Arrogant / Modest — 2.40

Ineffective Cooperatives
Bipolar Adjective Scales
(Phoenix Q-Analysis)

1. Passive / Aggressive — 4.93
2. Defended / Attacked — 4.63
3. Passive / Active — 4.51
4. Disinterested in the needs of his client / Knew the needs of his client — 3.96
5. Dishonest / Honest — 3.89
6. Willing to stretch the facts / Unwilling to stretch the facts — 3.85
7. Min. prepared on factual elements of the case / Thoroughly prepared on the factual elements — 3.74
8. Formal / Informal — 3.63
9. Min. prepared on the legal elements of the case / Thoroughly prepared on the legal elements — 3.59
10. Unwilling to stretch the rules / Willing to stretch the rules — 3.56
11. Emotionally involved / Emotionally detached — 3.52
12. Disregarded customs & courtesies of the bar / Adhered to customs & courtesies of the bar — 3.42
13. Did own factual investigation & preparation / Hired an investigator for investigation — 3.41
14. Revealed information gradually / Revealed information early — 3.33
15. Discourteous / Courteous — 3.26
16. Not careful about timing & sequence of actions / Careful about timing & sequence of actions — 3.11
17. Unintelligent / Intelligent — 3.04
18. Used take it or leave it / Did not use take it or leave it — 2.96
19. Unconcerned about how I would look in the eyes of my client / Concerned about how I would look — 2.96
20. Used threats / Did not use threats — 2.96
21. Emotional / Logical — 2.93
22. Ineffective trial attorney / Effective trial attorney — 2.89
23. Took one position and refused to move from it / Was willing to move from original position — 2.89
24. Distrustful / Trustful — 2.85
25. Unfriendly / Friendly — 2.85
26. Disinterested in my position / Probed my position — 2.81
27. Obstructed / Facilitated — 2.74
28. Unsure of the value of the case / Accurately estimated the value of the case — 2.74
29. Devious / Forthright — 2.70
30. Disinterested in my personality / Got to know my personality — 2.70
31. Unwilling to share information / Willing to share information — 2.67
32. Insincere / Sincere — 2.52
33. Tactless / Tactful — 2.41
34. Made a high opening demand / Made a low opening demand — 2.37
35. Unskilful in reading my cues / Skilful in reading my cues — 2.19
36. Rigid / Flexible — 2.19
37. Arrogant / Modest — 2.19
38. Did not consider my needs / Considered my needs — 1.96
39. Uncooperative / Cooperative — 1.93
40. Narrow range of bargaining strategies / Wide range of bargaining strategies — 1.85
41. Disinterested in the needs of my client / Knew the needs of my client — 1.81
42. Unreasonable / Reasonable — 1.74
43. Took an unrealistic initial position / Took a realistic initial position — 1.74

Ineffective Aggressives
Bipolar Adjective Scales
(Phoenix Q-Analysis)

1. Dishonest / Honest — 6.89
2. Devious / Forthright — 6.44
3. Distrustful / Trustful — 6.33
4. Unwilling to share information / Willing to share information — 6.33
5. Discourteous / Courteous — 6.11
6. Disregarded customs & courtesies of the bar / Adhered to customs & courtesies of the bar — 6.11
7. Insincere / Sincere — 6.00
8. Unfriendly / Friendly — 6.00
9. Uncooperative / Cooperative — 5.89
10. Disinterested in the needs of his client / Knew the needs of his client — 5.89
11. Emotional / Logical — 5.67
12. Used threats / Did not use threats — 5.56
13. Obstructed / Facilitated — 5.44
14. Tactless / Tactful — 5.44
15. Took one position and refused to move from it / Was willing to move from original position — 5.33
16. Unintelligent / Intelligent — 5.22
17. Unreasonable / Reasonable — 5.22
18. Disinterested in my personality / Got to know my personality — 5.11
19. Min. prepared on factual elements of the case / Thoroughly prepared on the factual elements — 5.11
20. Rigid / Flexible — 5.11
21. Formal / Informal — 5.11
22. Emotionally involved / Emotionally detached — 5.00
23. Disinterested in my position / Probed my position — 5.00
24. Revealed information gradually / Revealed information early — 4.78
25. Arrogant / Modest — 4.67
26. Unsure of the value of the case / Accurately estimated the value of the case — 4.67
27. Took an unrealistic initial position / Took a realistic initial position — 4.56
28. Willing to stretch the facts / Unwilling to stretch the facts — 4.56
29. Min. prepared on legal elements of the case / Thoroughly prepared on the legal elements — 4.56
30. Used take it or leave it / Did not use take it or leave it — 4.22
31. Not careful about timing & sequence of actions / Careful about timing & sequence of actions — 4.22
32. Disinterested in the needs of my client / Knew the needs of my client — 4.11
33. Unskilful in reading my cues / Skilful in reading my cues — 4.11
34. Did not consider my needs / Considered my needs — 4.11
35. Ineffective trial attorney / Effective trial attorney — 3.78
36. Made a high opening demand / Made a low opening demand — 3.56
37. Unwilling to stretch the rules / Willing to stretch the rules — 3.56
38. Defended / Attacked — 3.44
39. Passive / Active — 2.89
40. Narrow range of bargaining strategies / Wide range of bargaining strategies — 2.78
41. Unconcerned about how I would look in the eyes of my client / Concerned about how I would look — 2.78
42. Passive / Aggressive — 2.56
43. Did own factual investigation & preparation / Hired an investigator for investigation — 2.11

THE MOTIVATIONAL OBJECTIVES

There were 12 items in the motivational objectives list, which also asked for ratings on a scale of 1 to 7. All ratings above 4.0 (i.e. all positive characteristics) were used in this analysis. The highest rated attributes from each list are given in tables accompanying the discussion of each level of negotiator effectiveness.

Effective Cooperatives Objectives (Phoenix Q–Analysis)

1.	Conducting himself ethically	6.09
2.	Maximizing settlement for his client	5.58
3.	Getting a fair settlement	5.24
4.	Meeting his client's needs	4.97
5.	Satisfaction in exercise of legal skills	4.84
6.	Avoiding litigation	4.54
7.	Maintaining or establishing good personal relations with you	4.50
8.	Improving reputation with you	3.25
9.	Obtaining profitable fee for himself	3.05
10.	Improving reputation in his Firm	3.04
11.	Improving reputation among bar members	2.83
12.	Outdoing or outmaneuvering you	2.77

Effective Competitives Objectives (Phoenix Q–Analysis)

1.	Maximizing settlement for his client	5.86
2.	Obtaining profitable fee for himself	4.67
3.	Outdoing or outmaneuvering you	4.59
4.	Conducting himself ethically	4.32
5.	Satisfaction in exercise of legal skills	4.01
6.	Meeting his client's needs	3.68
7.	Getting a fair settlement	3.68
8.	Improving reputation with his Firm	3.31
9.	Improving reputation among bar members	3.05
10.	maintaining or establishing good personal relations with you	2.69
11.	Avoiding litigation	2.59
12.	Improving reputation with you	2.55

Average Cooperatives Objectives (Phoenix Q–Analysis)

1.	Maximizing settlement for his client	5.35
2.	Conducting himself ethically	5.09
3.	Getting a fair settlement	4.65
4.	Meeting his client's needs	4.27
5.	Maintaining or establishing good personal relations with you	4.02
6.	Avoiding litigation	4.00
7.	Satisfaction in exercise of legal skills	3.63
8.	Obtaining profitable fee for himself	3.20
9.	Improving reputation in his Firm	3.15
10.	Outdoing or outmaneuvering you	3.11
11.	Improving reputation with you	3.07
12.	Improving reputation among bar members	2.61

Average Competitives Objectives (Phoenix Q–Analysis)

1.	Maximizing settlement for his client	5.83
2.	Outdoing or outmaneuvering you	4.97
3.	Meeting his client's needs	4.23
4.	Obtaining profitable fee for himself	4.17
5.	Improving reputation in his Firm	3.97
6.	Satisfaction in exercise of legal skills	3.84
7.	Conducting himself ethically	3.49
8.	Getting a fair settlement	3.34
9.	Avoiding litigation	3.14
10.	Improving reputation among bar members	2.80
11.	maintaining or establishing good personal relations with you	2.54
12.	Improving reputation with you	2.38

Ineffective Cooperatives
Objectives
(Phoenix Q–Analysis)

1.	Conducting himself ethically	5.56
2.	Maximizing settlement for his client	5.33
3.	Meeting his client's needs	4.44
4.	Getting a fair settlement	4.33
5.	Maintaining or establishing good personal relations with you	4.33
6.	Satisfaction in exercise of legal skills	4.22
7.	Obtaining profitable fee for himself	3.56
8.	Avoiding litigation	3.44
9.	Outdoing or outmaneuvering you	2.78
10.	Improving reputation with you	2.67
11.	Improving reputation among bar members	2.67
12.	Improving reputation in his Firm	1.86

Ineffective Competitives
Objectives
(Phoenix Q–Analysis)

1.	Maximizing settlement for his client	4.96
2.	Outdoing or outmaneuvering you	4.81
3.	Obtaining profitable fee for himself	4.50
4.	Improving reputation in his Firm	3.42
5.	Conducting himself ethically	3.26
6.	Meeting his client's needs	3.23
7.	Satisfaction in exercise of legal skills	2.63
8.	Improving reputation among bar members	2.48
9.	Getting a fair settlement	2.37
10.	Avoiding litigation	2.19
11.	Maintaining or establishing good personal relations with you	2.19
12.	Improving reputation with you	1.96

*

Appendix III

TRANSCRIPTS OF STUDENT SEXUAL HARASSMENT AND PERSONAL INJURY NEGOTIATIONS[1]

To provide interesting examples of legal negotiations, we occasionally ask practicing attorneys to work on negotiations exercises. We video tape these interactions and show them to our classes after our students have negotiated the same exercises. In this section, we include four transcripts from negotiations conducted by four Clinical Law Professors at George Washington University: Susan Jones, Charles Masner, Peter Meyers, and Joan Strand. We are deeply indebted to them for their gracious participation.

The first two transcripts involve a Sexual Harassment Exercise involving a first year law student who claims to have been propositioned by her Tort Law professor. The third and fourth transcripts involve a Personal Injury Exercise. These interactions were completely unscripted. Although the outcomes of the two Sexual Harassment Exercise negotiations were quite different, it is amazing that both pairs reached the identical agreement with respect to the Personal Injury Exercise negotiations.

We provide the Sexual Harassment Exercise followed by the two separate negotiation transcripts dealing with this exercise. We then provide the Personal Injury Exercise followed by the two negotiation transcripts pertaining to this exercise.

GENERAL INFORMATION—SEXUAL
HARASSMENT EXERCISE

Last year, Jane Doe was a first year law student at the Yalebridge Law School, which is part of Yalebridge University, a private, nonsectarian institution. Ms. Doe was a student in Professor Alexander Palsgraf's Tort Law class.

During the first semester, Professor Palsgraf made sexually suggestive comments to Ms. Doe on several occasions. These comments were always made outside of the classroom and when no other individuals were present. Ms. Doe unequivocally indicated her personal revulsion toward Professor Palsgraf's remarks and informed him that they were entirely improper and unappreciated.

During the latter part of the second semester, Professor Palsgraf suggested to Ms. Doe in his private office that she have sexual relations with him. Ms. Doe immediately rejected his suggestion and told Professor Palsgraf that he was "a degenerate and disgusting old man who was a disgrace to the teaching profession."

Last June, Ms. Doe received her first year law school grades. She received one "A", two "A-", one "B+", and one "D", the latter grade pertaining to her Tort Law class. She immediately went to see Professor Palsgraf to ask him about her low grade. He said that he was sorry about her "D", but indicated that the result might well have been different had she only acquiesced in his request for sexual favors.

Ms. Doe then had Professor Irving Prosser, who also teaches Tort Law at Yalebridge, review her exam. He said that it was a "most respectable paper" which should certainly have earned her an "A-" or "B+", and possibly even an "A".

Ms. Doe has sued Professor Palsgraf in state court for $250,000 based upon three separate causes of action: (1) sexual harassment in violation of Title IX of the Education Amendments of 1972; (2) intentional infliction of emotional distress; and (3) fraud. Professor Palsgraf has a net worth of $450,000, including the $350,000 equity in his house and a $50,000 library of ancient Gilbert's outlines.

CONFIDENTIAL INFORMATION—JANE DOE

Your client wants to obtain several forms of relief from Professor Palsgraf: (1) a grade of "A" or "A-" in Tort Law; (2) the resignation of Professor Palsgraf from the Yalebridge Law School; and (3) a sufficiently large sum of money to deter such offensive conduct by other professors in the future.

(I) Score **plus 35 points** if Professor Palsgraf agrees to change Ms. Doe's Tort Law grade to "A-", and **plus 50 points** if he agrees to change her grade to "A".

(II) Score **plus 200 points** if Professor Palsgraf agrees to resign from the Yalebridge Law School faculty. If Professor Palsgraf does not resign, but agrees to take a one-year leave of absence **or** a one-year sabbatical leave from the Law School during the *coming* academic year (*i.e.*, Ms. Doe's second year), score **plus 50 points**. If Professor Palsgraf agrees to take a leave of absence and/or sabbatical leave during the coming year *and* the following year (*i.e.*, Ms. Doe's final two years of law school), score **plus 75 points**.

(III) If Professor Palsgraf does not resign, but he does agree to seek psychiatric counseling *and* personally apologize to Ms. Doe, score **plus 50 points**.

(IV) Score **plus 2 points** for *each $1,000*, or part thereof, Professor Palsgraf agrees to immediately pay Ms. Doe in settlement of her suit.

(V) Ms. Doe is concerned about the publicity surrounding this matter and the impact that publicity may have on her future employment opportunities. Score **plus 50 points** for a clause guaranteeing the confidentiality of any settlement reached with Professor Palsgraf.

Since Ms. Doe wishes to have this matter resolved now so that she may concentrate fully on her legal education, you will automatically be placed at the **bottom** of your group if no settlement agreement is achieved.

CONFIDENTIAL INFORMATION—PROFESSOR PALSGRAF

Your client realizes that his conduct was entirely inappropriate, and he is deeply sorry for the difficulty he has caused Ms. Doe. He would thus be willing to submit to psychiatric counseling and to personally apologize to Ms. Doe. Should you agree to either or both of these requirements, you **lose no points**.

Professor Palsgraf fears that Ms. Doe may ask for his resignation from the Yalebridge Law School, and he would rather lose everything before he would forfeit his Yalebridge position. Should you agree to have Professor Palsgraf resign his Yalebridge professorship, you must **deduct 500 points**.

Your client recognizes that he will have to provide Ms. Doe with the grade she should have received. He is readily willing to change her grade to "A-", and you lose **no points** for agreeing to an "A-". Professor Palsgraf does not think that Ms. Doe's exam performance was really worthy of an "A". You thus **lose 50 points** if you agree to have Ms. Doe's Tort Law grade changed to an "A".

Professor Palsgraf is currently eligible for a one-year, paid "sabbatical leave." He has been saving this leave to enable him to go to Cambridge University in two years. If you agree to have Professor Palsgraf take that "sabbatical leave" during either of the next two academic years, you **lose 25 points**. Should you agree to have him take a "leave of absence" during either of the next two academic years, which, unlike a "sabbatical leave," would not involve a continuation of his salary, you **lose 100 points**. (If you agree to both a one-year sabbatical *and* a one-year leave of absence, you **lose** a total of **125 points**.)

Professor Palsgraf will almost certainly have to provide Ms. Doe with monetary compensation for the wrong he committed. You **lose 3 points** for *each $1,000*, or part thereof, you agree to pay Ms. Doe. Any agreement regarding the payment of money must be operative immediately—no form of future compensation may be included.

Professor Palsgraf is concerned about the publicity surrounding this tragic affair. Score **plus 50 points** for a clause guaranteeing the confidentiality of any settlement reached.

Since Professor Palsgraf believes that the continuation of this law suit may ruin his outstanding legal career, you will automatically be placed at the **bottom** of your group if no settlement is achieved.

SEXUAL HARASSMENT EXERCISE EFFICIENCY

I. A- is **More Efficient** grade than A [Net Gain of 35 pts. for A- vs. 0 pts. for A]

> A- generates +35 pts. for Doe at No Cost to Palsgraf

> A generates +50 for Doe, but at cost of –50 to Palsgraf

If Doe accepts A- and saves Palsgraf 50 pts., Palsgraf can afford to give Doe an additional $10,000 to $15,000—costing Palsgraf fewer than 50 pts. while generating extra 20 to 30 pts. for Doe which, when added to +35 for A-, results in more than +50 Doe would get for A alone.

II. Personal Apology **and** Psychological Counseling generate +50 for Doe at No Cost to Palsgraf.

By giving Doe +50 here, Doe could reduce her Monetary Demand by $10,000, $15,000, or even $20,000 and still gain more than +50 pts.—reduction of $10,000, $15,000, or $20,000 saves Palsgraf –30, –45, or –60 pts.

III. Resignation generates Net Loss of 300 pts.—Doe gets +200, but Palsgraf loses 500 pts.

If Palsgraf willing to lose 500 pts., Doe should seek the $167,000 that would cost Palsgraf 501 pts. while generating +334 for Doe.

IV. Sabbatical Leave generates Net Gain of 25 pts.—Plus 50 for Doe with only –25 for Palsgraf—allowing Doe to reduce her monetary demand by up to $10,000, $15,000, or $20,000.

V. Leave of Absence generates Net Loss of 50—Plus 50 pts. for Doe, but –100 for Palsgraf.

VI. Confidentiality Clause generates +50 for *each* party. When first party requests this clause, should opponent immediately agree to it or use it as False Issue in effort to obtain additional concession for same Confidentiality Clause it also wants?

VII. Money is Net Loser—Each $1000 gets +2 pts. for Doe, while costing Palsgraf –3 pts.

TRANSCRIPT I

PLAINTIFF: Hi, ___. How are you?

DEFENDANT: Fine.

PLAINTIFF: Good to see you again.

DEFENDANT: You too.

PLAINTIFF: You know that we're here to discuss the Doe–Palsgraf case?

DEFENDANT: Yes.

PLAINTIFF: Perhaps the best way to proceed is to review the facts a little bit to make sure that we're sort of speaking the same language or at least thinking in the same way.

DEFENDANT: That'd be fine with me.

PLAINTIFF: I'd say this has been pretty troubling. For me; as you are aware my client has just completed her first year in law school, is about to be a second year law student. And she alleges in her complaint, in her $250,000 law suit, that your client sexually harassed her and made advances toward her. And the situation is quite egregious. This has got to be the most vulnerable time, as we all remember from first year law school, and to have a professor come on to you, as it were, is just overwhelming. A settlement here is gonna really have to be substantial to avoid, I think, a lot of embarrassment. And my client wants this behind her. I mean she's got two years of law school to get through. So, we'd like to try to accomplish that — not to mention this grade that she was given of a D — when independent torts professor says this is clearly A work.

DEFENDANT: Well, it is a troubling case. And, it's something which, if it's possible, to resolve, he would like to. I think, in terms of going to trial, I think probably for both of them, you know — if we can work this thing out and reach an agreement, I think it's probably better for both of them.

PLAINTIFF: Absolutely.

DEFENDANT: One of the things which I just think we need to focus on, from my perspective is, whether or not, the money's the most important thing to put in the mix, adjusting the grade, which is certainly possible, and other things which are important to her. You know, it is a terrible situation and so we would certainly like to settle it. And if we can reach an agreement, we would. There are problems, I think a number of problems, in terms of trying to take this case to trial from her perspective. Let me tell you what some of those problems are as I see them. First, I think if it came down to it, it's a hard case to prove. All of these incidents have no corroborating details — and I'm not saying that it didn't happen, and I'm not saying he doesn't feel remorse and regret for what happened here. I'm not

170

saying that. I'm just saying that if it comes down to it and it comes down to a jury, it's a difficult thing for both of them to get up there and talk about. It's a hard case to prove. All these allegations are his word against hers, if need be. There's no corroborating information. They are always alone when this is supposed to have happened. And, I'm not saying that I view it like this, but I mean it's possible, if it goes to trial, to characterize her as somebody who, in retaliation for getting her only bad grade in school, is either making up or exaggerating or something. I'm not saying even making up, that there wasn't some kernel that lead to this thing. But you know, she could be portrayed as somebody who is so disgusted and disappointed about getting her one low grade that she is, perhaps exaggerating or perhaps going overboard in terms of describing incidents which may or may not have happened.

PLAINTIFF: I think that the major difficulty with that is the grade. I mean this is a stellar student. How do you explain a D in the torts class when all of her other grades were As and Bs? And clearly there's another issue here. And the other issue is the fact that we've had an independent torts professor review the examination, a very well respected professor, and in his opinion, clearly this would have been an A grade.

DEFENDANT: Well the information I've received is slightly different from that. What I've been informed was that in his view it's clearly a B+ or an A− —but possibly an A. You know as well as I do—we've been through law school—you get the grades and you look at essay exams. As I say, I know that Professor Palsgraf is willing to — if it's important to her as part of a settlement — make a substantial boost in that grade. He's willing to do that. But in terms of a jury, you and I know from law school, that one professor reads an essay exam and that looks like an A to him, another it looks like C, so even with good professors, assuming everybody is being honest, you get grade variances between how good a grade a professor thinks there is. So I think having your independent professor's view is worth something, but the other side of it is again that different experts and professors often see things very differently. But I say to you, if we can reach a settlement, I know that he would be willing to, again as I understand it even if the other professor didn't say it was an A— B+, A− —so I think let's take the lower range. I think B+ if that's what's important to her, those types of things, rather than getting the maximum amount of money, I think that could be part of the deal.

PLAINTIFF: OK, what's important to my client is not only the grade but deterring this kind of conduct in the future.

171

	The reality is that being a law professor is a tremendous responsibility. I mean clearly that person is training somebody, teaching somebody, educating somebody to be a member of a very noble profession, and when someone performs in this fashion that is simply unacceptable. Now there are several issues that I think we need to discuss generally. I mean frankly, we'd like to consider (1) some cloud of confidentiality around this. I mean my client wants to get on with her life, and I would imagine that your client wants to do exactly the same thing.
DEFENDANT:	I think they're interests are the same on that.
PLAINTIFF:	Right. The other thing is that maybe it's time for your client to take a little time out and do a little reflection. And one way to do that is psychological counseling and maybe a sabbatical or a leave of absence.
DEFENDANT:	I think both of those are possible. As part of a mix here, in addition to increasing her grade — again I'm thinking of in the nature of a B+ something like that.
PLAINTIFF:	Let's stay on that point for just a minute because I'm thinking that based on two things. One is clearly her grade point average thus far. Her grades have all been As and Bs. Clearly the high end there would be more appropriate. So I would strongly suggest an A− there as opposed to a B+.
DEFENDANT:	I've spoken to the professor. If we can reach agreement on the other things, that's something which the professor thinks is not unreasonable so that could be part of the mix — A−.
PLAINTIFF:	OK, A−.
DEFENDANT:	Let me also respond. Counseling. I've also discussed that with him before coming here today. Not only apologizing to her and making that clear that he regrets what happened and how sorry he is for it, …
PLAINTIFF:	But, during the apology we won't leave them alone. We'll make sure that somebody is there to witness the apology.
DEFENDANT:	Oh absolutely, we can structure that as you think's appropriate. We certainly would want it to be a healing for both of them rather than any further complications. Your suggestion about mandatory counseling, a therapeutic type of thing, to deal with this in the future so that it doesn't happen, I think not only is it important from your client's perspective, but I think that would also be useful for him. I mean that's something that could also go into the mix as part of this agreement. So I've spoken with him, that certainly could be part of the agreement as well.
PLAINTIFF:	So what I hear thus far is that we've reached agreement in at least in two, I think, very important areas, but we have two very important areas still remaining. One is really time away from the University. This

172

woman has actually been traumatized by this professor. She has two more years in law school and I'd clearly like to suggest that he not be there for the remainder of the time that she is in school — that he take either a leave of absence or a sabbatical.

DEFENDANT: This is something which I've spoken to him about as well in detail. And it is possible to work out, from his perspective, the details of something that she could be comfortable with. Two years away from the University is asking too much. It would be possible, again in terms of making these offers to you, that the grade, the therapy, the apology and staying away, all of this is premised, because when we finish this we're going to get to the money. All of this is premised, is that these types of things are what's most important to her rather than reaching a high monetary settlement. Because the mix would be different. But let me tell you in terms of if we go on that assumption, that these things are more important, because if they're less important, let's trade these off and give her some more money if that's really what she cares more about. But leaving for two years is impossible. What is possible, and I'll put it right on the table — a sabbatical for the first year, he's gone. Next year when she comes back in September she doesn't have to see him there, he's not going to be there. He will be out of town one year. And then for the second year, even though he'd be on the campus, you work out the language of conditions that he would avoid her, that he would make no contact with her — kind of a stay-away order that you see in the criminal cases or child custody. If you see her walking down the street, turn the other way; initiate no contact and totally stay away from her for the second year. So again, if you're saying to me, What's the maximum he could do? That would be a promise to take the sabbatical for the first year starting in a couple of weeks. Be gone from the campus so she'd never have to see him. Give her the year, again, of him not being there just to have that peace of mind. And then the second year, even though he is on campus, a promise to totally avoid and stay away from her.

PLAINTIFF: Right. And I think that that would be acceptable, but that's not in lieu of money, and I want to make that perfectly clear.

DEFENDANT: I'm not saying in lieu of money, but it's just a question of all of these major things you're asking him to make and he's willing to do. Major, major changes in his life to accommodate her and I'm not saying totally no money for that. I'm not saying that. But I'm saying, to me it's a balanced scale. If you're asking for all of these big, big things, major changes to say to her, I'm sorry, not only will I apologize now, I will take these actions

173

that it doesn't happen again. I will change my life
entirely as a way of paying you back and making your
life as easy as possible the next two years here. All I'm
saying is that's not no money. And I'm not saying zero.
But it's a question of if you want all those things, from
his perspective is, look how much I'm doing.

PLAINTIFF: The flip side of that is look how much he has done.
And this is something that will affect this woman for
her entire life. Let's talk about money at this point.
And I think something substantial must occur in terms
of a monetary settlement in order to deter this kind of
conduct from occurring in the future. And in addition
to that, my client has to have the option of being able
to get past this with psychological counseling, if she
chooses to do that. This has had a devastating impact
on her and getting through first year of law school is
enough, but being sexually harassed on top of it and
then having to go through two years more of school is
quite a bit. Let's talk some numbers. Our lawsuit is for
$250,000. I'd be willing to start the discussion around
$175,000.

DEFENDANT: To me that is way, way out of line. If you want these
other things — that's impossible. Let me give you my
perspective. You're talking first of all, I mean you can
ask for whatever you want in a lawsuit. Nothing pre-
vents you from doing that. It's just a number. First of
all, look at your three courses of action. Again I think
that, putting aside the problems with proof that we
talked about before that you know if you get into no
corroboration, perhaps his word against hers. Perhaps
somebody who is just angry and retaliating for getting
her one low grade, all I'm saying is you run some risk
by going to trial. That they could say no liability. But I
would think there are problems with the legal theories.
Let me talk about that for one second. Three legal
theories. Again, which I think at least have some
problems. Title IX of the educational amendments, I
think that you're gonna have a problem here that
we're talking about a private rather than a public
university. Fraud, well again, he may have done something to her, you know, but whether as a legal matter
that constitutes fraud . . .

PLAINTIFF: I think even the torts professor would agree to that
one.

DEFENDANT: Intentional infliction of emotional stress. Maybe, all
I'm saying is perhaps we could kick out two. You know
maybe even some hope. I don't know what the chances
are. Perhaps we can kick out all three causes of action.
So I factor this in, in terms of advising him. Neither of
the clients wants to have to fight this thing to the
bitter end. But you have a case which is potentially
difficult to prove. A case in which the legal theories are

to some extent weak. Perhaps two—if we're really lucky, a pretrial motion gets rid of all three. So it seems to me if you're talking about making accommodations to her, and this is what the professor says to me, to say I'm sorry, do these things and change my life plus give you money for counseling and that, if that's what you're talking about, that is within the ballpark. But if you're talking $175,000, well then lets talk money and then let's not talk about the other stuff. That's my perspective.

PLAINTIFF: I think clearly it's a complete package. I disagree with some of your perspectives about the viability of the lawsuit. I mean here we have a vulnerable first year law student who is sexually harassed by an older torts professor. Unfortunately, this kind of activity happens all too often. There is a fair amount of controversy going on about this generally and the world, I think, has been recently been heightened, particularly after Anita Hill, to the world of sexual harassment and how subtle it is.

DEFENDANT: Yeah, but the Anita Hill case also shows the risks of taking this to trial. If your client is not believed, then you've got to factor in the fact that she could get nothing and she could come out of this thing just like Anita Hill did. The person who lied.

PLAINTIFF: Absolutely. But the flip side of that as well is the reality that your client has a very substantial reputation to protect.

DEFENDANT: Exactly.

PLAINTIFF: So.

DEFENDANT: We don't want to risk that.

PLAINTIFF: And that's the goal. So let's hear a counter offer. What does your client have that he'd be willing to put up in terms of a monetary settlement.

DEFENDANT: If you want, and again I've given you the Cadillac of everything you've offered on the other side. I don't need to list them all again. Everything you've said in terms of . . .

PLAINTIFF: I don't know about the Cadillac characterization, but we've reached some agreements.

DEFENDANT: An A-, he's going to be away, we're going to keep everything confidential, he's going to apologize to her, he's going to go to therapy, he's going to leave campus for a year and avoid her for the next year. I mean everything to try to make her life easy, and to try to say I'm sorry.

PLAINTIFF: And protecting his reputation. So what's the number.

DEFENDANT: But you see, if you want all that, I think we're talking whatever it costs for therapy. If you're talking 10–, 15–, 20 thousand dollars for therapy, that's what you're talking about.

175

PLAINTIFF: That I think is wholly unworkable. I mean we're moving from 10, 15 thousand dollars . . .

DEFENDANT: Whatever therapy is.

PLAINTIFF: That's nominal. I mean clearly that is not substantial enough to deter this kind of activity. And we have to make it absolutely clear to your client that this can never happen again. And it's gonna cost. It hurts. So, frankly, his exposure is—the equity in his house is from what I understand somewhere around $350,000.

DEFENDANT: Yes. A substantial amount of equity.

PLAINTIFF: I'd be willing to consider something in the nature of a hundred thousand dollars for my client based on our discussions. And there are several factors, I think, that impact that figure. One is the length of therapy. Therapy is extremely expensive, so I think that frankly your 15 to 20 thousand dollar characterization is a drop in the bucket. If there's any leak of this, my client still has to go out and get a job after law school. And the long range impact of something like this is totally unpredictable. Not to mention the fact that the settlement figure here should deter this kind of activity from occurring in the future. And I think, frankly, a hundred thousand dollar figure, in addition to the concessions that we've already talked about, seems appropriate.

DEFENDANT: Well if you want to use the money then to punish and then if you expect us to come up. OK, let's say we're willing to come up to $40,000, $45,000, well then let's eliminate the punishment of him leaving campus. Let's eliminate that from what we've said. He can remain on campus, he can continue to teach his classes—avoiding her but staying on campus—both years. Look what that costs him to leave campus.

PLAINTIFF: But as an advocate for your client it's also important to think about the benefits to your client. And clearly the activity indicates the potential for a larger problem which should properly be examined and taking some time out to examine that, not only to be away from the University to reflect, but also to get the counseling. I think it's an important part of the bargain for benefit of your client long term.

DEFENDANT: Counseling, again, I'm not going to take that off the table because I see that as something both sides have an interest in. That's not something I want to trade off for money, leave that there but you can do that as many people do and still remain and continue to work in your job and you don't have to leave. And I'd say that's worth more than, you know, the type of money you're talking about. If he can stay there, again, I think we could be talking about 40, 45 thousand dollars in addition to everything else if he can stay at the

	school. If it's more important for him to be out of there then we have to talk lower.
PLAINTIFF:	I still think that the $50,000 figure that you're suggesting is a bit low. Clearly something in the nature of $75,000 I think would be acceptable. And I think that an appropriately drafted stay-away order might be a viable alternative for both years.
DEFENDANT:	For both years.
PLAINTIFF:	For both years. For both years. In addition to the counseling that your client will undergo.
DEFENDANT:	You know I think we're getting close. I've spoken to him. We have like a limit in terms of —75 is above the limit — in terms of what he can afford to do. I mean it's true there's equity in the house. But then you know you're talking a mortgage. Equity in your house is one thing. But cash and your ability to spend money is another. But I think we're getting close, at least, in terms of our agreements here. I can go up to $50 with all the other provisions that you're talking about. I mean if it's a package, and it's 50, that's something we can do.
PLAINTIFF:	I'd like to suggest a counter in a package at $65 and let's call it quits. And what that will frankly do is allow my client to get psychological counseling and get through law school. And your client has already substantially impacted her ability to do that with some degree of comfort. So if you would take 65 back to your client with these other concessions I think that that would be a good place to be.
DEFENDANT:	Well, we're real close that's for sure. I'm authorized with the package you've done to say 60 thousand, and we could have a deal right now with the other provisions that you've already said.
DEFENDANT:	O.K. I think we've got a deal.
DEFENDANT:	Shall we make sure that we all agree on what the terms of that is?
PLAINTIFF:	Yes. Please, let's review them carefully.
DEFENDANT:	You want to do that or me.
PLAINTIFF:	As I understand those terms we are talking about an A— grade.
DEFENDANT:	Yes.
PLAINTIFF:	A stay away order for two years.
DEFENDANT:	Yes.
PLAINTIFF:	$60,000 in a settlement.
DEFENDANT:	Paid to her immediately.
PLAINTIFF:	Paid to her immediately. Your client will undergo substantial psychological counseling. And there is also an agreement regarding confidentiality of our settlement.
DEFENDANT:	Neither client will divulge it in any public way.
PLAINTIFF:	That's correct.

177

DEFENDANT: I think the only thing you haven't included, which also
              we agreed to, is an apology to her in a way that you
              find appropriate.
PLAINTIFF: Thank you.
DEFENDANT: Thank you.

TRANSCRIPT II

DEFENDANT: Hi ___. How're you doing?

PLAINTIFF: Hi ___. Nice to see you.

DEFENDANT: Nice to see you too.

PLAINTIFF: Wish it could be under more pleasant circumstances.

DEFENDANT: Well, that's what being a lawyer is all about isn't it?

PLAINTIFF: I guess so.

DEFENDANT: I've read over your client's complaint in this case and I don't know, I mean I think that, I guess what I'd really like to know from you is what she's really looking for here. The complaint asks for $250,000 in damages and my client is not a rich person and if what she really wants is to have a full open trial and to seek a lot of damages from him then that might be what we have to do but if there are some other things that we can talk about and maybe if you could itemize for me what some of her damages are then I think there might be a possibility that we could resolve it. So I'd really be interested in hearing from you what your view of the case is from your client's view point.

PLAINTIFF: O.K. Well I'll do my best to do that. We have one point of agreement at least already. My client's not a rich person either. As a student at Yalebridge Law School, she's piled up quite a bit of debt. So there're really a couple of principles, from my client's perspective that are important here. One is that she wants to be treated fairly herself for the work that she did in Professor Palsgraf's class. And, the other principle that's at stake for her here is that—and it's really two parts—she wants to make sure that she doesn't suffer any more at the hands of Professor Palsgraf and that she does whatever she can to make sure that no other law student at the law school suffer at the hands of Professor Palsgraf. So, that's what's at stake for her behind the figures that are indicated in her prayer for relief.

DEFENDANT: O.K. So what you're suggesting is that if there are some other things that we can come to an agreement on that that might be a way to resolve the case? Is that what I'm getting from you?

PLAINTIFF: I'm suggesting that money is only part of the solution to the problem and money is representative of other problems that she wants resolved as well.

DEFENDANT: O.K. Well, I think we can start addressing some of her concerns specifically and just see where some areas of agreement might lie. One thing I would like to say at the beginning though is I think this has been an embarrassing incident for my client and assuming that we can meet some of her other concerns I think it's important to him that if we can reach an agreement that the terms of the agreement be confidential and I think that might be an advantage for your client as

179

well given that she's just about to embark upon a legal career.

PLAINTIFF: Well all I can say is certainly she has no reason to want to make it public if a satisfactory agreement can otherwise be reached. I suppose that remains to be seen. Obviously, if we go to trial a lot of things will be public.

DEFENDANT: Right.

PLAINTIFF: But, assuming that we could otherwise reach an agreement here today then probably we could make that agreement confidential.

DEFENDANT: O.K. Well then beginning with your client's interest in seeing that she is treated fairly, I think that your reference there is probably to the grade that she received in the course, is that right?

PLAINTIFF: Yes.

DEFENDANT: O.K. That's something that I have talked about with my client and he would be willing to give her the grade of A−,—that she squarely deserves based on her paper.

PLAINTIFF: O.K. We'll accept that.

DEFENDANT: All right. The next thing that you discussed was what could be done to make sure that this didn't happen again. Is that right?

PLAINTIFF: Make sure that it doesn't again to her or to anyone else.

DEFENDANT: I think that there may be a couple of ways to look at doing that. One is, my client would be agreeable to getting counseling and I think that it's not something that he would view as something he just has to do to comply with the settlement. I think he seriously is willing to recognize that he has a problem and he needs treatment for it; so he would definitely be willing to do that. And, with regard to your client making sure that it doesn't happen to her again, he is willing to have no contact with her. He is willing to agree that he will not seek her out in any way. That he will not contact her in writing, by telephone or in person during her remaining two years at Yalebridge.

PLAINTIFF: I'm glad to hear that he's sensitive to her concerns. However, obviously she's going to be a second year law student—it takes three years to graduate from law school—and even with best efforts if he's there that's going to create a problem.

DEFENDANT: Why?

PLAINTIFF: Because his presence will always be a reminder to her of the injury that she's suffered.

DEFENDANT: Even if she's not seeing him?

PLAINTIFF: She'll see him there. How's she going to not see him? He's a part of the faculty.

DEFENDANT: It's a big school. It's not like she's going to be taking a class from him. There are lots of professors that other professors and other students don't see if they're not

	taking their courses. I just think if he makes a concerted effort not to contact her any form, that it shouldn't be a problem.
PLAINTIFF:	However we resolve it, I think it is going to be a problem because, again, there's just no way if he sees her this is going to be a reminder. The other think is would he be willing to take a brief leave of absence from the school?
DEFENDANT:	I don't think he'd be willing to take a leave of absence. There's a possibility that he might be willing to take an early sabbatical but it would only be for one year. That's a possibility depending upon how we can work out some other things.
PLAINTIFF:	Is he willing to apologize to my client.
DEFENDANT:	Oh yes. Absolutely. Absolutely.
PLAINTIFF:	Let's assume for the moment, assuming we can reach agreement on what remains, if he was willing to get counseling, to apologize to my client, and take an early sabbatical for at least a year, that would satisfy her concerns—but as I say—for other students. Okay.
DEFENDANT:	For the time being.
PLAINTIFF:	Okay.
DEFENDANT:	Let's keep that on the table.
PLAINTIFF:	Well, the final item is money.
DEFENDANT:	Uh huh.
PLAINTIFF:	And she's asked for $250,000. And I guess my question to you is how much does he think is fair. She's indicated that that's what she thinks would be a fair amount.
DEFENDANT:	Uh huh.
PLAINTIFF:	And if you say [chuckling] $250,000 we can settle this and go home now.
DEFENDANT:	I'm sure we could. [chuckle].
PLAINTIFF:	But I assume you're not going to say that.
DEFENDANT:	I think from my client's point of view that by doing these other things he is really remedying the harm that may have been caused her. I don't think there's really going to be any monetary effect on her career or any other long-term aspects here. I think what he would be willing to pay is in the range of nominal damages in terms of a couple thousand dollars.
PLAINTIFF:	Well, with all due respect, that wouldn't even be sufficient to pay her attorney's fees.
DEFENDANT:	Well we're at the beginning of the case. I mean come on, _____, you just filed the complaint. We haven't even done discovery yet.
PLAINTIFF:	Well, two thousand isn't going to be enough. I think she'd be willing to come down from $250,000 because a part of what's at stake here is that again we're not at trial, and obviously if we were at trial all this would come out, and so I understand that is part of the agreement—your client is not admitting anything—but from my client's perspective she's been injured. This

	happened. So by getting a grade of A− and by your client getting counseling and taking a sabbatical he's doing nothing more in her view than he should do.
DEFENDANT:	Well, which makes her whole though, essentially. If the point is to make her whole then that's what he's trying to do here.
PLAINTIFF:	How about $10,000?
DEFENDANT:	I think that's still going to be hard for him especially if he agrees to take the sabbatical and is going to have to walk away from some things that he had been planning to do here. I would say that maybe more like $7500.
PLAINTIFF:	Done. Now are we agreed on the counseling. No contact with her and a sabbatical. She gets an A− and she gets $7500.
DEFENDANT:	Right. All right.
PLAINTIFF:	Thank you.

GENERAL INFORMATION—PETERSON v. DENVER

At approximately 11:30 p.m. on a rainy and dark Friday evening last November, accountant Jim Denver was driving his Continental up Powell Street in San Francisco. He had just completed a long and acrimonious dinner meeting with a difficult, but important, client. Although he had consumed three or four Martinis during the course of his lengthy discussions, he felt in complete control of his faculties when he concluded the meeting.

As a result of the emergency session with his client, Denver was forced to miss a prestigious social event that his wife had been eagerly anticipating. He realized she would be very angry over the situation, and he was in a great hurry to return home to assuage her feelings. As Denver was heading up a particularly steep portion of Powell Street, he swerved toward the middle of the road to avoid a double-parked car, and he drove precariously close to an oncoming cable car on which Norma Peterson was riding.

Denver's mind was on both the problems with his client and his wife's ire, and he did not see Peterson, who was clumsily dismounting from the cable car in front of him. Peterson slipped on the wet pavement into the path of Denver's automobile, and she was directly struck before Denver could even apply his brakes.

Peterson suffered a broken back resulting in paralysis from the waist down. She was 40 years old at the time of the mishap. Peterson, who was a successful patent attorney at the time of the accident with Denver, has adapted herself well to her present condition and she is currently able to conduct her business as effectively as ever. However, one month ago, her husband instituted marital dissolution proceedings. She contends that this was brought on by her paralyzed condition.

Peterson has sued Denver for $5,000,000. Her medical expenses and lost earnings total about $250,000. The State of California is a comparative negligence jurisdiction. Any settlement figure agreed upon must be paid to Peterson immediately.

CONFIDENTIAL INFORMATION—PETERSON ATTORNEYS

You are aware that on the night of the accident, Peterson had been drinking heavily at a bar with a favorite male associate from her office. She had not intended to leave the cable car where she did, but, in her intoxicated state, had fallen off the car and slipped on the wet pavement into the path of Denver's automobile. Nevertheless, you have located an apparently reliable witness who is positive that Denver was speeding and swerving sharply at the moment he struck Peterson. You have suspicions that Denver may have consumed several drinks too many before he commenced his drive home, but you have not been able to substantiate this fact.

You have been informed that Mr. Peterson had been planning to dissolve his marriage prior to the accident due to his wife's extra-marital affairs, and you know that her injury did not precipitate this action. In fact, Peterson's disability may have precluded his filing for dissolution at an earlier time.

Peterson, who is reputed to be a solid citizen, is terrified of the adverse consequences that might be caused to her lucrative practice should her clients learn of her drinking and "dating" proclivities. She has thus decided *not* to press her suit against Denver to trial. She would like to recover at least $250,000 to cover her medical expenses and lost earnings, and would be pleased to recover any amount above that figure. She is presently earning $175,000 per year.

Since Peterson does not wish to take this case to trial, you will automatically be placed at the **bottom** of Plaintiff groups if you fail to reach any agreement. If you achieve a settlement, your group placement will be determined by the amount of money Peterson is to receive.

CONFIDENTIAL INFORMATION—DENVER ATTORNEYS

You know that your client had been drinking on the night in question, but you doubt that this adversely influenced his driving ability. However, you suspect that he was driving too fast for such a damp and dark night on busy Powell Street. You also realize that Denver's mind was on his client and wife at the moment it should have been concentrating on the traffic, and you believe that a jury could conclude that he had driven negligently.

You have learned of the excellent reputation which Peterson has in the community, and you have been led to believe that her paralysis has caused her husband to sue for dissolution after 15 years of apparently blissful marriage. You have discovered from investigation that Peterson had visited a bar with one of her male associates prior to the time she had boarded the cable car on Powell Street, but she has stated that she had only stopped off after work to help him celebrate his birthday. She has denied any heavy drinking. Although you believe that she had been out quite late to have merely been engaged in a friendly birthday celebration, you have no hard evidence to refute Peterson's story.

Your client is worried about the effect any adverse publicity could have on his business, and he would like to settle the case as soon as possible. Denver has a $1,000,000 automobile insurance policy, and has the personal assets to cover an additional $1,000,000. The insurance carrier has authorized you to pay the entire $1,000,000 policy limit, and Denver has said that he is willing to provide an additional $1,000,000 cash, if necessary. He is hoping, however, that you will be able to settle this matter within the scope of his insurance coverage.

If you reach a settlement, your group placement will be determined by the amount of money you agree to pay to Peterson. If you do not achieve any settlement, you will be treated as if you lost a $2,000,000 judgment, with that $2,000,000 figure being used to determine your group placement.

TRANSCRIPT I

PLAINTIFF: So, ___, I haven't seen you in a long time. How've you been?

DEFENDANT: Fine thanks.

PLAINTIFF: Well good, good. It's been a while since we've had a case against one another hasn't it?

DEFENDANT: It really has. You're looking good.

PLAINTIFF: Well thanks, thanks. How's your family?

DEFENDANT: Fine.

PLAINTIFF: Now I know we've settled cases with one another in the past, so I was glad that we're able to meet together today because hopefully this is another one that we'll be able to resolve.

DEFENDANT: I think so. I think we should be able to get together. I think it's a case we should settle. I'm just not sure there's really much money that we should be paying, but I agree we should settle it but I think there's real problems with your case. Just let me start from the top. Is it negligent? A jury could well find there's negligence here, but I think even that's questionable. Here it is what he's doing is kind of swerving to get out of the way to get out of the way of a double parked car.

PLAINTIFF: Well and speeding too. He was going at a pretty high speed.

DEFENDANT: Yes. But whether or not he's actually negligent, I think a jury probably—I won't fight you about that—probably there's negligence, probably. I don't think it's clear. I'm more concerned that if he was negligent I think the jury could very well find that she was negligent as well. Our investigation indicates that she was drinking, getting off the trolley in kind of a sloppy manner; that to some extent—maybe fifty/fifty even—she was responsible for what happened even if he was partially responsible as well.

PLAINTIFF: Well I'm not sure I'd say it was fifty/fifty. There may be some responsibility on her part but even so I think that your client—we do have a witness who will say that your client was speeding. You know we also, after we do discovery, may find out that he had been drinking too. There are just a lot of things I think can go both ways here. But I also think that even if there was some negligence on her part it's still a case that when the jury views it, she's going to be the sympathetic party. She was the person who was injured and the sympathy's going to lie with her. Her whole life has been changed by what happened on that day. I think that's what we have to talk about compensating her for. There have just been drastic changes and what the rest of her life is going to be like. And, she was only 40

186

	when it happened so she's got quite a lifespan left here to deal with.
DEFENDANT:	I really don't disagree with that really. A payment I think is appropriate here. She would be the more sympathetic person in general. I don't think we're talking about whether we should be making any settlement but really a question of how much. Now in terms of what her damages are. From what I can understand, she had a temporary loss of business but as I understand, at least, that she's pretty much able to conduct the business as she did before. So certainly whatever lost income she had as a result of the accident, however many thousands of dollars, we would be willing to put that into the mix. So that's one thing. You also allege in the complaint, and this is really one of the big areas that we have a real concern about, that the accident somehow led to her husband filing dissolution of the marriage complaint. Our preliminary investigation indicates that may well have been something totally different and relating to what she was doing that night. Here she was very late at night, up to like 11:30 at night, out there drinking herself so if he ...
PLAINTIFF:	We can probably cut that short a little bit. She does have that claim in the complaint. I think you're right there will be a factual dispute if the case goes to trial as to what happened there, but I really see that as one of the smaller components of her damages. I think it's true that her life is very different, that she is by herself now and for someone in the type of handicapped state that she's in, I think that in and of itself kind of has an effect on how these damages affect her. But I really think the bulk of the damages here lie in what happened to her, her pain and suffering and what the rest of her life is going to be like; so I really don't think we need to spend a lot of time talking about exactly what happened on that part of it. I think the rest of the damages is what she's looking for here.
DEFENDANT:	I think we are in agreement, essentially, on what the heart of the damage is, but I think this is also relevant for her to settle from our perspective; that at least we have information, again, that she was out drinking with a male friend late at night—so therefore, both in terms of contributing to her own negligence—that she was drinking prior to this time—plus, if this thing has to go to go trial, the whole circumstances of that could impact even on the dissolution. The information we've developed could negatively hurt her in terms of when she has to deal with that proceeding as well. Even though it's not the damages we're talking about, I think that whole situation is better if we can settle it so that all of that whole situation doesn't come out here.

187

PLAINTIFF: There would be a fact question about that if it went to trial, and nobody likes to have that kind of stuff brought out if you think you could put on evidence or testimony about that but on the other hand if she is getting divorced and if that had been leading up to some thing like that for a while. She's entitled to her own life too, so as I said that's not really where we're looking for the bulk of the damages here I don't think. But, admittedly, just as with your client, testimony that he had been out drinking and driving wouldn't be good public relations for him either.

DEFENDANT: That's why I think we agree on a lot of this, but it's a two-way street—that's my whole point. We want to settle it. We'd like to resolve the thing so we see something where we don't want to have to take this case to trial. We're certainly willing to make an offer. We're certainly willing to compensate her for particularly, as you say—lost business, pain and suffering, what she's been through—and we want to be fair about that. Do you have an amount that's in your mind about what you would settle for?

PLAINTIFF: I think if the case went to the jury it could be worth a couple of million dollars. You see cases like this where someone has this kind of severe injury and juries want to compensate. They, I think in a case like this, would want to award her substantial damages and I think it could clearly be in the 2 million dollar range.

DEFENDANT: Well but again it could also be a lot less. I see this thing very different from that. I see this thing as something which it's possible that a jury could be granting two million dollars, you know in that range, but it could also be factoring in whatever percentage they think she's responsible whether they reduce whatever injuries she has by 50 percent or 30 percent, that she becomes less sympathetic if we're able to totally develop this evidence that she is also not exemplary in this manner; that she's been able to keep up her business the same as before—that that's a temporary loss.

PLAINTIFF: I think that's true but I also think there are other life time damages that could even be monetary. For example, the house that she's in now, there were certain modifications that had to be made to accommodate her but it's certainly not an ideal situation for her. She's probably going to have to find some place that's just more accessible to her. Transportation is a big problem. It's much more expensive for her just to carry out the normal daily living activities. And I agree she has adjusted well. Not everybody could adjust the way that she has adjusted in terms of her work but that still leaves a lot out there to be compensated for.

DEFENDANT: And I agree with that in terms of those types of adjustments. If we're going to reach a settlement, we should fairly compensate her for that, but I'm more thinking in the range of three or four hundred thousand dollars—reflecting lost business, a multiple of what her medical expenses had been so far and the fact that even if there is, hypothetically, if a jury found there was two million dollars worth of damages and you even factor that down by the comparative negligence standard—you know if they say 50 percent—you're looking at perhaps tops or even a million taking your chances at a jury trial with all the hassle that would be to her as well as our client, I agree with you on that. So we do have a strong desire to settle it, but I think—we think—more of the three, four, perhaps five hundred thousand dollar range not the two million dollar range.

PLAINTIFF: I think when you're talking down anything $500,000 dollars or below, it's hard for me to even talk to her about that at this point. Given the out-of-pocket damages that she's had and the other modifications that it's likely that she will have to make, I think that that figure doesn't come close to what she would really deserve to get out of this. So I mean I think you're going to have to do better than that.

DEFENDANT: Five hundred is not our final number. I'm authorized to go somewhat above that but two million dollars is out of the ballpark of what I can do. We can go above that. If we can get somewhere in that ballpark—$600,000, $665,000—in that type of ballpark—if you push me $700,000 that's the type of thing I am authorized to do. We could do a deal on that basis.

PLAINTIFF: I just think it's going to be a bit difficult. When I talk to her, I told her that I think that a couple million is what a jury might come back with; and explained to her that there may be some facts that would come out, perhaps negatively impacting on her case, and there could be some kind of sharing of the negligence award, but I really think taking all of those things into account for her to get $1.5 million would not be unreasonable.

DEFENDANT: Well you know I think we are getting close to what we can do. I can put even a million on the table right now in terms of what we could do. We're getting real close. Again, a million and a half is just—when you factor in everything you've said—it seems a little high. I think we're getting close. Is there a bottom line that we could actually wrap this thing up with? I could go a $1 million, $1.1 million.

PLAINTIFF: Well, the old lawyer's remedy for everything—split the difference, $1,250,000.

DEFENDANT: [Nods affirmatively and shakes Plaintiff's hand.]

189

TRANSCRIPT II

PLAINTIFF: Hi _____. It's good to see you again. How are you doing?

DEFENDANT: Nice to see you, _____.

PLAINTIFF: Trust that maybe we can reach some resolution in the Peterson/Denver case today. Trusting that can maybe talk about a possible settlement.

DEFENDANT: My client has authorized me to come and listen in the hope that we can reach some sort of agreement. Obviously I'll have to talk with my client about it afterwards, but I'm fairly certain that my client would accept any recommendation that I made. So, I'd be happy to listen to any proposal you have to make.

PLAINTIFF: Terrific. I think it would be useful at this point to review the facts a little bit here. And, as you are aware, given our extensive conversations, my client—Ms. Peterson—who is a practicing patent attorney, was and is permanently paralyzed from the waist down as a result of being hit by the defendant in his automobile. The defendant's automobile in fact hit my client and resulted in her becoming a paraplegic. Needless to say, this has been pretty difficult for her. She has extensive medical expenses and also substantial lost earnings. The specials here are $25,000 [$250,000?] and I think the other thing that we're going to need factor in here is what her life looks like down the line. The reality is she will probably have to have personal care attendants, perhaps an automobile equipped for her use and there's a total revamping of her life that will have to occur. This has even impacted her marriage quite substantially. Her husband has filed for dissolution of the marriage, as a result, she believes, of her physical condition. So, in light of that, you know that our complaint is for $5 million, and I, frankly, don't see going too far below that in looking at a settlement. I don't know what your thoughts are about that but we can certainly chat some more about your perspectives.

DEFENDANT: You say you don't consider going too far below that. How far below that do you consider going?

PLAINTIFF: Well, frankly, I think that we're probably looking, realistically—given the extensive possible future medicals—at about $4 million realistically.

DEFENDANT: Let me write that down, because I don't want to forget that. Let me just characterize the facts as I understand them so that we can maybe make sure, as much as possible, that we have the same facts because, obviously, if we end up in trial the facts are going to come out for our respective clients ...

PLAINTIFF: Without a doubt true.

DEFENDANT: ... the best that we can have them come out. It is true that your client has been injured and it is true that my

190

client was driving the car which collided with your client and resulted in the injury. However, the rest of it seems, to me, entirely unclear as to first, how much my client—as opposed to your client—was at fault. It's my understanding that your client actually slipped and fell in the path of my client's car, so it's not as if she was walking across the street within a legally confined crosswalk and he ran through the crosswalk and ran her down. That's not what happened. Also, and perhaps more importantly in this case were it to go to trial, is the rather messy question as to what damages she would be entitled to beyond medical expenses and lost earnings. As I understand it, while she has suffered injury from this accident, it is also true that she continues to work at her profession which is that of an attorney and continues to make money just as well as she did before, so I have a hard time seeing that she's going to suffer any in terms of lost earnings in the future. As to the issue of her relationship with her husband, that seems to me to be the really messy part because it's less than clear to me that whatever she's lost with her husband was that solid to begin with. Now, again, I don't know the information your client shared with you. It's my understanding that she was out—it was a social evening—and she was out rather late with a gentleman that she worked with and we have not done any discovery yet and that hasn't been gone into but it certainly appears to me that the marriage that she had with her husband wasn't all that sound, and perhaps she hasn't lost all that much. Now we're sitting here in negotiations—just between you and me . . .

PLAINTIFF: Sure.

DEFENDANT: talking about this and we're not at a trial but, obviously, if we were at a trial all that would come out. So those are kind of the facts as I see them and seeing them in that way, as I say, that leads me to believe that were we to end up at trial it would be a very messy business for both sides.

PLAINTIFF: I agree with you that the goal here is that a trial should be avoided if it is at all possible. And, it's obviously a little bit difficult because we've not had the opportunity to do a complete discovery. But, our research does reveal that there is at least one possible very reliable witness that would testify, we believe, that the defendant was speeding when he traveled up the hill and that he also swerved sharply before actually striking Ms. Peterson. And it also appears that he was attempting to avoid a car that was doubled parked and it seems to me, that under the circumstances, going up a steep portion of Powell Street on a Friday night—it was dark, in the rain—that greater precaution could have been taken on the part of your client to proceed with caution in approaching the cable car. The other issue, I think, with respect to the damages here, I think really the emphasis really should be placed on the fact that my client is in fact paralyzed from the waist down, which is obviously very traumatic. The impact on her life is extraordinary—quite extreme. And the fact that she continues to practice her profession, I don't think really has that big of a bearing and I think we would probably both agree that loosing the lower part of your body is just unimaginable. And we don't know what the future holds for her. And she will, in fact, need to have a quality of care—not to mention—unanticipated consequences as a result of the injury. So we are clearly, clearly looking at a substantial settlement here, I think. And what that number is, is certainly left up to further discussion but I don't see this as an insubstantial settlement matter.

DEFENDANT: So are you saying then that if you don't obtain the $4 million that you've just indicated here that your client is prepared to go to trial and have all of this come out at trial?

PLAINTIFF: I think there are a couple of things. My client clearly would like to avoid a trial. She wants this behind her.

DEFENDANT: Why is that?

PLAINTIFF: Needless to say, she's already been through quite a substantial medical ordeal. In addition to that, she would like to continue practicing her profession and would simply not like to spend the time involved in trial with all of the possible testimony, unknown, coming out. I mean that's just not, I think, a plausible way to address this matter. I think that there's another way to deal with it. At the same time, we have to be able to factor in what the future looks like for her. And that's simply what I'm attempting to do. So I'm not suggesting that we're locked in at $4 million, but you know I've clearly indicated that I think something substantial is going to be required now. What that means, I think, is subject to discussion. As it relates to the actually liability, I think that the reality is, and I think the evidence would bear out, that the defendant is, in fact, liable here. And, but for his actions, this accident—and my client's subsequent paralysis—would never have occurred.

DEFENDANT: We're in a comparative negligence jurisdiction. You're not saying that my client is 100% liable, are you?

PLAINTIFF: Well, it's hard to take a position otherwise, not knowing entirely the other circumstances; however, there is some evidence to suggest that my client may have slipped upon exiting the cable car. But the other perspective, with respect to that, is did the defendant have an opportunity to avert the accident? For the purposes of discussion, if we assume that the defendant may be,

PLAINTIFF: excuse me, that the plaintiff may be responsible in some way, I would say that that is not terribly significant, I mean given the comparative negligence circumstance; and 10, 15%, at the most.

DEFENDANT: Well, we're far apart there, because I would say it's at a minimum 50–50. And that's certainly the way I would approach it if I was going to trial.

PLAINTIFF: What's the basis for your 50–50 calculation?

DEFENDANT: All my client was doing was driving his car, even as if as you say, he swerved to miss another automobile. There doesn't seem to be anything wrong with that. You're client would not have been injured had she'd been more careful and not slipped and fallen from whatever it was she was riding on, I forget—the trolley, the

PLAINTIFF: The cable car.

DEFENDANT: the cable car. So there would have been no injury at all. So it's hard for me to see how my client could be more than 50% liable. I'll tell you what. Go ahead.

PLAINTIFF: The flip side of that for me is just sort of understanding that your client is going up a hill, averts a doubly parked car, sees a trolley coming—a cable car coming—and wouldn't be more careful. I somehow have difficulty with the 50–50 comparison. I would be willing to consider even a 70–30 option but 50–50 under the circumstances just seems quite extreme to me.

DEFENDANT: Well, obviously, you would hope that you got a juror who would see it your way; and I would hope that I got a juror that would see it mine; and what we're trying to do here today, I guess, is avoid having a trial if we can and maybe we're not going to be able to do that. Certainly, $4 million is way too high. My client—here's what my client would be willing to do in addition to the $250,000, which is given in medical expenses and lost earnings—is a million on top of that. If we can come to that as an agreement, I can recommend to my client and we can settle it today.

PLAINTIFF: I'd like to consider a brief counter to that, given the fact that we're a little bit apart on this comparative negligence issue. And I think I'd like to counter that at a million and a quarter above. So, at this point I think we're looking at a million and a half if my calculation is correct. I don't know if that's something that you can take back to your client but I think that that would be . . .

DEFENDANT: One and a half million?

PLAINTIFF: Right.

DEFENDANT: O.K. Now, are you saying? I mean I feel like my client should have some—I mean even if we go the 70–30 route, in terms of the comparative fault—I feel like my

	client, there should be some recognition that my client wasn't totally at fault.
PLAINTIFF:	Well, I think the 30–70 accomplishes that goal.
DEFENDANT:	O.K. So you think that at a million and a half we have accomplished the 70–30 goal. How about a million and a quarter?
PLAINTIFF:	I will certainly take that to my client.
DEFENDANT:	O.K. And I can recommend that to my client too.
PLAINTIFF:	O.K. Thank you.

BIBLIOGRAPHY

ACKERMAN, H., *Disputing Together: Conflict Resolution and the Search for Community*, 18 Ohio St. J. Disp. Res. 27 (2002).

ACUFF, Frank L., *How to Negotiate Anything with Anyone Anywhere Around the World* (American Management Assn. 1997).

ADLER, R., *Flawed Thinking: Addressing Decision Biases in Negotiation*, 20 Ohio St. J. Disp. Res. 683 (2005).

ADLER, R. & E. Silverstein, *When David Meets Goliath: Dealing with Power Differentials in Negotiations*, 5 Harv. Negot. L. Rev. 1 (2000).

ALLRED, K., *Distinguishing Best and Strategic Practices: A Framework for Managing the Dilemma Between Creating and Claiming*, 16 Negot. J. 387 (Oct. 2000).

ANDERSON, David, *Dispute Resolution: Bridging the Settlement Gap* (JAI Press 1996).

ANDERSON, Peter, *The Complete Idiot's Guide to Body Language* (ALPHA 2004).

AMERICAN BAR ASSOCIATION, *Model Code of Professional Responsibility* (1969, 1980).

ARMATO, L., *Offers of Judgment and Compromise: Turning the Tables on Your Opponent*, 55 Cal.St.B.J. 286 (July 1980).

ARROW, Kenneth, Robert Mnookin, Lee Ross, Amos Tversky & Robert Wilson, eds., *Barriers to Conflict Resolution* (W.W. Norton & Co. 1995).

AUBERT, V., *Competition and Dissensus: Two Types of Conflict and Conflict Resolution*, 7 J. Conflict Res. 26 (1963).

AXELROD, Robert, *The Evolution of Cooperation* (Basic Books 1984).

AYRES, I. & B. Nalebuff, *Common Knowledge as a Barrier to Negotiation*, 44 U.C.L.A. L. Rev. 1631 (1997).

BABCOCK, Linda & Sara Laschever, *Women Don't Ask* (Princeton Univ. Press 2003).

BACHARACH, Samuel B. & Edward J. Lawler, *Bargaining: Power, Tactics, and Outcomes* (Jossey–Bass Inc. 1981).

BAER, Harold & Aaron J. Broder, *How to Prepare and Negotiate Cases for Settlement* (Prentice–Hall, Inc. 1967).

BALACHANDRA, L., R. Bordone, C. Menkel–Meadow, P. Ringstrom & E. Sarath, *Improvisation and Negotiation: Expecting the Unexpected*, 21 Negot. J. 415 (2005).

BARKAI, J., *Teaching Negotiation and ADR: The Savvy Samurai Meets the Devil*, 75 Univ. Neb. L. Rev. 704 (1996).

BARNARD, Phyllis & Bryant Garth, *Dispute Resolution Ethics: A Comprehensive Guide* (A.B.A. Section of Disp. Res. 2002).

BARNETT, L., *Deductibility of Attorneys' Fees: New Developments,* 59 A.B.A. Jour. 661 (1973).

BARTOS, O., *How Predictable are Negotiations?* 2 J. Conflict Res. 481 (1967).

BARTOS, Otomar J., *Process and Outcome of Negotiations* (Columbia Univ. Press 1974).

BARTOS, Otomar, *Simple Model of Negotiation: A Sociological Point of View* in I. W. Zartman, *The Negotiation Process* 13 (Sage 1978).

BAZERMAN, Max & Margaret Neale, *Negotiating Rationally* (Free Press 1992).

BEIER, Ernst & Evans Valens, *People Reading* (Warner 1975).

BELLOW, Gary, *Conflict Resolution and the Lawyering Process: Materials for Clinical Teaching of Law* (1971).

BELLOW, Gary & Bea Moulton, *The Lawyering Process: Materials for Clinical Instruction in Advocacy* (Foundation Press 1978).

BELLOW, Gary & Bea Moulton, *Negotiation* (Foundation Press 1981).

BENNETT, W. Lance & Martha S. Feldman, *Reconstructing Reality in the Courtroom: Justice and Judgment in American Culture* (Rutgers Univ. Press 1981).

BERLO, D., J.B. Lemert & R.J. Mertz, *Evaluating the Acceptability of Message Sources*, 33 Pub.Op. Q. 563 (1970).

BERMANT, Gordon, Charlan Nemeth & Neil Vidmar, ed., *Psychology and the Law* (D.C. Heath and Co. 1976).

BIRDWHISTELL, Ray L., *Kinesics and Context: Essays on Body Motion Communication* (Univ. of Pennsylvania Press 1970).

BIRKE, R. & C. Fox, *Psychological Principles in Negotiating Civil Settlements*, 4 Harv. Negot. L. Rev. 1 (1999).

BLACKMUN, H., *Thoughts About Ethics*, 24 Emory L.J. 1 (1975).

BLAUSTEIN, Albert P. & Charles O. Porter, *The American Lawyer: A Summary of the Survey of the Legal Profession* (Greenwood Press 1954).

BODIN, H. S., *Civil Litigation and Trial Techniques* (Practicing Law Institute 1976).

BODINE, L., *The Case Against Guaranteed Verdict Agreements*, 29 Defense L.J. 232 (1980).

BOND, James E., *Plea Bargaining and Guilty Pleas* (Clark Boardman Co. 1978).

BORDONE, R., *Fitting the Ethics to the Forum: A Proposal for Process–Enabling Ethical Codes*, 21 Ohio St. J. Disp. Res. 1 (2005).

BORDONE, R., *Teaching Interpersonal Skills for Negotiation and for Life*, Negot. J. 377 (Oct. 2000).

BOWLES, H.R., L. Babcock & K. McGinn, *Constraints and Triggers: Situational Mechanics of Gender in Negotiation*, 89 J. Personality & Soc. Psych. 951 (2005).

BRAND, J. & J. PALMER, *Relevancy and Its Limits*, 48 Miss. L.J. 935 (1977).

BRANTON, J., *Settlement Strategy, Evaluation, and Brochures*, 12 St. Mary's L.J. 407 (1980).

BRAZIL, W., *Civil Discovery: Lawyers' Views of Its Effectiveness, Its Principal Problems and Abuses*, Amer. Bar Foundation Res. J. No. 4, 787 (1980).

BRAZIL, W., *Settling Civil Cases: What Lawyers Want From Judges*, 23 Judges J. 14 (1984).

BRETT, Jeanne, *Negotiating Globally* (Jossey–Bass 2001)

BRETT, J., W. Adair, A. Lempereur, T. Okumura, P. Skikhirev, C. Tinsley & A. Lytle, *Culture and Joint Gains in Negotiation*, 14 Negot. J. 61 (1998).

BRIGHAM, Eugene, *Financial Management Theory and Practice* (Dryden 2nd ed. 1979).

BROCKNER, Joel & Jeffrey Rubin, *Entrapment in Escalating Conflicts: A Social Psychological Analysis* (Springer–Verlag 1985).

BRODT, S. & L. Thompson, *Negotiating Teams: A Levels of Analysis Approach*, 5 Group Dynamics: Theory, Research, and Practice 208 (2001).

BROWN, B., *The Effects of Need to Maintain Face in Interpersonal Bargaining*, 4 J. Experimental Social Psych. 107 (1968).

BROWN, J., *Creativity and Problem–Solving*, 87 Marquette L. Rev. 697 (2004).

BROWN, J., *The Role of Apology in Negotiation*, 87 Marquette L. Rev. 665 (2004).

BROWN, J., *The Role of Hope in Negotiation*, 44 U.C.L.A. L. Rev. 1661 (1997).

BROWN, R., *Some Applications of the Rules of Legal Ethics* 6 Minn. L.Rev. 427 (1922).

BROWN, Steven R., *Political Subjectivity: Applications of Q Methodology in Political Science* (Yale Univ. Press 1980).

BUECHNER, Sliding Scale Agreements and the Good Faith Requirement of Settlement Negotiations, 12 Pacific L.J. 121 (1980).

BURGOON, Judee, David Buller & W. Gill Woodall, *Nonverbal Communication: The Unspoken Dialogue* (McGraw–Hill 1996).

BURTON, Lloyd, Larry Farmer, Elizabeth D. Gee, Lorie Johnson & Gerald R. Williams, *Feminist Theory, Professional Ethics, and Gender-Related Distinctions in Attorney Negotiating Styles,* 1991 J. Disp. Res. 199 (1991).

CALERO, Henry, *The Power of Nonverbal Communication* (Silver Lake Publishing 2005).

CAMP, Jim, *Start with No* (Crown Bus. 2002).

CARLIN, Jerome E., *Lawyers on Their Own: A Study of Individual Practitioners in Chicago* (Rutgers University Press 1962).

CARLIN, Jerome E., *Lawyers' Ethics: A Survey of the New York City Bar* (Russell Sage Foundation 1966).

CHURCH, Thomas W., Jr., *The Pace of Litigation in Urban Trial Courts* (National Center for State Courts 1978).

CIALDINI, Robert, *Influence: The Psychology of Persuasion* (William Morrow 1993).

Civil Trial Manual (R. M. Figg, R. C. McCollough II & J. L. Underwood reporters, updated through Jan. 1, 1976) (Joint Project of American College of Trial Lawyers and ALI–ABA Committee on Continuing Professional Education).

COCHRAN, W.T., *The Obligation to Settle Within Policy Limits*, 41 Miss.L.J. 398 (1970).

COFFIN, Royce A., *The Negotiator: A Manual for Winners* (AMACOM 1973).

COHEN, Herb, *Negotiate This* (Warner Bus. Books 2003).

COHEN, Herb, *You Can Negotiate Anything: How To Get What You Want* (Lyle Stuart, Inc. 1980).

COHEN, L. Jonathan, *The Probable and the Provable* (Clarendon Press 1977).

COHEN, L., *When People are the Means: Negotiating with Respect*, 14 Geo. J. Legal Ethics 739 (2001).

COHN, Roy, *How to Stand Up For Your Rights and Win* (Simon and Schuster 1981).

COLEMAN, N., *Teaching the Theory and Practice of Bargaining to Lawyers and Students*, 30 J. Legal Educ. (1980).

COLOSI, Thomas, *On and Off the Record: Colosi on Negotiation* (Amer. Arb. Assn. 2d ed. 2001).

COMMENT, *Avoidance of Tort Releases*, 13 West. Res. L. Rev. 768 (1962).

COMMENT, *Games Lawyers Play*, 10 Trial Lawyer's Guide 5 (Nov., 1966).

CONARD, Alfred F., James N. Morgan, Robert W. Pratt, Jr., Charles E. Voltz, & Robert L. Bombaugh, *Automobile Accident Costs and Payments: Studies in the Economics of Injury Reparation* (Univ. of Mich. Press 1964).

CONDLIN, R., *Bargaining in the Dark: The Normative Incoherence of Lawyer Dispute Bargaining Role*, 51 Md. L. Rev. 1 (1992).

CONDLIN, R., *Cases on Both Sides: Patterns of Argument in Legal Dispute–Negotiation*, 44 Md. L. Rev. 65 (1985).

COOK, Michael L. & Marcia L. Goldstein, *Settling with the Bankruptcy Trustee: More or Less Litigation?* 5 Litigation 19–22 (1978).

COULSON, Robert, *How to Stay Out of Court* (Crown Publishers, Inc. 1968).

CRAVER, C., *Clinical Negotiating Achievement as a Function of Traditional Law School Success and as a Predictor of Future Negotiating Performance*, 1986 Mo. J. Disp. Res. 63 (1986).

CRAVER, Charles B., *Effective Legal Negotiation and Settlement* (LEXIS 5th ed. 2005).

CRAVER, C., *The Impact of Gender on Clinical Negotiating Achievement*, 6 Ohio St. J. Disp. Res. 1 (1990).

CRAVER, C., *The Impact of a Pass/Fail Option of Negotiation Course Performance*, 48 J. Legal Educ. 176 (1998).

CRAVER, C., *The Impact of Student GPAs and a Pass/Fail Option on Clinical Negotiation Course Performance*, 15 Ohio St. J. Disp. Res. 373 (2000).

CRAVER, Charles, *The Intelligent Negotiator* (Prima/Crown 2002).

CRAVER, C., *Negotiation as a Distinct Area of Specialization*, 9 Amer. J. Trial Ad. 377 (1986).

CRAVER, C., *Negotiating Ethics: How to be Deceptive Without Being Dishonest/How to be Assertive Without Being Offensive*, 38 S. Tex. L. Rev. 713 (1997).

CRAVER, C., *The Negotiation Process*, 27 Amer. J. Trial Ad. 271 (2003).

CRAVER, C., *Negotiation Styles: The Impact on Bargaining Transactions*, Disp. Res. J. 48 (Feb.-Apr. 2003).

CRAVER, C., *Negotiation Techniques*, 24 Trial 65 (June 1988).

CRAVER, C., *Race and Negotiation Performance*, Disp. Res. Mag. 22 (Fall 2001).

CRAVER, C., *When Parties Can't Settle*, Judges J. 4 (Winter 1987).

CRAVER, C. & D. Barnes, *Gender, Risk Taking, and Negotiation Performance*, 5 Mich. J. Gender & Law 299 (1999).

CROSBY, Philip, *The Art of Getting Your Own Sweet Way* (McGraw–Hill 1981).

CROWLEY, Thomas, *Settle It Out of Court* (John Wiley & Sons 1994).

CURTIS, C., *The Ethics of Advocacy*, 4 Stanford L. Rev. 3 (1951).

DAVIDSON, M. N. & L. Greenhalgh, *The Role of Emotion in Negotiation: The Impact of Anger and Race*, 7 Research on Negot. In Organizations 5 (1999).

DAVIS, C., *Comparative Negligence, Comparative Contribution, and Equal Protection in the Trial and Settlement of Multiple Defendant Product Cases*, 10 Ind. L.Rev. 831 (1977).

DAWSON, Roger, *Secrets of Power Negotiating* (Career Press 2d ed. 2001).

DAWSON, Roger, *You Can Get Anything You Want* (Simon & Schuster 1985).

DEAUX, Kay, *The Behavior of Women and Men* (Wadsworth Publishing Co. 1976).

DEELEY, E., *Denying Contribution Between Tortfeasors in Arizona: A Call for Change*, 1977 Ariz. St. L.J. 673 (1977).

DEUTSCH, M., *Trust and Suspicion*, 2 J. Conflict Res. 265 (1958).

DIETMEYER, Brian & Rob Kaplan, *Strategic Negotiation* (Dearborn Trade Pub. 2004).

DIMITRIUS, Jo–Ellan & Mark Mazzarella, *Reading People* (Random House 1998).

DINWIDDY, Caroline, *Elementary Mathematics for Economists* (Oxford 1967).

DOBBS, D.B., *Conclusiveness of Personal Injury Settlements: Basic Problems*, 47 N.C. L. Rev. 665 (1963).

DOLE, R., *The Settlement of Class Actions for Damages*, 71 Colum. L. Rev. 971 (1971).

DOUGLAS, Ann, *Industrial Peacemaking* (Columbia Univ. Press 1962).

DOUGLASS, John Jay, ed., *Ethical Considerations in Prosecution* (The National College of District Attorneys, Inc. 1977).

DRINKER, H. S., *Legal Ethics* (Columbia Univ. Press 1962).

DRUCKMAN, D., *Departures in Negotiation: Extensions and New Directions*, 20 Negot. J. 185 (April 2004).

DRUCKMAN, D., *Prenegotiation Experience and Dyadic Conflict Resolution in a Bargaining Situation*, 4 J. Experimental Social Psych. 367 (1968).

DRUCKMAN, Daniel, *Negotiations: Social Psychological Perspectives* (Sage Publications 1977).

DRUCKMAN, Daniel, *Boundary Role Conflict: Negotiation as Dual Responsiveness* in I.W. Zartman, *The Negotiation Process* (1978).

DRUCKMAN, D., R. Rozelle & J. Baxter, *Nonverbal Communication* (Sage 1982).

DUPLACK, R., *Post-Accident Repairs and Offers of Compromise: Shaping Exclusionary Rules to Public Policy*, 10 Loyola Univ. of Chi. L. J. 487 (1979).

EDGAR, J. H., *Procedural Aspects of Settlement: An Overview of Texas Law*, 12 St. Mary's L.J. 279 (1980).

EDWARDS, Harry & James J. White, *The Lawyer as a Negotiator* (West Publishing Co. 1977).

EISENBERG, M., *Private Ordering Through Negotiation: Dispute–Settlement and Rulemaking*, 89 Harv. L.Rev. 4 (1976).

EISER, J. Richard, *Cooperation and Competition Between Individuals* in *Introducing Social Psychology*, (Henri Tajfel & Colin Fraser, eds., Penguin 1978).

EKMAN, Paul, *Telling Lies* (Norton 1992).

EPSTEIN, L., *Cyber E–Mail Negotiation vs. Traditional Negotiation: Will Cyber Technology Supplant Traditional Means of Settling Litigation?* 36 Tulsa L.J. 839 (2001).

ERICKSON, W., *New Directions in the Administration of Justice: Responses to the Pound Conference*, 64 A.B.A.J. 48 (Jan. 1978).

FARAGO, J., *Intractable Cases: The Role of Uncertainty in the Concept of Law*, 55 N.Y. U. L. Rev. 157 (1980).

FASSINA, N., *Constraining a Principal's Choice: Outcome Versus Behavior Contingent Agency Contracts in Representative Negotiations*, 20 Negot. J. 435 (2004).

FAST, Julius, *Body Language* (Simon & Schuster 1970).

FAURE, Guy & Jeffrey Rubin, *Culture and Negotiation* (Sage Publications 1993).

FELDER, Raoul, *Bare-Knuckle Negotiation* (John Wiley & Sons 2004).

FINKELSTEIN, Michael O., *Quantitative Methods in Law: Studies in the Application of Mathematical Probability and Statistics to Legal Problems* (The Free Press 1978).

FIRTH, Alan, *The Discourse of Negotiation* (Pergamon 1995).

FISHER, Roger & Daniel Shapiro, *Beyond Reason: Using Emotions as You Negotiate* (Viking 2005).

FISHER, Roger, William Ury, and Bruce Patton, *Getting To Yes: Negotiating Agreement Without Giving In* (Penguin 1991).

FISHER, Roger, Elizabeth Kopelman & Andrea Schneider, *Beyond Machiavelli* (Harv. Univ. Press 1994).

FISHER, Walter R. & Edward M. Sayles, *Perspectives on Argumentation* (Scott, Foresman & Co. 1966).

FISS, O., *Against Settlement*, 93 Yale L.J. 1073 (1984).

FOLBERG, Jay & Dwight Golann, *Lawyer Negotiation Theory, Practice, and Law* (Aspen 2006).

FORDE, K., *Settlement of the Class Action*, 5 Litigation 23 (Fall, 1978).

FORESTER, J., *Responding to Critical Moments with Humor, Recognition, and Hope*, 20 Negot. J. 221 (April 2004).

FORGAS. J., *On Feeling Good and Getting Your Way: Mood Effects on Negotiator Cognition and Bargaining Strategies*, 74 J. Personality & Soc. Psych. 565 (1998).

FOSKETT, David, *The Law and Practice of Compromise* (Sweet & Maxwell 1980).

FOTHERINGHAM, Wallace C., *Perspectives on Persuasion* (Allyn and Bacon Inc. 1966).

FOX, *Settlement: Helping the Lawyers to Fulfill Their Responsibility*, 53 F.R.D. 129 (1971).

FRANKEL, M., *The Reform of the Adversary Process*, 48 Univ. Chicago L. Rev. 478 (1981).

FRANKLIN, M., R. Chanin & I. Mark, *Accidents, Money, and the Law: A Study of the Economics of Personal Injury Litigation*, 61 Colum. L. Rev. 1 (1961).

FRESHMAN, C., A. Hayes & G. Feldman, *The Lawyer–Negotiator as Mood Scientist: What We Know and Don't Know About How Mood Relates to Successful Negotiation*, 2992 J. Disp. Res. 13 (2002).

FREUND, James, *Smart Negotiating* (Simon & Schuster 1992).

FRICKE, Charles W., *Planning and Trying Cases* (West Publishing Co. 1957).

FRIEDMAN, R. & D. Shapiro, *Deception and Mutual Gains Bargaining: Are They Mutually Exclusive?* 11 Negot. J. 243 (1995).

GALANTER, M., *A World Without Trials?* 2006 J. Disp. Res. 7 (2006).

GALINSKY, A. & T. Mussweiler, *First Offers as Anchors: The Role of Perspective–Taking and Negotiator Focus*, 81 J. Personality & Soc. Psych. 657 (2001).

GAMSON, William, *Power and Discontent* (Dorsey Press 1968).

GELFAND, Michele & Jeanne Brett, *The Handbook of Negotiation and Culture* (Stanford Bus. Books 2004).

GERGEN, Kenneth, *The Psychology of Behavior Exchange* (Addison–Wesley 1969).

GIFFORD, D., *A Context–Based Theory of Strategy Selection in Legal Negotiation*, 46 Ohio St. L.J. 41 (1985).

GIFFORD, Donald, *Legal Negotiation: Theory and Applications* (West Publishing 1989).

GIFFORD, D., *The Synthesis of Legal Counseling and Negotiation Models: Preserving Client–Centered Advocacy in the Negotiation Context*, 34 U.C.L.A. L. Rev. 811 (1987).

GILSON, R. & R. Mnookin, *Disputing Through Agents: Cooperation and Conflict Between Lawyers in Litigation*, 94 Columbia L. Rev. 509 (1994).

GOLANN, D., *Death of a Claim: The Impact of Loss Reactions on Bargaining*, 20 Negot. J. 539 (2004).

GOLDMAN, Alvin, *Settling for More* (B.N.A. 1991).

GOLDSTEIN, C. & S. Weber, *The Art of Negotiating*, 37 N.Y. Law School L. Rev. 325 (1992).

GOLEMAN, Daniel, *Emotional Intelligence* (Bantam 1995).

GOODPASTER, Gary, *A Guide to Negotiation and Mediation* (Transnational 1997).

GOODPASTER, G., *A Primer on Competitive Bargaining*, 1996 J. Disp. Res. 325 (1996).

GOSNEY, C., *How Insurance Companies Can Reduce Litigation Costs*, F.I.C. Quarterly (Spring 1981).

GOULDNER, Alvin W., *The Norm of Reciprocity: A Preliminary Statement*, 25 Amer. Sociological Rev. 2 (1960).

GRANELLI, J., *Structuring the Settlement: Piecemeal Payments Gain in Popularity*, National Law Journal (Feb. 16, 1981).

GRAY, B., *Negotiating with Your Nemesis*, 19 Negot. J. 299 (2003).

GREENHALGH, L., *The Case Against Winning in Negotiations*, 3 Negot. J. 167 (1987).

GROSS, S. & K. Syverud, *Getting to No: A Study of Settlement Negotiations and the Selection of Cases for Trial*, 90 Mich. L. Rev. 319 (1991).

GUERNSEY, Thomas, *A Practical Guide to Negotiation* (NITA 1996).

GULLIVER, P. H., *Negotiations as a Mode of Dispute Settlement: Towards a General Model*, 7 Law & Society Rev. 669 (1973).

GUTHRIE, C., *Better Settle than Sorry: The Regret Aversion Theory of Litigation Behavior*, 1999 Univ. of Illinois L. Rev. 43 (1999).

GUTHRIE, C., *Framing Frivolous Litigation: A Psychological Theory*, 67 Univ. of Chicago L. Rev. 163 (2000).

GUTHRIE, C., *Panacea or Pandora's Box: The Costs of Options in Negotiation*, 88 Iowa L. Rev. 601 (2003).

GUTHRIE, C., *Principles of Influence in Negotiation*, 87 Marquette L. Rev. 829 (2004).

GUTHRIE, C., *Prospect Theory, Risk Preference, and the Law*, 97 Northwestern Univ. L. Rev. 1115 (2003).

GUTHRIE, C. & D. Sally, *The Impact of the Impact Bias on Negotiation*, 87 Marquette L. Rev. 817 (2004).

GUTTERMAN, Sheila, ed., *Collaborative Law: A New Model for Dispute Resolution* (Bradford Publishing 2004).

HALL, Edward, *The Hidden Dimension* (Anchor 1966).

HALL, Edward, *Silent Language* (Anchor 1973).

HAMMOND, John, Ralph Keeney & Howard Raifffa, *Smart Choices* (Harvard Bus. School Press 1999).

HARDINGHAM, I.J., *Setting Aside Agreements of Compromise*, 8 Melb.U. L. Rev. 151 (1971).

HARNETT, D., L. Cummings & W. Hamner, *Personality, Bargaining Style and Payoff on Bilateral Monopoly Bargaining Among European Managers*, 36 Sociometry 325 (1973).

HARPER, Robert G., Arthur N. Weins & Joseph D. Matarazzo, *Nonverbal Communication: The State of the Art* (John Wiley & Sons 1978).

HARTWELL, S., *Understanding and Dealing with Deception in Legal Negotiation*, 6 Ohio St. J. Disp. Res. 171 (1991).

HARVARD BUSINESS ESSENTIALS, *Negotiation* (Harv. Bus. School Press 2003).

HAUSSMANN, B., *The ABA Ethical Guidelines for Settlement Negotiations: Exceeding the Limits of the Adversarial Ethic*, 89 Cornell L. Rev. 1218 (2004).

HAVIGHURST, H., *Problems Concerning Settlement Agreements*, 50 N.W.U. L. Rev. 599 (1958).

HAVIGHURST, H., *The Effect upon Settlements of Mutual Mistake as to Injuries*, 12 Defense L.J. 1 (1963).

HAVIGHURST, H., *Principles of Construction and the Parol Evidence Rule Applied to Releases*, 60 N.W.U. L. Rev. 599 (1965).

HENDERSON, R., *Periodic Payments of Bodily Injury Awards*, 66 A.B.A. J. (June 1980).

HERMAN, G. Nicholas, *Plea Bargaining* (Lexis Nexis 2d ed. 2004).

HERMAN, G. Nicholas, Jean Cary & Joseph Kennedy, *Legal Counseling and Negotiating: A Practical Approach* (Lexis Nexis 2001).

HERMANN, Philip J., *Better Settlements Through Leverage* (Aqueduct Books 1965).

HERMAN, M. & N. Kogan, *Effects of Negotiators' Personalities on Negotiating Behavior* in *Negotiations: Psychological Perspectives* 247 (D. Druckman, ed., Sage Publications 1977).

HERRINGTON, *Compromise v. Contest in Legal Controversies*, 16 A.B.A. J. 795 (1938).

HINDE, Robert A., ed., *Non-Verbal Communication* (Cambridge Univ. Press 1972).

HOGAN, Kevin, *The Psychology of Persuasion* (Pelican Publishing 1996).

HOLTOM, Robert B. *Restraints on Underwriting: Risk Selection, Discrimination and the Law* (The National Underwriter Co. 1979).

HORNWOOD, Sanford, *Systematic Settlements* (Lawyers Cooperative Publishing Co., Bancroft–Whitney Co. 1972).

HYMAN, J., *Trial Advocacy and Methods of Negotiation: Can Good Trial Advocates Be Wise Negotiators?* 34 U.C.L.A. L. Rev. 863 (1987).

IKLE, Fred Charles, *Every War Must End* (Columbia University Press 1971).

IKLE, Fred Charles, *How Nations Negotiate* (Harper and Row 1964).

ILICH, John, *The Art and Skill of Successful Negotiation* (Prentice–Hall, Inc. 1973).

ILICH, John, *Dealbreakers and Breakthroughs* (John Wiley & Sons 1992).

ILICH, John, *Power Negotiating* (Addison–Wesley 1980).

JANDT, Fred, *Win-Win Negotiating: Turning Conflict into Agreement* (John Wiley & Sons 1985).

JOHNSTONE, Quintin & Dan Hopson, Jr., *Lawyers and Their Work: An Analysis of the Legal Profession in the United States and England* (Bobbs–Merrill Co. 1967).

KAHN, A. & J. Kohls, *Determinants of Toughness in Dyadic Bargaining*, 35 Sociometry 305 (1972).

KAHNEMAN, D., *New Challenges to the Rationality Assumption*, 3 Legal Theory 105 (1997).

KAHNEMAN, D. & A. Tversky, *Prospect Theory: An Analysis of Decision Under Risk*, 47 Econometrica 263 (1979).

KAPLOW, Louis & Steven Shavell, *Decision Analysis, Game Theory, and Information* (Foundation Press 2004).

KARRASS, Chester L., *Give & Take: The Complete Guide To Negotiating Strategies and Tactics* (Thomas Y. Crowell Co. 1974).

KARRASS, Chester L., *The Negotiating Game* (World Publishing Co. 1970).

KARRASS, Chester L., *A Study of the Relationship of Negotiator Skill and Power as Determinants of Negotiation Outcome* (Xerox University Microfilms 1968).

KELNER, Milton, *What is Truth?* 24 Trial Law. Guide 264 (Summer 1980).

KEMPF, D., *Rule 68 Offers of Judgment: An Underused Tool*, 7 Litigation, No. 3, 39 (1981).

KENNEDY, Gavin, *Kennedy on Negotiation* (Gower 1998).

KING, E. & D. SEARS, *The Ethical Aspects of Compromise, Settlement and Arbitration*, 25 Rocky Mountain L. Rev. 454 (1952).

KNIGHT, Frank H., *Risk, Uncertainty and Profit* (Univ. of Chicago Press 1921).

KOLB, D. & L. Putnam, *Negotiation Through a Gender Lens* in *The Handbook of Dispute Resolution* 136 (M. Moffitt & R. Bordone, eds.) (Jossey–Bass 2005).

KOLB, Deborah & Judith Williams, *Everyday Negotiation* (Jossey–Bass 2003).

KOLB, Deborah & Judith Williams, *The Shadow Negotiation* (Simon & Schuster 2000).

KOROBKIN, R., *A Positive Theory of Legal Negotiation*, 88 Georgetown L.J. 1789 (2000).

KOROBKIN, R., *Aspirations and Settlement*, 88 Cornell L. Rev. 1 (2002).

KOROBKIN, R., *The Endowment Effect and Legal Analysis*, 97 Northwestern Univ. L. Rev. 1227 (2003).

KOROBKIN, R., *The Role of Law in Settlement* in *The Handbook of Dispute Resolution* 254 (M. Moffitt & R. Bordone, eds.) (Jossey–Bass 2005).

KOROBKIN, R. & C. Guthrie, *Heuristics and Biases at the Bargaining Table*, 87 Marquette L. Rev. 795 (2004).

KOROBKIN, R. & C. Guthrie, *Opening Offers and Out of Court Settlement: A Little Moderation Might Not Go a Long Way*, 10 Ohio St. J. Disp. Res. 1 (1994).

KOROBKIN, R. & C. Guthrie, *Psychological Barriers to Litigation Settlement: An Experimental Approach*, 93 Mich. L. Rev. 107 (1994).

KOROBKIN, R., M. Moffitt & N. Welsh, *The Law of Bargaining*, 87 Marquette L. Rev. 839 (2004).

KRASH, A., *Professional Responsibility to Clients and the Public Interest*, 55 Chicago B. Rec. 31 (1974).

KRAY, L. & L. Babcock, *Gender in Negotiations: A Motivated Social Cognitive Analysis* in *Negotiation Theory and Research* 203 (L. Thompson, ed.) (Psychology Press 2006).

KRAUSE, C., *Structured Settlements for Tort Victims*, 66 A.B.A.J. (December 1980).

KRITZER, Herbert, *Let's Make a Deal* (Univ. of Wisconsin Press 1991).

KRIVIS, Jeffrey, *Improvisational Negotiation* (Jossey–Bass 2006).

KURTZBERG, T. & V.H. Medveck, *Can We Negotiate and Still Be Friends?* 15 Negot. J. 355 (1999).

LANDE, J., *Possibilities for Collaborative Law: Ethics and Practice of Lawyer Disqualification and Process Control in a New Model of Lawyering*, 64 Ohio St. L. J. 1315 (2003).

LANDSMAN, S., *The Decline of the Adversary System: How the Rhetoric of Swift and Certain Justice has Affected Adjudication in American Courts*, 29 Buffalo L. Rev. 487 (1980).

LATZ, Martin, *Gain the Edge: Negotiating to Get What You Want* (St. Martin's Press 2004).

LAWLESS, W., *Why Litigants Hate Lawyers*, 17 Judges J., No. 3, 4 (Summer 1978).

LAX, David & James Sebenius, *3–D Negotiation* (Harvard Bus. School Press 2006).

LAX, David & James Sebenius, *The Manager as Negotiator: Bargaining for Cooperation and Competitive Gain* (Free Press 1986).

LEBOW, Richard, *The Art of Bargaining* (Johns Hopkins Univ. Press 1996).

LEHMAN, W., *The Pursuit of a Client's Interest*, 77 Mich. L. Rev. 1078 (1979).

Le POOLE, Samfrits, *Never Take No For an Answer* (Kogan Page 1991).

LEVIN, Edward, *Negotiating Tactics* (Fawcett 1980).

LEVIN, S., *Practical, Ethical, and Legal Considerations Involved in the Settlement of Cases in Which Statutory Attorney's Fees are Authorized*, 1980 Clearinghouse Review 515 (1980).

LEVINSON, Conrad, Mark Smith & Orvel Wilson, *Guerilla Negotiating* (John Wiley & Sons 1999).

LEWICKI, Roy, Joseph Litterer, John Minton & David Saunders, *Negotiation* (Irwin 1994).

LEWIS, David, *Power Negotiating Tactics and Techniques* (Prentice–Hall 1981).

LINDSEY, R., *Documentation of Settlements*, 27 Ark. L. Rev. 27 (1973).

LINDSKOLD, S., *Trust Development, the GRIT Proposal, and the Effects of Conciliatory Acts on Conflict and Cooperation*, 85 Psychological Bull. 4 (1978).

LISNEK, Paul, *A Lawyer's Guide to Effective Negotiation and Mediation* (West Publishing 1993).

LIVINGSTON, A., *Settlements in Multiple Tortfeasor Controversies—Texas Law*, 10 St. Mary's L.J. 75 (1978).

LONDON, Harvey & John E. Exner, Jr., eds., *Dimensions of Personality* (John Wiley & Sons, Inc. 1978).

LONGENECKER, R. R., *Some Hints on the Trial of a Lawsuit* (Lawyer's Cooperative Publishing Co. 1927).

LOWENTHAL, G., *A General Theory of Negotiation Process, Strategy, and Behavior*, 31 Kansas L. Rev. 69 (1982).

LYNCH, E., *Settlement of Civil Cases: A View from the Bench*, 5 Litigation 57 (1978).

LYTTLE, A., J. Brett & D. Shapiro, *The Strategic Use of Interests, Rights, and Power to Resolve Disputes*, 15 Negot. J. 31 (1999).

MACAULAY, Stewart & Elaine Walster, *Legal Structures and Restoring Equity* in *Law, Justice and the Individual in Society,* (Tapp, June Lovin & Levine, Felice J., eds., Holt, Rinehart and Winston 1977).

MACAULAY, S., *Non-Contractual Relations in Business: A Preliminary Study*, 28 Am.Soc.Rev. 55 (1963).

MACCOBY, Michael, *The Gamesman* (Bantam 1977, 1978).

MACDUFF, I., *Your Place or Mine? Culture, Time, and Negotiation* 22 Negot. J. 31 (2006).

MACHIAVELLI, Niccolo, *The Prince and the Discourses* (Random House, Inc., 1950).

MACK, W., *Settlement Procedures in the U.S. Court of Appeals: A Proposal*, 1 Justice System J. 17 (March 1975).

MACNEIL, I., *Primer on Contract Planning*, 48 So. Cal. L. Rev. 627 (1975).

MALONE, Michael, *Psychetypes* (Pocket Books 1977).

MARU, Olavi, *Research on the Legal Profession: A Review of Work Done* (Amer. Bar Foundation 1972).

MATHENY, A., *Negotiation and Plea Bargaining Models: An Organizational Perspective*, 2 Law & Policy Quarterly 267 (July 1980).

MATHEWS, R., *Negotiation: A Pedagogical Challenge*, 6 J. Legal Ed. 93 (1953).

MAYNARD, Douglas, *Inside Plea Bargaining* (Plenum 1984).

McCARTER, C. & B. Greenley, *Business Valuations*, 16 Tulsa L.J. 41 (1980).

McCORMICK, Charles Tilford, *Evidence* (West Publishing Co., 2d ed. by E. W. Cleary 1972).

McCORMICK, Mark., *On Negotiating* (Dove Books 1995).

208

McILVAINE, *The Value of an Effective Pretrial Conference*, 28 F.R.D. 158 (1961).

McWHINNEY, Edward, *Conflict and Compromise: International Law and World Order in a Revolutionary Age* (Holmes & Meier Publishers, Inc., 1981).

MELLINGER, G., *Interpersonal Trust as a Factor in Communication*, 52 J. Abnormal Soc. Psych. 304 (1956).

MELTSNER, Michael & P. G. Schrag, *Public Interest Advocacy: Materials For Clinical Legal Education* (Little, Brown & Co. 1974).

MENDELSOHN, G., *Lawyers as Negotiators*, 1 Harv. Negot. L. Rev. 139 (1996).

MENKEL–MEADOW, C., *The Art and Science of Problem–Solving Negotiation*, Trial 48 (June 1999).

MENKEL–MEADOW, C., *Toward Another View of Legal Negotiation: The Structure of Problem Solving*, 31 U.C.L.A. L. Rev. 754 (1984).

MENKEL–MEADOW, C. & M. Wheeler, *What's Fair: Ethics for Negotiators* (Jossey–Bass 2004).

MILLER, Lee & Jessica Miller, *A Woman's Guide to Successful Negotiating* (McGraw–Hill 2002).

MISHAN, Edward, *Economics For Social Decisions* (Praeger 1972).

MNOOKIN, R., *Strategic Barriers to Dispute Resolution: A Comparison of Bilateral and Multilateral Negotiations*, 8 Harv. Negot. L. Rev. 1 (2003).

MNOOKIN, Robert, Scott Peppet & Andrew Tulumello, *Beyond Winning: Negotiating to Create Value in Deals and Disputes* (Harvard Univ. Press/Belknap 2000).

MNOOKIN, R., S. Peppet & A. Tulumello, *The Tension Between Empathy and Assertiveness*, 12 Negot. J. 217 (1996).

MOFFITT, M., *Contingent Agreements: Agreeing to Disagree About the Future*, 87 Marquette L. Rev. 691 (2004).

MOORE, D. & J. Tomlinson, *The Use of Simulated Negotiation to Teach Substantive Law*, 21 J. Legal Ed. 579 (1969).

MORLEY, Ian & Geoffrey Stephenson, *The Social Psychology of Bargaining* (George Allen & Unwin Publishers Ltd. 1977).

MORRIS, Desmond, *Bodytalk* (Crown 1994).

MURNIGHAN, J. Kieth, *Bargaining Games* (William Morrow 1992).

NADLER, J. & D. Shestowsky, *Negotiation, Information Technology, and the Problem of the Faceless Other* in *Negotiation Research and Theory* 145 (Leigh Thompson, ed. 2006).

NADLER, J., *Rapport in Negotiation and Conflict Resolution*, 87 Marquette L. Rev. 875 (2004).

NADLER, J., *Rapport in Legal Negotiation: How Small Talk Can Facilitate E–Mail Dealmaking*, 9 Harv. Negot. L. Rev. 223 (2004).

NAGEL, S., *Attorney Time Per Case: Finding an Optimum Level*, 32 Univ. of Florida L. Rev. 424 (1980).

NAGEL, S., *The Legal Process and Decision Theory: Some Introductory Comments*, 2 Law & Policy Quarterly, 261–66 (July 1980).

NEALE, M. & A. Fragale, *Social Cognition, Attribution, and Perception in Negotiation: The Role of Uncertainty in Shaping Negotiation Processes and Outcomes* in *Negotiation Theory and Research* 27 (Leigh Thompson, ed., Psychology Press 2006).

NEAL, Richard G., *Bargaining Tactics: A Reference Manual For Public Sector Labor Negotiations* (Richard Neal Associates 1980).

NELKEN, Melissa, *Understanding Negotiation* (Anderson Publishing 2001).

NICOLSON, Sir Harold, *Diplomacy* (Oxford Univ. Press 1963).

NIERENBERG, Gerard I., *The Art of Negotiating: Psychological Strategies For Gaining Advantageous Bargains* (Cornerstone Library 1968).

NIERENBERG, Gerald I., *The Complete Negotiator* (Barnes & Noble 1996).

NIERENBERG, Gerard I., *Fundamentals of Negotiating* (Hawthorn Books, Inc. 1973).

NIERENBERG, Gerard I. & Henry H. Calero, *How To Read A Person Like A Book* (Simon & Schuster 1971).

NIERENBERG, Juliet & Irene Ross, *Women and the Art of Negotiating* (Simon & Schuster 1985).

NORTON, E., *Bargaining and the Ethic of Process*, 64 N.Y.U. L. Rev. 493 (1989).

NOTE, *Rule 68: "A 'New' Tool for Litigation,"* 1978 Duke L.J. 889 (1978).

NOTE, *An Analysis of Settlement*, 22 Stanford L.Rev. 67 (1969).

O'CONNELL, J., *Harnessing the Liability Lottery: Elective First–Party No–Fault Insurance Financed by Third–Party Tort Claims*, 1978 Wash. Univ. L. Quarterly 693 (1978).

O'DEA, D., *The Lawyer–Client Relationship Reconsidered: Methods for Avoiding Conflicts of Interest, Malpractice Liability, and Disqualification*, 48 Geo. Wash. L. Rev. 693 (1980).

O'HARA, E. & D. Yarn, *On Apology and Conscience*, 77 Wash. L. Rev. 1121 (2002).

ORR, D. & C. Guthrie, *Anchoring, Information, Expertise, and Negotiation: New Insights from Meta–Analysis*, 21 Ohio St. J. Disp. Res. 597 (2006).

OSGOOD, C., *An Alternative to War or Surrender* (Univ. of Illinois Press 1962).

PARKER, D., *Rhetoric, Ethics and Manipulation*, 5 Philosophy and Rhetoric 69 (1972).

PEASE, Allan & Barbara Pease, *The Definitive Book of Body Language* (Bantam Books 2006).

PECK, Cornelius, *Cases and Materials on Negotiation* (B.N.A. 1972).

PECK, C. and R. Fletcher, *A Course on the Subject of Negotiation*, 21 J. Legal Ed. 196 (1968).

PEPPET, S., *Lawyers' Bargaining Ethics, Contract, and Collaboration: The End of the Legal Profession and the Beginning of Professional Pluralism*, 90 Iowa L. Rev. 475 (2005).

PERDUE, J., *Is Your Case Worth Pursuing?* Case & Comment (Nov.-Dec. 1980).

PERKINS, A., *Are Two Heads Better Than One?* 71 Harv. Bus. Rev. 13 (Nov.-Dec. 1993).

PERSCHBACHER, R., *Regulating Lawyers' Negotiations*, 27 Arizona L. Rev. 75 (1985).

PETERS, *The Use of Lies in Negotiation*, 48 Ohio St. L.J. 1 (1987).

PINKLEY, Robin & Gregory Northcraft, *Get Paid What You're Worth* (St. Martins Press 2000).

PITULLA, J., T*he Ethics of Secretly Taping Phone Conversations*, A.B.A. J. 102 (Feb. 1994).

PLINER, Patricia, Lester Krames, and Thomas Alloway, eds., *Advances in the Study of Communication and Affect*, Vol. 2: *NonVerbal Communication of Aggression* (New York: Plenum Press 1975).

POSNER, Richard A., *Economic Analysis of Law* (Little, Brown and Company 1972).

PRICE, M. and H. Bitner, *Effective Legal Research* (Augustus M. Kelley 1969).

PRUITT, Dean, *Negotiation Behavior* (Academic Press 1981).

PRUITT, Dean & Jeffrey Rubin, *Social Conflict* (Random House 1986).

PUTNEM, L., *Transformations and Critical Moments in Negotiations*, 20 Negot. J. 275 (April 2004).

QUILLIAM, Susan, *Body Language* (Firefly Books 2004).

RACHLINSKI, J., *Gains, Losses, and the Psychology of Litigation*, 70 S. Cal. L. Rev. 113 (1996).

RADFORD, K. J., *Managerial Decision Making* (Reston Publishing Co. 1975).

RAIFFA, Howard, *The Art and Science of Negotiation* (Belknap/Harvard Univ. Press 1982).

RAIFFA, Howard (with J. Richardson & D. Metcalfe), *Negotiation Analysis* (Belknap/Harvard Univ. Press 2003).

RAMBERG, Bennet, *Tactical Advantages of Opening Positioning Strategies* in I. William Zartman, *The Negotiation Process* 133 (1978).

REARDON, Kathleen, *The Skilled Negotiator* (Jossey–Bass 2004).

RENFREW, C. B., *Negotiations and Judicial Scrutiny in Civil and Criminal Antitrust Cases*, 57 Chi. B. Rec. 130 (1975).

REILLY, P., *Teaching Law Students How to Feel: Using Negotiations Training to Increase Emotional Intelligence*, 21 Negot. J. 301 (2005).

RIEKE, Richard D. & Malcolm O. Sillars, *Argumentation and The Decision Making Process* (John Wiley & Sons, Inc. 1975).

RINGER, Robert, *To Be or Not To Be Intimidated? That is the Question* (M. Evans & Co. 2004).

RINGER, Robert J., *Winning Through Intimidation* (Fawcett Publications 1974).

ROBBENNOLT, J., *Apologies and Legal Settlement: An Empirical Examination*, 102 Mich. L. Rev. 460 (2003).

ROSENBERG, Maurice, *The Pretrial Conference and Effective Justice: A Controlled Test In Personal Injury Litigation* (Columbia Univ. Press 1964).

ROSENTHAL, Douglas E., *Lawyer and Client: Who's In Charge* (Russell Sage Foundation 1974).

ROSETT, Arthur and Donald R. Cressey, *Justice By Consent: Plea Bargains in the American Courthouse* (J. B. Lippincott Co. 1976).

ROSS, H. Laurence, *Settled Out of Court: The Social Process of Insurance Claims Adjustment* (Aldine Publishing Co. 2d ed. 1980).

ROSS, Raymond S., *Persuasion: Communication and Interpersonal Relations* (Prentice–Hall, Inc. 1974).

ROSSITER, Charles M., Jr. & W. Barnett Pearce, *Communicating Personally: A Theory of Interpersonal Communication and Human Relationships* (Bobbs–Merrill Co.1975).

RUBIN, Jeffrey Z., & Bert R. Brown, *The Social Psychology of Bargaining and Negotiation* (Academic Press 1975).

RUBIN, A., *A Causerie on Lawyers' Ethics in Negotiations*, 35 La. L. Rev. 577 (1975).

RUBIN, M. & S. Stroschein, *The Ethics of Negotiations: Are There Any?*, 56 La. L. Rev. 447 (1995).

RYAN, E., *The Discourse Beneath: Emotional Epistemology in Legal Deliberation and Negotiation*, 10 Harv. Negot. L. Rev. 231 (2005).

RYCKMAN, Richard M., *Theories of Personality* (Litton Educational Publishing, Inc. 1978).

SAHAKIAN, William S., *Learning: Systems, Models and Theories* (Rand McNally College Publishing Co. 1970, 1976).

SALACUSE, Jeswald, *The Global Negotiator* (Palgrave 2003).

SALACUES, Jeswald, *Making Global Deals* (Houghton Mifflin 1991).

SALES, J., *Contribution and Indemnity Between Negligent and Strictly Liable Tortfeasors*, 12 St. Mary's L.J. 323 (1980).

SAMBORN, H., *The Vanishing Trial*, A.B.A. J. 24 (Oct. 2002).

SCHATZKI, Michael, *Negotiation: The Art of Getting What You Want* (The New American Library, Inc. 1981).

SCHELLING, Thomas C., *The Strategy of Conflict* (Harvard Univ. Press 1960, 1980).

SCHNEIDER, A., *Effective Responses to Offensive Comments*, 10 Negot. J. 107 (April 1994).

SCHNEIDER, A., *Shattering Negotiation Myths: Empirical Evidence on the Effectiveness of Negotiation Style*, 7 Harv. Negot. L. Rev. 143 (2002).

SCHNEIDER, A., *Aspirations in Negotiation*, 87 Marquette L. Rev. 675 (2004).

SCHNEIDER, Andrea & Christopher Honeyman, eds., *The Negotiator's Fieldbook* (A.B.A. Section of Disp. Res. 2006).

SCHOONMAKER, Alan, *Negotiate to Win: Gaining the Psychological Edge* (Prentice Hall 1989).

SCHWARTZ, Barry, *The Paradox of Choice: Why More is Less* (Harper Collins 2004).

SCOTT, L.W., *Lawyers' Forum: Settlements—New Perspectives*, 12 St. Mary's L.J. 275 (1980).

SENGER, J., *Decision Analysis in Negotiation*, 87 Marquette L. Rev. 723 (2004).

SHAPIRO, D., *Negotiating Emotions*, 20 Conflict Res. Quarterly 67 (2002).

SHAPIRO, Ronald & Mark Jankowski, *The Power of Nice* (John Wiley & Sons 2001).

SHARSWOOD, G., *Professional Ethics* (1854).

SHELL, G. Richard, *Bargaining for Advantage* (Viking 1999).

SHURE, G., R. Meeker & E. Hansford, *The Effectiveness of Pacifist Strategies in Bargaining Games*, IX Conflict Resolution 106 (1965).

SIEGEL, Sidney and Lawrence Fouraker, *Bargaining and Group Decision Making* (McGraw–Hill 1960).

SIMMONS, Robert L., *Winning Before Trial: How To Prepare Cases for the Best Settlement or Trial Result* (Executive Reports Corp. 1974) (2 vols.).

SMITH, Jeffrey M., *Preventing Legal Malpractice* (West Publishing Co. 1981).

SPIEGEL, M., *The New Model Rules of Professional Conduct: Lawyer–Client Decision Making and the Role of Rules in Structuring the Lawyer–Client Dialogue*, 4 American Bar Found. Res. J. 921 (1980).

STARK, Peter & Jane Flaherty, *The Only Negotiating Guide You'll Ever Need* (Broadway Books 2003).

STELLE, W., *Deceptive Negotiating and High–Toned Morality*, 39 Vanderbilt L. Rev. 1387 (1986).

STEPHENSON, R. & JOHNSON, R., *Drafting Settlement Agreements, Negotiation and Settlement—Oregon State Bar* 121 (1980).

STRAUSS, Anselm, *Negotiations: Varieties, Contexts, Processes, and Social Order* (Jossey–Bass 1978).

SUMMERS, R., *"Good Faith" in General Contract Law and the Sales Provisions of the Uniform Commercial Code*, 54 Va. L. Rev. 195 (1968).

SWINGLE, Paul, ed., *The Structure of Conflict* (Academic Press 1970).

TEMKIN, B., *Misrepresentation by Omission in Settlement Negotiations: Should there be a Silent Safe Harbor?*, 18 Georgetown J. Legal Ethics 179 (2004).

TEPLEY, Larry, *Legal Negotiation in a Nutshell* (West Publishing 2d ed. 2005).

THIELENS, Wagner, Jr., *The Socialization of Law Students: A Case Study in Three Parts* (Arno Press 1980).

THOMAS, Jim, *Negotiate to Win: The 21 Rules for Successful Negotiation* (Collins 2005).

THOMPSON, Leigh, ed., *Negotiation Theory and Research* (Psychology Press 2006).

THOMPSON, Leigh, *The Mind and Heart of the Negotiator* (Prentice Hall 3d ed. 2005).

THOMPSON, L. & T. DeHarpport, *Social Judgment, Feedback, and Interpersonal Learning in Negotiation*, 58 Organ. Behavior & Human Decision Processes 327 (1994).

THOMPSON, L. & J. Nadler, *Negotiating Via Information Technology: Theory and Application*, 58 J. Social Issues 109 (2002).

THURMAN, Samuel, Ellis Phillips & Elliott Cheatham, *Cases and Material on the Legal Profession* (1970).

TINSLEY, C., K. O'Connor & B. Sullivan, *Tough Guys Finish Last: The Perils of a Distributive Reputation*, 88 Organ. Behavior & Human Decision Processes 621 (2002).

TRAYNOR, M., *Lawsuits: First Resort or Last*, 4 Utah L. Rev. 635 (1978).

Trial Manual 3 For the Defense of Criminal Cases (Amsterdam, Segal & Miller, reporters) (ALI–ABA 1974).

TVERSKY, A. & D. Kahneman, *The Framing of Decisions and the Psychology of Choice*, 211 Science 453 (1981).

URY, William, *Getting Past No* (Bantam Books 1991).

VAN BOVEN, L., T. Gilovich & V. Medvec, *The Illusion of Transparency in Negotiations*, 19 Negot. J. 117 (2003).

VERBECK, M. & S. Michaels, *Structured Settlements and the Uniform Periodic Payments Act*, Fed'n. Insur. Coun. Quarterly 17 (Fall 1978).

VOLKEMA, Roger, *Leverage: How to Get It and How to Keep It in Any Negotiation* (AMACOM 2006).

VOLKEMA, Roger, *The Negotiation Toolkit* (AMACOM 1999).

VOORHEES, T., *Law Office Training: The Art of Negotiation*, 60 Practical Lawyer 61 (1967).

VRIJ, Aldert, *Detecting Lies and Deceit* (John Wiley & Sons 2000).

WAAS, D., *Expanding the Insurer's Duty to Attempt Settlement*, 49 U. Colo. L. Rev. 251 (1978).

WALD, R., *FTC Settlement Procedures*, 5 Litigation 8 (Spring 1979).

Wall Street Journal, More Law Firms Put Computers to Work to Find Cases, Print Filings, Bill Clients (December 23, 1980).

WALSTER, Elaine, G. William Walster & Ellen Berscheid, *Equity: Theory & Research* (Allyn & Bacon, Inc. 1978).

WALTON, Richard & Robert McKersie, *A Behavioral Theory of Labor Negotiations* (McGraw–Hill 1965).

WALTZ, J. R. & J.P. Huston, *The Rules of Evidence in Settlement*, 5 Litigation 11 (Fall 1981).

WARSCHAW, Tessa Albert, *Winning By Negotiation* (Berkley Books 1981).

WATKINS, Michael, *Shaping the Game* (Harvard Bus. School Press 2006).

WELSH, N., *Perceptions of Fairness in Negotiation*, 87 Marquette L. Rev. 753 (2004).

WENKE, Robert, *The Art of Negotiation for Lawyers* (Richter 1985).

WETLAUFER, G., *The Ethics of Lying in Negotiations*, 75 Iowa L. Rev. 1219 (1990).

WETLAUFER, G., *The Limits of Integrative Bargaining*, 85 Georgetown L.J. 369 (1996).

WHITE, J.J., *The Lawyer as a Negotiator: An Adventure in Understanding and Teaching the Art of Negotiation*, 19 J. Legal Ed. 337 (1967).

WHITE, J.J., *Machiavelli and the Bar: Ethical Limitations on Lying in Negotiation*, 1980 Amer. Bar Found. Research J. 926 (1980).

WILL, Hubert L., Robert R. Merhige, Jr. & Alvin B. Rubin, *The Role of the Judge in the Settlement Process* (Federal Judicial Center 1976).

WILLIAMS, England, Farmer & Blumenthal, *Effectiveness in Legal Negotiation* in Harry T. Edwards & James J. White, *The Lawyer as a Negotiator* 8 (West 1977).

WILLIAMS, Gerald & Joseph M. Geis, *Negotiation Skills Training in the Law School Curriculum* in *Teaching Negotiation: Ideas and Innovations* 203 (Michael Wheeler, ed.) (PON Books 2000).

WILLIAMS, Gerald, *Negotiation as a Healing Process*, 1996 J. Disp. Res. 1 (1996).

WILLIAMS, Gerald, *Style and Effectiveness in Negotiation* in *Changing Tactics: Negotiating for Mutual Gain* (Lavinia Hall, ed.) (National Institute for Dispute Resolution 1991).

WILLIAMS, Gerald, *Using Simulation Exercises in Negotiation and Other Dispute Resolution Courses*, 34 J. Legal Educ. 307 (1984).

WILLISTON, Samuel, *Williston on Contracts* (W. Jaeger 3d ed. 1970).

WISE, R. L., *Legal Ethics* (Matthew Bender 2d ed. 1970).

WRIGHT, Charles Alan & Arthur Miller, *Federal Practice and Procedure* (West Publishing Co. 1973).

WRIGHT, J. Skelly, *The Pretrial Conference*, 28 F.R.D. 141 (1960).

YOUNG, Oran R., *Bargaining: Formal Theories of Negotiation* (Univ. of Illinois Press 1975).

ZARTMAN, I. William, *The 50% Solution: How to Bargain Successfully With Hijackers, Strikers, Bosses, Oil Magnates, Arabs, Russians, and Other Worthy Opponents in This Modern World* (Anchor Press/Doubleday 1976).

ZARTMAN, I. William, ed., *The Negotiation Process: Theories and Applications* (Sage Publications 1978).

ZARTMAN, I. William & Jeffrey Rubin, *Power and Negotiation* (Univ. of Mich. Press 2002).

ZEMANS, Frances Kahn & Victor G. Rosenblum, *The Making of a Public Professional* (American Bar Foundation 1981).

Index

References are to Pages

ABSTRACT REASONING ABILITY (IQ) vs. EMOTIONAL INTELLIGENCE (EI)
Generally, 131-136
Null and alternative hypotheses, 132, 133
P-value, 133
Spearman rank-order coefficients, 133-135
Statistical findings, 132-136
Student GPA and a pass/fail option on clinical negotiation course performance, impact of, 132-136

ACCUSATIONS
Competitive/adversarial negotiating, 61

ADMISSIBILITY OF EVIDENCE
Rules of evidence, 109

ADVERSARIAL NEGOTIATING
Competitive/Adversarial Negotiating, this index
Law of negotiation and settlement, 61
Prof. Schneider's 1999 Study, this index

AGREEMENT AND FINAL BREAKDOWN (STAGE 5)
Stages of Negotiation Process, this index

ANCHORING IMPACT
Initial offers, economic and psychological factors, 126

ANDREA KUPFER SCHNEIDER
Prof. Schneider's 1999 Study, this index

ANNUITY
Objective economic method for case evaluation, 122

ARGUMENTATION (STAGE 3)
Stages of Negotiation Process, this index

ASPIRATION LEVELS
Stages of negotiation process, 75

ATTITUDINAL BARGAINING
Race and negotiation performance, 149

ATTORNEY-CLIENT RELATIONSHIP
Generally, 65-67
Classification, conflicting styles between attorneys and clients, 67

ATTORNEY-CLIENT RELATIONSHIP —Cont'd
Communication—Cont'd
Client participation, importance of, 66
Communication
Effectiveness of communication by attorney, 65
Offers of settlement, communication with client, 97
Conflicts between attorneys and clients generally, 67-69
Classification, conflicting styles between attorneys and clients, 67
Stylistic differences between attorneys and clients, 68
Win-lose results, 68
WIN-win results, 68
Win-win results, 67
Decision-making process, negotiation as, 65
Developments of case, keeping clients informed of, 67
Ethical Consideration 7-8, 67
Legal process, helping client understand, 66
Manipulation, issue of, 65
Misunderstandings which lead to trial, 65
Model Rules 1.4 and 1.2, 67
Mutual understandings between attorney and client, 66
Participation, importance of client, 66
Preparation of case, client involvement in, 66
Responsibilities of clients, discussion of, 67
Stylistic differences between attorneys and clients, 68
Understanding of legal process, helping client to gain, 66
Win-lose results, attorney-client conflicts, 68
WIN-win and win-win results, attorney-client conflicts, 68

ATTORNEYS FEES
FRCP Rule 68, payment of attorney's fees by losing party under, 104

AVERAGE/COMPETITIVE NEGOTIATORS
Prof. Williams 1976 legal negotiation research project, characteristics, 26, 27

AVERAGE/COOPERATIVE NEGOTIATORS
Prof. Williams 1976 Legal Negotiation Research Project, this index

BAD FAITH
Defined, special rules applicable to insurers, 108

BARGAINING
Contract law, use of threats in bargaining, 96

BATNA'S
Best Alternatives to Negotiated Agreements (BATNA's), below

BEST ALTERNATIVES TO NEGOTIATED AGREEMENTS (BATNA'S)
Preparation (Stage 1), 79
Stages of negotiation process, 75

BIPOLAR RATINGS
Prof. Schneider's 1999 study, 36
Prof. Williams 1976 legal negotiation research project, similarities between effective/cooperative and effective/competitive negotiators, 22

BLUFFING
Competitive/adversarial negotiating, 61
Law of negotiation and settlement, 8, 98

BUSINESS DISPUTES
Stages of negotiation process, interplay between legal proceedings and negotiation process, 89, 90

CHARACTERISTICS OF NEGOTIATORS
Prof. Williams 1976 Legal Negotiation Research Project, this index

CIVIL DISPUTES
Transactions, distinguished, 3

CLASS ACTION SETTLEMENTS
Court supervision and approval of settlements, 105

CLIENT LIABILITY
Law of negotiation and settlement, client liability due to attorney misrepresentation, 99, 100

CLIENT RELATIONS AND NEGOTIATION
Attorney-Client Relationship, this index

"COLLATERAL USE"
Rules of evidence, exception, 110

COMMUNICATION
Attorney-Client Relationship, this index
Competitive/adversarial negotiating, distortion of communication, 62

COMPETENCY OF LAWYER
Adequacy of training in negotiation skills, 4

COMPETENCY OF LAWYER—Cont'd
Des Moines negotiations results, 6

COMPETITIVE/ADVERSARIAL NEGOTIATING
Generally, 60-64
Accusations, 61
Bargaining breakdown, 62, 63
Bluffs, 61
Communication distortion between parties, 62
Dynamics, 58-74
Exaggerations, 61
High demands, 61
Impasse, danger of, 63
Ineffective competitors, 63
Ineffective cooperatives, 63
Lack of preparation by ineffective competitive/adversarial negotiators, 62
Law of negotiation and settlement, 61
Limitations, 62
Long-term relationships, damage of, 64
Mistrust between negotiators as problem, 62
Misunderstandings, 62
Perception of parties, effect of toughness on, 63
Ridicule, 61
Settlement value, maximization of, 61
Siegel & Fouraker, experiments by, 61
Strategy, 60-64
Tactic, 61
Tension and mistrust between negotiators as problem, 62
Threats, 61
Toughness in bargaining, 61

COMPETITIVE/PROBLEM-SOLVING NEGOTIATION
Generally, 53, 54
Maximization of benefits to opponent, 64
Strategy, 64, 65
"Win-win attorneys," 64

CONCESSIONS
Stages of Negotiation Process, this index

CONFLICT OF INTEREST
Insurers, special rules applicable to, 108

CONFLICTS
Attorney-Client Relationship, this index

CONFLICTS OF LAW
Law of negotiation and settlement, 103

CONSENT JUDGMENTS
Law of negotiation and settlement, 101

CONSIDERATION
Law of negotiation and settlement, 100

CONTRACT LAW
Law of Negotiation and Settlement, this index

"CONTRACT" THEORY
Rules of evidence, 108

COOPERATIVE/PROBLEM-SOLVING NEGOTIATING
Disadvantages, 59
Dynamics, 58-74
Fairness, commitment to, 59
Limitations, 59
Strategy, 59, 60
Unilateral concessions, use of, 59
Vulnerability to exploitation, 59
Weakness, appearance of, 59

COURTS
Law of Negotiation and Settlement, this index

CRIMINAL CASES
Plea bargaining, 3, 4

CRISES
Stages of Negotiation Process, this index

DEADLINES
Stages of Negotiation Process, this index

DECISION TREES
Economic and psychological factors, factoring relevant considerations and calculation of case values, 119

DECISION-MAKING INFLUENCES
Economic and Psychological Factors, this index

DEFECTS
Law of Negotiation and Settlement, this index

DES MOINES NEGOTIATIONS
Competency of lawyer, 6

DEVELOPMENTS OF CASE
Attorney-client relationship, keeping clients informed of case developments, 67

DISMISSAL WITH PREJUDICE
Law of negotiation and settlement, 101

ECONOMIC AND PSYCHOLOGICAL FACTORS
Generally, 111-130
Anchoring impact of initial offers, 126
Annuity, objective economic method for case evaluation, 122
Appropriate rate of interest for time-value calculation, objective economic method for case evaluation, 122
Combined formula components, Simmons formula of case value evaluation, 117, 118
Decision trees, factoring relevant considerations and calculation of case values, 119
Decision-making influences
    generally, 124-130
    Anchoring impact of initial offers, 126

ECONOMIC AND PSYCHOLOGICAL FACTORS—Cont'd
Decision-making influences—Cont'd
    Egocentric/self-serving bias, 125, 126
    Fixed pie assumption, 124
    Gain-loss framing, 127, 128
    Non-zero-sum negotiations, 125
    Reactive devaluation, 128, 129
    Regret aversion, 129
    Zero-sum money disputes, 125
Economic analysis of cases
    generally, 111-115
    Methods of economic case evaluations, below
    Missing lawyer skill, below
    Objective economic method for case evaluation, below
Egocentric/self-serving bias as decision-making influence, 125, 126
Electronic calculators, use in computing time value of money, 121
Expenses, consideration in calculations, 118
Financial calculators, use in calculation of present or future value, 122
Fixed pie assumption as decision-making influence, 124
Formulas and rules of convenience, use in personal injury cases, 116
Gain-loss framing as decision-making influence, 127, 128
Impact of factors, 111-130
Intangibles, consideration in economic case evaluation calculations, 118
Jury verdict report services, use of, 116
Lost earnings, consideration in economic case evaluations, 118
Methods of economic case evaluations
    generally, 116-120
    Combined formula components, Simmons formula of case value evaluation, 117, 118
    Decision trees to factor relevant considerations and calculation of case values, 119
    Expenses, consideration in calculations, 118
    Formulas and rules of convenience, use in personal injury cases, 116
    Intangibles, consideration in calculations, 118
    Jury verdict report services, use of, 116
    Lost earning, use in calculations, 118
    Probabilities, consideration in calculations, 118
    Simmons formula of case value evaluation, 117, 118
    "Three times special damages," 116
Missing lawyer skill
    generally, 111-115
    Calculating case values, 112, 113
    Facts, importance of, 112
Non-zero-sum negotiations as decision-making influence, 125

ECONOMIC AND PSYCHOLOGICAL FACTORS—Cont'd
Objective economic method for case evaluation
    generally, 120-124
  Annuity, 122
  Appropriate rate of interest for time-value calculation use, 122
  Electronic calculators, use in computing time value of money, 121
  Financial calculators, use in calculation of present or future value, 122
  Tables, calculation of present and future values using, 121
  Tax aspects of settlement, 123
  Time value calculation of money, 121
Personal injury cases, use of formulas and rules of convenience in, 116
Probabilities, consideration in economic case evaluations, 118
Reactive devaluation as decision-making influence, 128, 129
Regret aversion as decision-making influence, 129
Rules of convenience, use of, 116
Simmons formula of case value evaluation, 117, 118
Tables, calculation of present and future values using, 121
Tax aspects of settlement, objective economic method for case evaluation, 123
"Three times special damages," methods of economic case evaluations, 116
Time value calculation of money, objective economic method for case evaluation, 121
Zero-sum money disputes as decision-making influence, 125

EFFECTIVE/COMPETITIVE NEGOTIATORS
Prof. Williams 1976 Legal Negotiation Research Project, this index

EFFECTIVE/COOPERATIVE NEGOTIATORS
Prof. Williams 1976 Legal Negotiation Research Project, this index

EFFECTIVENESS IN LEGAL NEGOTIATION
Defined, 7

EGOCENTRIC/SELF-SERVING BIAS
Decision-making influence, 125, 126

EI
Abstract Reasoning Ability (IQ) vs. Emotional Intelligence (EI), this index

ELECTRONIC CALCULATORS
Economic and psychological factors, computation of time value of money, 121

"EMBELLISHMENT" BY OPPONENTS
Law of negotiation and settlement, 98

EMERGENCIES AND CRISIS (STAGE 4)
Stages of Negotiation Process, this index

EMOTIONAL INTELLIGENCE
Abstract Reasoning Ability (IQ) vs. Emotional Intelligence (EI), this index

ENFORCEMENT OF SETTLEMENT AGREEMENTS
Law of Negotiation and Settlement, this index

"ENGLISH" THEORY
Rules of evidence, 108

EQUITABLE POSITIONING
Stages of Negotiation Process, this index

ETHICAL CONSIDERATIONS AND CONSTRAINTS
Attorney-client relationship, Ethical Consideration 7-8, 67
Law of Negotiation and Settlement, this index

EVIDENCE RULES
Rules of Evidence, this index

EXAGGERATIONS
Competitive/adversarial negotiating, 61

EXCEPTIONS
Law of negotiation and settlement, 101

EXPECTATIONS
Stages of Negotiation Process, this index

EXTRINSIC EVIDENCE
Law of negotiation and settlement, 102

FAIRNESS
Cooperative/problem-solving negotiating, commitment to fairness, 59

FEDERAL RULES OF CIVIL PROCEDURE
Offers of compromise under Rule 68, 103, 104

FINAL BREAKDOWN
Stages of Negotiation Process, this index

FINANCIAL CALCULATORS
Economic and psychological factors, use of financial calculators in calculation of present or future value, 122

FIXED PIE ASSUMPTION
Decision-making influence, 124

FORMATION OF SETTLEMENT AGREEMENTS
Law of Negotiation and Settlement, this index

FRAUD, MISREPRESENTATION AND MIS-TAKE
Law of negotiation and settlement, 106

GAIN-LOSS FRAMING
Decision-making influence, 127, 128

GENDER AND NEGOTIATION PERFORMANCE
Generally, 136-144
Confidence, influences on, 140
Equal exchanges vs. equitable distributions, 140
Finding implications, 142
Gender-based competitive differences, 140
Real and perceived gender-based differences, 137-142
Statistical results, 141
Stereotypes based on gender, 137-142

GOOD FAITH
Labor/management negotiations, 3
Law of Negotiation and Settlement, this index

GOVERNING LAW
Law of negotiation and settlement, 103

HARD BARGAINING
Law of negotiation and settlement, contract law, 95

HIGH DEMANDS
Competitive/adversarial negotiating, 61

IMPASSE
Competitive/adversarial negotiating, danger of impasse, 63

INEFFECTIVE/COMPETITIVE NEGOTIATORS
Prof. Williams 1976 legal negotiation research project, characteristics, 30-33

INEFFECTIVE/COOPERATIVE NEGOTIATORS
Prof. Williams 1976 Legal Negotiation Research Project, this index

INSURANCE
Law of Negotiation and Settlement, this index

INTANGIBLES
Economic and psychological factors, consideration in economic case evaluation calculations, 118

INTEGRATIVE POSITIONING
Stages of Negotiation Process, this index

INTENT OF PARTIES
Law of negotiation and settlement, 102

INTERPERSONAL ORIENTATION (IO) FACTOR
Race and negotiation performance, 146

INTERPRETATION OF SETTLEMENT AGREEMENTS
Law of Negotiation and Settlement, this index

IQ
Abstract Reasoning Ability (IQ) vs. Emotional Intelligence (EI), this index

JOINT TORTFEASORS
Law of negotiation and settlement, release problems, 102

JURY VERDICT REPORT SERVICES
Economic and psychological factors, 116

LABOR/MANAGEMENT NEGOTIATIONS
Generally, 3

LAW OF NEGOTIATION AND SETTLEMENT
Generally, 93-110
Advantages of
  Settlement, 8, 9
  Trial, 9, 10
Attorneys fees, issue of payment by losing party under FRCP Rule 68, 104
Bad faith, defined, special rules applicable to insurers, 108
Bargaining, use of threats in, contract law, 96
Benefits of settlements to litigation, 93, 94
Bluffing
  generally, 8
  Opponents, 98
Class action settlements, court supervision and approval of settlements, 105
Client liability due to attorney misrepresentation, 99, 100
Communication with clients as to offers of settlement, 97
Competitive/adversarial negotiating, 61
Compromise and settlement, general policy of law toward, 93, 94
Conflict of interest, special rules applicable to insurers, 108
Conflicts of law and governing law, 103
Consent judgments, 101
Consideration, 100
Contract law as source of negotiation law
  generally, 94-97
  Bargaining, use of threats in, 96
  Good faith
    Bargaining, notion of good faith in, 94, 95
    Threats to commence litigation, 96
  Hard bargaining, 95
  Threats, use in bargaining, 95, 96
"Costs" under FRCP Rule 68, 104
Courts
  Notification by court of settlement, requirement, 101

LAW OF NEGOTIATION AND SETTLE-MENT—Cont'd
Courts—Cont'd
  Supervision and approval of settlements by court, 105
Defects in compromise and settlement agreements
  Fraud, misrepresentation and mistake, 106
  Mary Carter agreements, 106, 107
Dismissal with prejudice, 101
"Embellishment" by opponents, 98
Enforcement and preservation of settlements, 93, 94
Ethical constraints on legal negotiators generally, 97-100
  Client liability due to attorney misrepresentation, 99, 100
  Communication with clients as to offers of settlement, 97
  "Puffing," "bluffing," and "embellishment" by opponents, 98
Evidence. Rules of Evidence, this index
Exceptions, 101
Extrinsic evidence, 102
Federal Rules of Civil Procedure, Rule 68 offers of compromise, 103, 104
Form of agreement, 101
Formalities. Writings and formalities, below
Formation, interpretation and enforcement of settlement agreements generally, 100-105
  Class action settlements, court supervision and approval of settlements, 105
  Consideration, 100
  Court supervision and approval of settlements, 105
  Formalities. Writings and formalities, below
  Interpretation of agreement, below
  Offer and acceptance, 100
  Statutes of limitations, effect of negotiations on, 106
  Writings and formalities, below
Fraud, misrepresentation and mistake, 106
Good faith
  Bargaining, notion of good faith in, 94, 95
  Defined, 108
  Insurers, special rules applicable to, 108
  Threats to commence litigation, 96
Governing law and conflicts of law, 103
Hard bargaining, contract law, 95
Insurers, special rules applicable to generally, 107, 108
  Bad faith, defined, 108
  Conflict of interest, 108
  Good faith, defined, 108
Intent of parties, 102
Interpretation of agreement generally, 102, 103

LAW OF NEGOTIATION AND SETTLE-MENT—Cont'd
Interpretation of agreement—Cont'd
  Attorneys fees, issue of payment by losing party under FRCP Rule 68, 104
  Conflicts of law and governing law, 103
  "Costs" under FRCP Rule 68, 104
  Extrinsic evidence, 102
  Federal Rules of Civil Procedure, Rule 68 offers of compromise, 103, 104
  Governing law and conflicts of law, 103
  Intent of parties, 102
  Joint tortfeasors, release problems, 102
  Procedural incentives to settle under Federal Rules of Civil Procedure, Rule 68 offers of compromise, 103
  Specific claims, exclusion in settlement, 102
  Uniform Contribution Among Tortfeasors Act, 102
Joint tortfeasors, release problems, 102
Mary Carter agreements, 106, 107
Objective economic method for case evaluation, tax aspects of settlement, 123
Offer and acceptance of settlement agreement, 100
Prejudice, dismissal with, 101
Procedural incentives to settle under Federal Rules of Civil Procedure, Rule 68 offers of compromise, 103
"Puffing" by opponents, 98
Rules of Evidence, this index
Specific claims, exclusion in settlement, 102
Statutes of limitations, effect of negotiations on, 106
Threats, use in bargaining, contract law, 95, 96
Uniform Contribution Among Tortfeasors Act, 102
Writings and formalities
  generally, 101, 102
  Consent judgments, 101
  Court notification of settlement, requirement, 101
  Dismissal with prejudice, 101
  Exceptions, 101
  Form of agreement, 101

LIMITATIONS
Competitive/adversarial negotiating, 62
Cooperative/problem-solving negotiating, 59

LOCAL CUSTOM
Stages of negotiation process, consideration in maximalist positioning, 81

LONG-TERM RELATIONSHIPS
Competitive/adversarial negotiating, damage to long-term relationships, 64

LOST EARNINGS
Economic and psychological factors, consideration of lost earnings in economic case evaluations, 118

MANIPULATION
Attorney-client relationship, issue of manipulation, 65

MARY CARTER AGREEMENTS
Law of negotiation and settlement, 106, 107

MAXIMALIST POSITIONING
Stages of Negotiation Process, this index

METHODS OF ECONOMIC CASE EVALUATIONS
Economic and Psychological Factors, this index

MISSING LAWYER SKILL
Economic and Psychological Factors, this index

MISUNDERSTANDINGS
Attorney-client relationship, misunderstandings which lead to trial, 65

MODEL CODE OF PROFESSIONAL RESPONSIBILITY
Prof. Williams 1976 legal negotiation research project, 23

MODEL RULES 1.4 AND 1.2
Attorney-client relationship, 67

MUTUAL UNDERSTANDINGS
Attorney-client relationship, 66

NON-ZERO-SUM NEGOTIATIONS
Economic and psychological factors, decision-making influence, 125

OBJECTIVE ECONOMIC METHOD FOR CASE EVALUATION
Economic and Psychological Factors, this index

OFFER AND ACCEPTANCE
Law of negotiation and settlement, 100

ORIENTATION (STAGE 2)
Stages of Negotiation Process, this index

"OTHERWISE DISCOVERABLE" EXCEPTION
Rules of evidence, 110

PARTICIPATION BY CLIENT
Attorney-client relationship, importance of client participation, 66

PATTERNS OF NEGOTIATING
Generally, 12-57
Competitive/Adversarial Negotiating, this index
Competitive/Problem-Solving Negotiation, this index

PATTERNS OF NEGOTIATING—Cont'd
Cooperative/Problem-Solving Negotiating, this index
Determination of negotiator style, 54-58
Prof. Williams 1976 Legal Negotiation Research Project, this index

PERCEPTION OF PARTIES
Competitive/adversarial negotiating, 63

PERSONAL FACTORS INFLUENCING NEGOTIATOR PERFORMANCE
Generally, 131-151
Abstract Reasoning Ability (IQ) vs. Emotional Intelligence (EI), this index
Gender and Negotiation Performance, this index
Race and Negotiation Performance, this index

PERSONAL INJURY CASES
Rules of convenience and formulas, use in personal injury cases, 116

POSITIONING (STAGE 2)
Stages of Negotiation Process, this index

PRE-BARGAINING DYNAMICS
Stages of Negotiation Process, this index

PREJUDICE, DISMISSAL WITH
Law of negotiation and settlement, 101

PREPARATION (STAGE 1)
Stages of Negotiation Process, this index

PRIVILEGED EXCEPTION THEORY
Rules of evidence, 108

PROBLEM-SOLVING NEGOTIATION
Competitive/Problem-Solving Negotiation, this index
Prof. Schneider's 1999 Study, this index

PROCEDURAL INCENTIVES
FRCP, Rule 68 offers of compromise, 103

PROF. SCHNEIDER'S 1999 STUDY
Generally, 33-51
Administration of survey, 35
Adversarial negotiating
Changes during past 25 years, 49, 50
Judging effectiveness of adversarial behavior, 42
Problem-solving and adversarial styles of negotiating, 35
Background and population characteristics, 35
Bipolar ratings, 36
Changes in effective negotiating during past 25 years, 48-52
Comparison of effectiveness ratings over time, 51
Effective adversarial, changes during past 25 years, 49, 50
Effective problem-solving, changes during past 25 years, 48, 49

PROF. SCHNEIDER'S 1999 STUDY
—Cont'd

Empirical evidence on effectiveness of negotiation style, 33-51

Measuring negotiation effectiveness, 34

Problem-solving negotiating
  generally, 35
  Changes during past 25 years, 48, 49
  Judging effectiveness, 39

Style, effectiveness regardless of, 51

Substantive results, 35

PROF. WILLIAMS 1976 LEGAL NEGOTIATION RESEARCH PROJECT
  Generally, 12-33

Adjective checklist, similarities between effective/cooperative and effective/competitive negotiators, 21

Average negotiators, characteristics, 25-27

Average/competitive negotiators, characteristics, 26, 27

Average/cooperative negotiators
  Average/competitive negotiators, similarities, 27
  Characteristics, 25, 26

Bipolar scales, similarities between effective/cooperative and effective/competitive negotiators, 22

Characteristics
  Average negotiators, 25-27
  Average/competitive negotiators, 26, 27
  Average/cooperative negotiators, 25, 26
  Effective/competitive negotiators, 19-21
  Effective/cooperative negotiators, 17-19
  Ineffective negotiators, 27-33
  Ineffective/competitive negotiators, 30-33
  Ineffective/cooperative negotiators, 28-38

Described, 12-14

Differences between effective and ineffective/cooperative negotiators, 29, 30

Effective/competitive negotiators
  Adjective checklist, 21
  Bipolar scales, 22
  Characteristics, 19-21
  Objectives, 22
  Similarities to effective/cooperative and, 21-25

Effective/cooperative negotiators
  Adjective checklist, 21
  Bipolar scales, 22
  Characteristics, 17-19
  Differences and similarities to ineffective/cooperative negotiators, 29, 30
  Objectives, 22
  Similarities to effective/competitive negotiators, 21-25

Empirical study findings, 12-33

How lawyers negotiate, lessons from attorneys, 14-33

Ineffective/competitive negotiators, characteristics, 30-33

PROF. WILLIAMS 1976 LEGAL NEGOTIATION RESEARCH PROJECT—Cont'd

Ineffective/cooperative negotiators
  Characteristics, 28-38
  Differences and similarities to effective/cooperative negotiators, 29, 30

Model Code of Professional Responsibility, 23

Objectives, similarities between effective/cooperative and effective/competitive negotiators, 22

Percentage of each negotiator type among practicing bar, 16

Similarities
  Average/cooperative and average/competitive negotiators, 27
  Effective and ineffective/cooperative negotiators, 29
  Effective/cooperative and effective/competitive negotiators, 21-25

PSYCHOLOGICAL FACTORS
Economic and Psychological Factors, this index

"PUFFING" BY OPPONENTS
Law of negotiation and settlement, 98

RACE AND NEGOTIATION PERFORMANCE
  Generally, 144-151
Attitudinal bargaining, 149
Implications, 148-150
Interpersonal orientation (IO) factor, 146
Real and perceived racial differences, 145-147
Statistical findings, 147, 148
Stereotypical beliefs, 146

REACTIVE DEVALUATION
Decision-making influence, 128, 129

REGRET AVERSION
Decision-making influence, 129

RELEVANCY THEORY
Rules of evidence, 108

RESPONSIBILITIES OF CLIENTS
Attorney-client relationship, 67

RIDICULE
Competitive/adversarial negotiating, 61

RULES OF CONVENIENCE
Economic and psychological factors, 116

RULES OF EVIDENCE
  Generally, 108-110
Admissibility of evidence, 109
"Collateral use" exception, 110
"English" or "contract" theory, 108
Exceptions to Rule 408 of Federal Evidence Rules, 110
"Otherwise discoverable" exception, 110
Privileged exception theory, 108

RULES OF EVIDENCE—Cont'd
Relevancy theory, 108
Rule 408, 109, 110
Rule 409, 110
Rule 410, 110
"Valuable consideration," 109

SCHNEIDER
Prof. Schneider's 1999 Study, this index

SELF-SERVING BIAS
Decision-making influence, 125, 126

SETTLEMENT
Law of Negotiation and Settlement, this index

SIEGEL & FOURAKER
Competitive/adversarial negotiating, experiments, 61

SIMMONS FORMULA OF CASE VALUE EVALUATION
Economic and psychological factors, 117, 118

SPEARMAN RANK-ORDER COEFFICIENTS
Abstract reasoning ability (IQ) vs. emotional intelligence (EI), 133-135

STAGES OF NEGOTIATION PROCESS
Generally, 74-93
Agreement and final breakdown (Stage 5)
   generally, 88, 89
   Agreement, 88
   Final accord, working out details of, 77
   Final breakdown, 88, 89
   Formalizing agreement, 77
   Justification and reinforcement about desirability of agreement, 77
Argumentation (Stage 3)
   Concessions
      Problem of making, 85, 86
      Simultaneous benefit to both parties, 76
   Discovery and reduction of real positions of other side, 76
   Expectations of each side, 76
   Overview, 84, 85
   Projective view of concession-making, 85
   Strategic presentation of case, 76
Aspiration levels, determination of, 75
Bargaining stalemates, increased risk with maximalist strategy, 80
Best Alternatives to Negotiated Agreements (BATNA's), determination of, 75, 79
Business dispute context, interplay between legal proceedings and negotiation process, 89, 90
Clues about additional concessions, 77
Concessions. Argumentation (Stage 3), above
Crises. Emergencies and crisis (Stage 4), below

STAGES OF NEGOTIATION PROCESS—Cont'd
Critical issues, determination during preparation, 79
Deadlines. Emergencies and crisis (Stage 4), below
Definition of issues at stake in bargaining, 91
Discovery and reduction of real positions of other side, 76
Emergencies and crisis (Stage 4)
   generally, 86-88
   Client, opposing party, and negotiation process, 87, 88
   Clues about additional concessions, 77
   Crisis, point of, 77
   Deadlines
      Effect of, 86, 87
      Pressures, 76
   Expectations of client v. attorney, 87
   Innovative alternatives, 77
   Realistic expectations for clients, creation by attorney of, 87
   Reinforcement to opposing party by attorney, 88
Equitable and economic approach to conflict resolution, 81
Equitable positioning
   generally, 81, 82
   Equitable and economic approach to conflict resolution, 81
   Trust, requirement of, 82
Estimation of underlying needs and interests of other side, 75
Expectations
   Client v. attorney, 87
   Each side's expectations, 76
Final accord, working out details of, 77
Final breakdown. Agreement and final breakdown (Stage 5), above
Formalizing agreement, 77
High demands of maximalist positioning, effectiveness of, 81
Inalterable commitments to opening positions, 83
Information gathering, 74, 78
Innovative alternatives, 77
Integrative positioning
   generally, 82, 83
   Positional bargaining alternative, 82
Interplay between legal proceedings and negotiation process
   generally, 89, 90
   Business dispute context, 89, 90
Inventory and collection of useful resources, 90
Justification and reinforcement about desirability of agreement, 77
Local custom, consideration in maximalist positioning, 81
Logical and objective arguments, development of, 75
Maximalist positioning
   generally, 80, 81

STAGES OF NEGOTIATION PROCESS
—Cont'd
Maximalist positioning—Cont'd
Advantages, 80
Bargaining stalemates, increased risk of, 80
High demands, effectiveness of, 81
Local custom, consideration of, 81
Orientation (Stage 2)
generally, 75, 76
Duration of stage 2, 83, 84
Dynamics, 79
Inalterable commitments to opening positions, 83
Positioning, below
Positioning (Stage 2)
generally, 76, 79-83, 80
Equitable positioning, above
Integrative positioning, above
Maximalist positioning, above
Pre-bargaining dynamics
generally, 90, 91
Definition of issues at stake in bargaining, 91
Inventory and collection of useful resources, 90
Reputations as negotiators and proficient litigators, development of, 90
Rules of bargaining, influence of, 91
Timing of bargaining, exercise of control over, 90
Preparation (Stage 1)
generally, 74, 75
Best Alternatives to Negotiated Agreements (BATNA's), determination of, 79
Client involvement in case preparation with attorney, 66
Critical issues, determination of, 79
Information gathering, 78
Underlying client needs and interests, determining and valuing, 78
Principled opening positions, development of, 75
Projective view of concession-making, 85
Realistic expectations for clients, creation by attorney of, 87
Reinforcement to opposing party by attorney, 88
Reputations as negotiators and proficient litigators, development of, 90
Rules of bargaining, influence of, 91
Stage 1. Preparation (Stage 1), above
Stage 2
Orientation, above
Positioning, above
Stage 3. Argumentation (Stage 3), above
Stage 4. Emergencies and crisis (Stage 4), above
Stage 5. Agreement and final breakdown (Stage 5), above
Stalemate in bargaining, increased risk with maximalist strategy, 80

STAGES OF NEGOTIATION PROCESS
—Cont'd
Strategic presentation of case, 76
Timing of bargaining, exercise of control over, 90
Trust, requirement of, 82
Underlying client needs and interests, determination of, 74, 75, 78

STALEMATES
Stages of negotiation process, increased risk of bargaining stalemate with maximalist strategy, 80

STATUTES OF LIMITATIONS
Law of negotiation and settlement, effect of negotiations on statute of limitations, 106

STEREOTYPES
Gender and negotiation performance, 137-142
Race and negotiation performance, 146

TAXES
Objective economic method for case evaluation, tax aspects of settlement, 123

THREATS
Competitive/adversarial negotiating, 61
Contract law, use of threats in bargaining, 95, 96

"THREE TIMES SPECIAL DAMAGES"
Economic case evaluations, methods, 116

TIME VALUE CALCULATION OF MONEY
Objective economic method for case evaluation, 121

TORTFEASORS
Uniform Contribution Among Tortfeasors Act, 102

TRANSACTIONS
Generally, 2

UNIFORM CONTRIBUTION AMONG TORTFEASORS ACT
Law of negotiation and settlement, 102

UNILATERAL CONCESSIONS
Cooperative/problem-solving negotiating, 59

"VALUABLE CONSIDERATION"
Rules of evidence, 109

WEAKNESS
Cooperative/problem-solving negotiating, appearance of weakness, 59

WILLIAMS
Prof. Williams 1976 Legal Negotiation Research Project, this index

WIN-LOSE RESULTS
Conflicts between attorneys and clients, 68

WIN-WIN RESULTS
Conflicts between attorneys and clients, 67, 68

WRITINGS AND FORMALITIES
Law of Negotiation and Settlement, this index

ZERO-SUM MONEY DISPUTES
Decision-making influence, 125

†